THE UNIVERSITY OF
WINCHESTER

Disability Studies:

Past, Present and Future

Edited by

**Len Barton
and Mike Oliver**

The Disability Press

Leeds

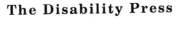

The Disability Press
The Disability Research Unit
The School of Sociology and Social Policy
The University of Leeds
Leeds LS2 9JT

Output from disk supplied and printed by University Print Services, a division of Media Services at Leeds.

British Library Cataloguing in Publication Data
A catalogue record for this book is available from the British Library.

Library of Congress Cataloguing in Publication Data
A catalogue record of this book has been requested.

ISBN 0 9528450 1 6

Contents

Acknowledgements

We would like to express our thanks to all the members of the editorial board and contributors who over the years have enabled the Journal to establish and maintain its high international reputation.

We are particularly grateful to Colin Barnes and the students on the Disability Studies course at the University of Leeds, for their helpful suggestions concerning what we should publish in sections 2 and 3 of this book. Of course, we remain solely responsible for the final decision over the published articles.

We are grateful to Carfax Publishing Company for their agreement to publish the past papers from the Journal *Disability and Society* (formerly, *Disability, Handicap and Society*).

The Disability Press

The Disability Press seeks to provide an alternative outlet for work in the field of disability studies. The Disability Press acknowledges and draws inspiration from the work of all those countless disabled individuals and their allies who have, over the years, struggled to put this particular issue on to the political agenda. Its establishment is a testament to the growing recognition of 'disability' as an equal opportunities and human rights issue within the social sciences.

Funding for this second volume from the Disability Press has been provided by the Disability Research Unit. The editors also wish to record their thanks for the support and encouragement of the School of Sociology and Social Policy at the University of Leeds.

Contributors

Paul Abberley
1 Rew Lea Cottages,
Rew Road,
ASHBURTON,
Devon TQ13 7EL
U.K.

Colin Barnes
The Disability Research Unit,
The School of Sociology and Social Policy,
University of Leeds,
LEEDS LS2 9JT
U.K.

Len Barton
Division of Education,
University of Sheffield,
388 Glossop Road,
SHEFFIELD S10 2JA
U.K.

Anne Borsay
Department of History,
University of Wales Lampeter,
LAMPETER,
Dyfed, SA48 7ED
U.K.

Mike Bury
Department of Social Policy and
Social Science,
Royal Holloway,
University of London,
EGHAM,
Surrey TW20 0EX
U.K.

Jane Campbell
7 Holmwood House,
South Place,
Alpha Road,
SURBITON,
Surrey KT5 8TB,
U.K.

Anne Chappell
Buckinghamshire College,
Faculty of Applied Social Sciences,
Queen Alexandra Road,
HIGH WYCOMBE,
Bucks HP11 2IZ,
U.K.

Jenny Corbett
University of London,
Institute of Education,
Department of Psychology and
Special Needs,
25 Woburn Square,
LONDON WC1H 0AA
U.K.

Marie Johnston
School of Psychology,
University of St. Andrews,
FIFE
KY16 9JU,
Scotland,
U.K.

CONTRIBUTORS

Helen Liggett
Department of Planning,
Public Policy and Management,
University of Oregon,
Eugene,
OREGON 97403,
U.S.A.

Mike Oliver
Department of Sociology,
University of Greenwich,
Brontë Building,
Avery Hill Road,
Southwood Site, Eltham,
LONDON SE9 2UG
U.K.

Ruth Pinder
CSHSD,
Department of Human Sciences,
Brunel: The University of
West London,
UXBRIDGE,
Middlesex UB8 3PH,
U.K.

Marcia Rioux
Roeher Institute,
Kinsmen Building,
York University,
4700 Keele Street,
North York,
ONTARIO M3J 1P3
Canada.

Tom Shakespeare
University of Leeds,
Disability Research Unit,
School of Sociology and Social Policy,
LEEDS LS2 9JT
U.K.

Ayesha Vernon
Social Policy Research Unit,
University of York,
YORK YO1 5DD,
U.K.

Jan Walmsley
The Open University,
School of Health & Social Welfare,
Walton Hall,
MILTON KEYNES, ·
MK7 6AA
U.K.

Nicholas Watson
Department of Nursing Studies,
University of Edinburgh,
40 George Square,
EDINBURGH,
EH8 9LL,
U.K.

Gerry Zarb
Policy Studies Institute,
100 Park Village East,
LONDON,
NW1 3SR
U.K.

INTRODUCTION

The Birth of Disability Studies

Twenty years ago there was no such thing as disability studies. However there were a few stirrings of interest within the academic world. Disabled people were beginning to politicise themselves around issues such as their poverty and incarceration in residential establishments. They were also beginning to write about themselves in ways which transcended the usual autobiographical 'triumph over tragedy' accounts which were and still are common.

Partly as an attempt to capture this newly emerging consciousness and to move beyond the dominance of psychological and medical discourses on disability, the Open University produced a new course titled "The Handicapped Person in the Community" as part of its undergraduate programme in the 1970s. This proved to be enormously popular and subsequently the University of Kent introduced the first masters programme in what later came to be called disability studies.

Following on from these small beginnings and the steady and ever growing stream of writings emerging from disabled people themselves, disability studies began to find its way onto the academic curriculum at both undergraduate and postgraduate levels as well as professional training courses of all kinds. There was no academic journal to support these developments and so in 1986 **Disability and Society** was first published, initially under the title **Disability, Handicap and Society**.

THE HISTORICAL CONTEXT

Two major motivations were particularly significant in contributing to the creation of this Journal. On the one hand, there was a powerful desire to provide an alternative forum for the generation of ideas and the encouragement of dialogue and debate. This included establishing a serious and sustained critique of the medical model of disability which legitimated individualised and personal tragedy perspectives. On the other hand, was the intention to create a journal that would endeavour to develop a balance between academic and non-academic needs. This would cover, for example, issues of language, values and interests.

It was essential therefore, that disabled people who had some experience of research and writing were clearly represented on the editorial board. This was particularly important with regard to the small group of Executive Editors who play a major role in developing policy and monitoring the various aspects of the Journal's profile. Currently there are six members of the Executive Editors, four of whom are disabled academics.

One of the significant and largely unexpected growths of the Journal has been its gradual spread to international markets. Currently we have subscribers from 50 countries and we are increasingly publishing articles from people in a range of different countries. This comparative aspect of the Journal's profile is providing a much needed stimulus which is both informative and challenging in terms of new ways of thinking, different sets of presuppositions, questions and interpretations. Points of commonalty and difference are evident within a more general appreciation of the complexity of the issues involved both at the policy and practice levels of activity.

A journal reflects the interests and development of its editors. One illustration of this concerns that of language. Some of the earlier publications did contain disabilist language. This became an increasingly serious issue which resulted in the editorial board unanimously agreeing in 1993 to changing the name of the Journal and removing 'Handicap' from the title. An editorial statement (Vol. 8, No. 2, 1993) was published on the question of language. It was intended to be both a public declaration of where we had now come to in our collective thinking and development and would also be helpful to intending authors when producing their articles. Another aspect of development was the decision in 1988 to include a **Current Issues** section in the Journal. This was related to our intention to provide an outlet within the Journal for a range of styles of presentation and a means of encouraging controversial ideas. The initial Policy Statement reflects these concerns.

A particularly successful innovation was the introduction of **Special Issues** of the Journal. These covered key themes and were intended to offer both an indication of the existing ideas and understanding available as well as provide new insights, interpretations and questions for consideration. Special Issues have covered such topics as: 'Researching Disability' Vol. 7, No. 2, 1992, 'Representation and Disabled People' Vol. 9, No. 3, 1994, and 'Disability, Development in the Changing World' Vol. 11, No. 4, 1996.

Different Review Editors have been responsible for the development and improvement of the Reviews Section of the Journal. The intention is to cover a range of literature and offer different forms of review some of which are brief and others of a much more detailed examination.

We believe that the Journal has now achieved a degree of international reputation that places it at the forefront of developing ideas and establishing connections between disabled and non-disabled people in many societies who are involved in the identification and removal of the barriers of oppression including forms of impairment-led thinking and practice. Past and present editors are to be thanked for their efforts and support in this process of development.

On reflection we now look forward with optimism and a desire to see the quality and influence of the Journal increase beyond that of its first ten years of publication.

TEN YEARS ON

The idea for this book emerged out of the conference held in Ashford, Kent, in September 1996 to celebrate the first ten years of the Journal. The papers given and the speakers chosen were designed to reflect some (though not all) of the issues and themes that the Journal has been instrumental in both raising and developing.

This book is an attempt to make the original papers available to a wider audience (Part One), to include some of the important papers published in the Journal over these years (Part Two) and to offer insights into some of the controversies that have emerged (Part Three).

PART ONE

The theme of culture is one that has been discussed regularly throughout the Journal. Barnes in his contribution considers the importance of culture in shaping social attitudes to disabled people in pre-industrial societies and also suggests that contemporary attitudes can only be properly understood by reference to these cultural antecedents.

The development of theory has been an integral part of the history of the Journal. Abberley made a major contribution in his seminal discussion of oppression and here he argues that a truly liberatory theory of disablement needs to transcend the Marxism on which much current theory is based. He suggests that impairment will remain problematic in societies where notions of humanity and value ultimately depend on labour.

Other theoretical debates within the Journal have focused on the issue of normalisation. In this section Chappell provides a review and commentary on this developing critique as well as attempting to pose some difficult questions for disability theory; notably concerning the current exclusion and future inclusion of issues of learning difficulty in the mainstream of these debates.

Walmsley, in her chapter, takes up some of these issues and describes a project which attempts to involve people with learning difficulties as equal partners. She considers the potential and limitations of such collaboration before finally raising some more general questions for both theory and practice.

Disabled people's attempts to transform disability from a medical to a political issue have also featured prominently throughout the life of the Journal. Campbell in her chapter reviews this and discusses the ways in which the emerging collective consciousness of disabled people has developed into a full–blown social movement in Britain at least

An essential element in the politicisation of disability has been the recognition that the personal is political. Corbett uses this theme to discuss a series of papers she has written for the Journal over the years, documenting her changing understanding of issues of independence, difference and empowerment and showing how they made a contribution to the transformation of her own consciousness.

The rise of disability politics has had an important impact on research and this has been stimulated by and reflected in the Journal. Rioux, in the final chapter in this section, provides an overview of this, distinguishing between what she calls the individual and social pathology models of research. She reminds researchers of their ethical and political obligations as well as their scientific ones and concludes on a positive note in suggesting that, the emerging disability movement world–wide will force researchers to accept these obligations.

PART TWO

Selecting a few papers from the last ten years when the Journal has published more than 200 has been no easy task. We have tried to use the following criteria; (i) the paper has made an original contribution to disability studies, (ii) it fits in with the themes and issues discussed in Section 1, and (iii) the popularity of the papers amongst the readership. This is not to imply that the papers not included are deficient in one or more of these ways but the process of selection has been an extremely difficult one.

The papers by Borsay and Barton were important in that they attempted to apply newly emerging disability perspectives to social policy and education respectively. Borsay takes the social model of disability as her organising theme and Barton uses his own personal experience to inform debates about special, and indeed by implication, all forms of education.

Abberley and Liggett, in their papers made key contributions to the development of disability theory; the former drawing upon marxist, feminist and anti-racist perspectives and the latter utilising post-modernist perspectives and particularly the work of Foucault.

The next two papers look at the issue of politics. Oliver and Zarb provide a critique of existing models of political representation and suggest that new social movement theory is a better way of conceptualising disability politics. Shakespeare provides a similar critique of cultural representations of disabled people and argues that the negative imagery which predominates has to be challenged by developing a cultural politics of disability.

PART THREE

The Current Issues section posed similar problems in that since its inception it has served as a vehicle for debating a wide range of issues, for allowing disabled people a voice on issues that are important to them, for incorporating pieces from across the world and much more. Our selections here are chosen mainly to fit in with issues raised throughout the rest of the book in order to give it an overall coherence.

The first three papers appeared side by side and reflect a debate that began at an international conference held at the University of Leeds in 1995. All three provide differing views on the nature of the research enterprise and discuss issues that have been of concern throughout the life of the Journal.

INTRODUCTION

The paper by Vernon returns to the theme of oppression originally raised by Abberley and discussed subsequently by Stuart and Morris in the Special Edition on disability research already referred to.

The final three papers again appeared side by side and provide some of the latest thinking on debates around the social model of disability currently occurring both amongst disabled people themselves and within academic circles.

We hope this book will be widely read and provide a stimulus for reflection and debate and thereby contribute to the development of disability studies as a serious field of study and research.

PART ONE

CHAPTER 1

A Legacy of Oppression:

A History of Disability in Western Culture

By Colin Barnes

> *'The one duty we owe to history is to rewrite it'.*
>
> *(Oscar Wilde, 1890, The Critic as Artist).*

INTRODUCTION

Over the last few years interest in the social and political dimensions of disablement has intensified considerably both at the general level and in universities and academic institutions. The inclusion of disabled people – people with perceived impairments whether physical, sensory or intellectual – into the mainstream of economic and social life is now a major issue for policy makers and politicians in both rich and poor countries alike; indeed, many now have some form of legislative framework with which to combat discrimination on the grounds of impairment (Doyle, 1995; NOG, 1996; Stone, 1996).

This has had a significant impact within colleges of further and higher education – particularly in Canada and the USA (Pfeiffer and Yoshida, 1994). As a consequence, there is a growing literature on the various barriers to inclusion and the experience of disablement; recent examples include Barnes (1991), Hales (1996), Morris (1996), French (1994), and Zarb (1995). Yet relatively little has been written on the origins of these barriers; particularly, with reference to the period before industrialisation. This is important because to appreciate fully the extent and significance of the oppression* of disabled people an understanding of history and its relationship to western culture: the central value system around which western society is clustered, is vital (Barnes, 1990; 1991; 1996).

It is vital because for many, both disabled and non-disabled people, the biggest obstacle to disabled people's meaningful inclusion into mainstream community life is negative public attitudes. These range from overt prejudice and hostility, condescension and pity to ignorance and indifference, and in these diverse ways they influence how we think about both ourselves and other people. In the broadest sense there are two explanations for this phenomenon. The first, and the older of the two, suggests that cultural perceptions of impairment are shaped by deep rooted psychological fears of the abnormal and the unknown. The second, explains disabled people's oppression in terms of material considerations such as the economy and the way that it is organised or what is sometimes termed 'the mode of production'.

In this chapter I will present the case for the latter. I will suggest that contemporary attitudes toward people with perceived impairments have their roots in the ancient world of the Greeks and Romans, and that this can be explained with reference to material rather than metaphysical forces. It is divided into two distinct but inter-related sections. The first section, provides a brief overview of socio-political approaches to disability. The second part centres on cultural responses to people with perceived impairments in western society before the onset of industrialisation with particular reference to Britain – the birthplace of industrial capitalism (Marx, 1970). I conclude by suggesting that to eliminate oppression, in all its forms, we must confront the value system upon which western capitalism rests.

*For a full detailed discussion of the concept of oppression and the social theory of disability see Paul Abberley (1987).

SOCIAL THEORIES OF DISABILITY

It is important at the outset to distinguish between the traditional individualistic medical approach to disability and the socio/political approaches discussed below. Within the context of sociology, the former, recently termed the 'socio/medical model of disability' by Bury (1996), is rooted in the work of the American sociologist Parsons and his discussion of sickness and sickness related behaviour. Writing in the late 1940s, Parsons argued that the normal state of being in western developed societies is 'good health', consequently sickness, and by implication impairments, are deviations from 'normality'. Subsequently, sociologists, particularly medical sociologists, have focused almost exclusively on the experience of 'illness', whether chronic or acute, and the social consequences which flow from it rather than the environmental and social barriers faced by disabled people, and the politicisation of disability by disabled people and organisations controlled and run by them (Barnes and Mercer, 1996).

Yet in Britain the politicisation of disability by disabled people and their organisations can be traced back to the nineteenth century (Campbell and Oliver, 1996; Pagel, 1988) and the reconceptualisation of disability as a socio/political rather than an individual/medical problem has its roots in the work of disabled people themselves in the early 1960s (Miller and Gwynne 1972; Oliver, 1990; Finkelstein, 1991).

Moreover, socio/political theories of disability can be divided into two distinct but linked traditions; one American and the other British. The first draws heavily on American functionalism and deviance theory, and explains the 'social construction' of the problem of disability as an outcome of the evolution of contemporary society. The second is rooted on the materialist analysis of history associated with Marx (1970) and maintains that disability and dependence are the 'social creation' of industrial capitalism (see Oliver, 1990). Both approaches have been criticised for their neglect of the role of culture by a 'second generation' of British writers concerned primarily with the experience, rather than the production, of both impairment and disability.

I. DISABILITY AND THE EVOLUTION OF WESTERN SOCIETY

Drawing on the work of Parsons (1951) American sociologists during the 1960s explored the relationship between perceived impairment and disability.

By focusing on the process of stigmatisation and the social construction of dependence by rehabilitation professionals, writers such as Erving Goffman (1968) and Robert Scott (1970) challenged the orthodox view that the problems associated with disability were the inevitable outcome of individually based impairments and/or medical conditions. These insights coupled with the radicalisation of young disabled Americans in the Movement for Independent Living (ILM) led Gerben de Jong to proclaim that attitudinal and environmental factors are at least as important as impairment in the assessment of disability (de Jong, 1979).

Subsequently, through a largely historical account of social policy in America, Britain and Germany, Stone (1984) developed the argument further. She claims that all societies function through a complex system of commodity production and distribution; the principal means of allocation being work. However, because many people are unable or unwilling to work a second system based on perceptions of need emerges. Access to this needs based system is based on both medical and political considerations determined by medical and rehabilitation professionals. Consequently for Stone, the 'social construction of disability' is the result of the accumulation of power by the medical profession and the state's need to restrict access to the state sponsored welfare system.

Wolfensberger extends the analysis further. By focusing on the recent experience of western societies, he suggests that the social construction of disability and dependence is a latent function of the unprecedented growth of 'human service industries' in the post-1945 period. Although all these agencies have manifest or stated purposes or functions, it is the latent or unacknowledged functions which are the most powerful. These are the covert functions of human services that are achieved in subtle and indirect ways. Wolfensberger maintains that in a 'post-primary production economy' such as America or Britain where human service industries have become increasingly important, their unspecified function is to create and sustain large numbers of dependent and devalued people in order to secure employment for others. This is in marked contrast to their stated function which is to rehabilitate such people back into the community (Wolfensberger, 1989).

The argument is taken one stage further by Albrecht (1992). In contrast to perceptions of disability as a medical condition, a form of social deviance, and/or a political or minority group issue, Albrecht argues that 'disability' is produced by 'the disability business'. Using the limited anthropological and historical sources available, Albrecht shows how the kind of society in which people live produce certain types of disease, impairment and disability. He traces the ways in which the economy and how it is organised causes particular bio-physical conditions and effects social interpretations of impairment. Due to the growth of the human service industries and the politicisation of disability by the disabled people's movement, Albrecht asserts that in modern America 'disability' and 'rehabilitation' have been commodified and transformed into a commercial enterprise.

Clearly, each of the above represents, to varying degrees, an alternative to orthodox individualistic interpretations of disability, they each fail to address some of the key structural factors precipitating their application. Notably, Albrecht concedes that issues such as poverty, race, ethnicity, gender and age are significant factors in the construction and production of disability and dependence, but the central value system upon which western capitalism rests – liberal utilitarianism, competitive free enterprise, and uncontrolled consumerism, for example – goes unchallenged. In a later paper (1994) Wolfensberger addresses what he terms 'modernistic values' but these are the direct outcome of what he calls the collapse of western society in the latter half of the twentieth century (?).

For each of these writers, therefore, the problem of 'disability' is the outcome of the evolution of western industrial society.

II. DISABILITY AND INDUSTRIAL CAPITALISM

A more radical assessment can be found in the work of British authors; many of whom are disabled people themselves. In an important and often overlooked essay on the experience of disability entitled 'A Critical Condition' (1966), for example, the disabled activist Paul Hunt argues that because people with impairments are viewed as 'unfortunate, useless, different, oppressed and sick' they pose a direct challenge to commonly held western values.

For Hunt, people with impairments are 'unfortunate' because they are seen as unable to 'enjoy' the material and social benefits of modern society. Because of the centrality of work in western culture they are viewed as 'useless' since they are considered not able to contribute to the 'economic good of the community'. Such people are then marked out as members of a 'minority group' in a similar position to other oppressed groups such as black people or 'homosexuals' because, like them, they are perceived as 'abnormal' and 'different'. This led Hunt to the contention that disabled people encounter 'prejudice which expresses itself in discrimination and oppression' (p. 152).

Besides the inhuman treatment he had witnessed in British residential institutions, Hunt draws attention to discrimination against people with impairments in the wider community; notably, in employment, in restaurants, and in marital relationships. The final element of disabled people's 'challenge' to 'able bodied' values is that they are 'sick, suffering, diseased, in pain'; in short, they represent everything that the 'normal world' most fears – 'tragedy, loss, dark, and the unknown' (Hunt, 1966, p. 155). The relationship between material considerations and cultural perceptions of disabled people is central to Hunt's understanding of the experience of impairment and disability in western society.

Almost a decade later the Union of the Physically Impaired Against Segregation (UPIAS), of which Hunt was a member, made the important distinction between impairment and disability. The former, in common with the traditional medical approach, relates to individually based bio-physical conditions, but the latter is about the exclusion of disabled people from 'normal' or mainstream society. Thus, disability is

'the disadvantage or restriction of activity caused by a contemporary social organisation which takes no or little account of people who have physical impairments and thus excludes them from participation in the mainstream of social activities' (UPIAS, 1976, p. 14).

This definition was later broadened to accommodate all impairments – physical, sensory, and intellectual – by other organisations of disabled people such as the British Council of Disabled People (BCODP); Britain's national umbrella for organisations controlled and run by disabled people (Barnes, 1991) and the Disabled People's International; the international equivalent of the BCODP (Driedger, 1989). The disabled writer Mike Oliver (1983) later referred to this new found focus on the way society is organised as an explanation for the multiple deprivations encountered by disabled people as the 'social model of disability'.

However, a disabled South African exile and psychologist living in Britain, Vic Finkelstein (1980) – also a founder member of UPIAS – argued that disability is the direct result of the development of western industrial society. Using a largely materialist analysis Finkelstein divides history into three distinct sequential phases. The first, Phase One, broadly corresponds to the feudal period which preceded European industrialisation. Here economic activity consisted primarily of agrarian or cottage based industries; a 'mode of production', he maintains, which does not preclude people with perceived impairments from participation.

But in Phase Two, round about the nineteenth century, when industrialisation took hold, people with impairments were excluded from employment on the grounds that they were unable to keep pace with the new factory based work system. Hence, they were segregated from the mainstream of economic and social activity into a variety of residential institutions. Finkelstein's third Phase, which he maintains is only just beginning, will see the eventual liberation of disabled people from such oppression through the development and use of technology, and their working together with helpers and allies toward commonly held goals.

For Finkelstein, therefore, disability is a paradox emerging out of the development of western capitalist society. On the one hand, disability implies 'a personal tragedy, passivity and dependence' (Finkelstein, 1980, p.1). On the other, it can be seen as societal restriction and discrimination. In Phase One, people with impairments were dispersed throughout the community; but in Phase Two, due to the emergence of large scale industry with production lines geared to 'able bodied norms' and 'hospital based medicine' (p. 10), they were separated from their social origins into a clearly defined devalued group. Phase Three will witness the end of the paradox as disability will be recognised as social restriction only.

Although intended as an aid to understanding rather than an accurate historical statement, Finkelstein's analysis has been criticised for being over-simplistic and over-optimistic. It is over-simplistic in that it assumes a simple relationship between the mode of production and perceptions and experiences of disability. It is too optimistic in its assumption that technological development and professional involvement will integrate disabled people back into society. Technology for disabled people can be disempowering as well as empowering and, hitherto, professional vested interests have proved one of the biggest barriers to disabled people's empowerment (Barnes, 1990; Oliver, 1986; 1990; 1996).

A more extensive evaluation of the transition to capitalism and its implications for disabled people is provided (Oliver, 1990). Drawing on each of the above he provides a materialist account of the creation of disability which places 'ideology' – a set of values based on 'scientific rationality' rather than religious or common-sense interpretations which influence culture and popular beliefs – at the centre of his argument. Hence, economic development, the changing nature of ideas, and the need to maintain order during industrialisation influenced social responses to and, therefore, the experience of impairment. The rise of the institution as a means of both social provision and control coupled with the individualisation and medicalisation of 'social problems' under capitalism resulted in the emergence of the individualistic medical approach to disability. For Oliver this 'personal tragedy theory' of disability has, in turn, achieved 'ideological hegemony' (Gramsci, 1971) in that it has become translated into common sense and everyday assumptions and beliefs.

It is evident that unlike the work of their American counterparts these accounts suggest that the basis of disabled people's oppression is founded upon the material and ideological changes which occurred as a result of the emergence of capitalist society.

III. DISABILITY, IMPAIRMENT AND CULTURE

In recent years the determinist approach of Finkelstein and Oliver has been criticised for its neglect of the individual experiences of disabled people – notably with reference to gender (Morris, 1991; 1996), minority ethnic status (Stuart, 1993; Begum et al., 1994) and impairment (Crow, 1992; 1996; French, 1993; 1994; Shakespeare, 1994) by a new generation of writers working from within a mainly feminist or postmodernist framework. With little apparent regard for previous work in the field produced by both medical sociologists and disabled people themselves (Barnes, 1996a), these writers have called for the renewal of the 'social model' of disability to include the diversity of experiences within the disabled community. Echoing many of these concerns, the disabled sociologist Shakespeare (1994) has argued that this might best be achieved by a more rigorous analysis of the role of culture in the oppression of disabled people.

Following the work of the disabled feminist, Morris (1991), Shakespeare contends that people with perceived impairments are not simply disabled by material discrimination but also by prejudice. Not simply interpersonal, this prejudice is implicit in cultural representation, in language and in socialisation. Drawing on the work of other feminist writers such as Simone de Beauvoir (1976) he explains this prejudice with reference to the objectification of disabled people as 'other' or visible evidence of the limitations of the body. He cites historical images such as the court jester, the freak show, the asylum and the Nazi death camps as examples of this objectification (Shakespeare, 1994). For Shakespeare, the history of the oppression of people with accredited impairments can only be explained with reference to the work of cultural anthropologists like Mary Douglas (1966) and Robert Murphy (1987).

Responding to deep rooted psychological fears of the unknown, Douglas maintains, that 'primitive' societies respond to anomalies such as perceived impairment by reducing ambiguity, physically controlling it, avoiding it, labelling it dangerous, or adopting it as ritual (Douglas, 1966). Similarly, Robert Murphy utilises Victor Turner's (1967) concept of 'liminality' to explain the position of people with impairments in all societies. Hence, they live in a constant state of social suspension neither:

> 'sick' nor 'well', 'dead' nor 'alive', 'out of society nor wholly in it.... they exist in partial isolation from society as undefined, ambiguous people' (Murphy, 1987, p. 112).

Adopting a similar position to that of Susan Griffin (1984), who explains women's and black people's oppression, in terms of their relationship to the body, instinct and sensuality, rather than the economy and exploitation, Shakespeare extends the analysis to include disabled people, gay men and lesbians. Thus, it is not 'disability' that non-disabled people fear but impairment as 'disabled people remind non-disabled people of their own mortality'. They are, therefore, a threat – either, as Douglas (1966) suggests, to order, or, to the self perception of western humans who view themselves as 'perfectible, all knowing ... over and above all human beings'. Shakespeare concludes by suggesting that this 'ethic of invincibility' is linked directly to notions of masculinity and potency (Shakespeare, 1994, p. 298).

In terms of advancing our understanding of the significance of culture in the oppression of disabled people, particularly with respect to perceptions of impairment, Shakespeare's analysis may be seen as something of a step forward. He, rightly, suggests that the cultural roots of disabled people's oppression in western society pre-dates the emergence of capitalism. However, the main difficulty with his analysis is that by endorsing Douglas' and Murphy's largely phenomenological approach, like them, he implies that all cultures respond to impairment in essentially negative terms. In other words, prejudice against people with apparent impairments is, in one way or another, universal and, by implication, inevitable.

Now there are at least two major problems with this approach. First, there is ample anthropological evidence to show that all societies do not respond to apparent impairment in exactly the same way – some of which dates back to the turn of the twentieth century. Two notable examples are the Dalegura, a group of Australian Aborigines (Hastings, 1918-1921), and the Kenyan Masai.

In both societies life is routinely harsh by western standards, yet infanticide is prohibited, age is considered a sign of authority and respect, and individuals with impairments are not rejected or excluded. Indeed, the anthropologist Aud Talle writes:

> 'The fact that an individual is impaired in one way or another is just an aspect of his/her person, but does not make any difference in social and cultural terms. Certainly Masai notice 'disabilities' and look upon them as bad or unfortunate things... They both name the difference and mark it, but.... this indicates acceptance and lack of fear of the different or abnormal. To give birth to a disabled child is not culturally defined as a crisis requiring specific actions and precautions. It is part of life's experience' (Talle, 1995, p. 71).

Secondly, Shakespeare's approach reduces explanations for cultural perceptions of people with perceived impairments as abnormal to the level of metaphysics or thought processes. Besides successfully attracting attention away from economic and social conditions this analysis also implies that the marginalisation of those perceived in this way is somehow unavoidable – regardless of what we do. In other words, the struggle for real and meaningful change is doomed to failure.

The following section will provide an account of the history of the social oppression of people with perceived impairments in western society with particular emphasis on the British experience. I will suggest that the roots of disabled people's oppression lie in the ancient world of Greece and Rome, and that this oppression is culturally produced through the complex interaction between 'the mode of production and the central values of the society concerned' (Oliver, 1990, p. 34).

A MATERIALIST ACCOUNT OF THE ORIGINS OF DISABILITY IN WESTERN CULTURE

As mentioned earlier, until very recently relatively little has been written about the history of the oppression of disabled people within the context of western culture. It is likely that there are several explanations for this omission; including a general lack of accessible information, and/or a dearth of historians, disabled or otherwise, with a particular interest in the field. It is worth remembering too that history is usually sponsored, written, and/or invented, by the powerful (Hobsbawm and Ranger, 1983) and, therefore, has a tendency to reflect their interests rather than those of the powerless. Perhaps unsurprisingly then historical accounts of 'disability' and the lives of disabled people have been ignored or, more recently, been dominated by an overtly individualistic medical perspective (Lupton, 1994; Wear, 1992). Nonetheless, there is evidence of a consistent cultural bias against people with accredited impairments in the antecedents of what we now refer to as western society long before the emergence of industrial capitalism. Examples can be found in Greek culture, Judean/Christian religions and European drama and art since well before the Renaissance (Barnes, 1990; 1991; 1992; Thomas, 1982).

I. DISABILITY IN THE ANCIENT WORLD OF GREECE AND ROME

It is widely acknowledged that the foundations of western 'civilisation' were laid by the ancient Greeks. Their achievements in philosophy, the arts, and in architecture have had a profound effect on the culture of the entire western world (Devonport, 1995; Risbero, 1975). As Oscar Wilde so cogently pointed out in 1890

'Whatever, in fact, is modern in our life we owe to the Greeks' (Wilde, 1966, p. 1019).

It is often overlooked, however, that the Greek economy was built on slavery and it was an overtly patriarchal, hierarchical, and violent society. Whilst the Greeks are universally renowned for asserting citizenship rights and the dignity of the individual; these were only extended to Greek males – women and non-Greeks were considered inferior. This enables the 'civilised' man to justify oppression and exploitation. The Greeks were also a violent race ever prone to war – military service for Greek males was obligatory. Greek society was made up of a collection of semi-autonomous city states often at war with each other and or with their neighbours – to some extent this was necessary in order to maintain a constant supply of slaves. Further, ever pessimistic over the fate of the soul after death they asserted the importance of enjoyment of the pleasures of the physical world (Cahn, 1990; Russell, 1981).

In this type of society the pursuit of physical and intellectual fitness was essential; there was little room for people with any form of flaw or imperfection. The Greek obsession with bodily perfection, which can be traced back to 700-675 BC. (Dutton, 1996), found expression in prescribed infanticide for children with perceived imperfections, in education, the Gymnasium, and in competitive sports.

Infanticide in the form of exposure to the elements for sickly or weak infants was widespread and in some states mandatory (Tooley, 1983). A reflection of established Greek practice can be found in a section entitled 'How to recognise a child that is worth raising' in *Gynaecology* written by a Greek physician, Soranos, in the second century AD. The child:

> 'should be perfect in all its parts, limbs and senses, and have passages that are not obstructed, including the ears, nose, throat urethra and anus. Its natural movements be neither slow nor feeble, its limbs bend and stretch, its size and shape should be appropriate, and it should respond to natural stimuli (Garland, 1995, p. 14).

Greek males were expected to compete both individually and collectively in the pursuit of physical and intellectual excellence in gymnasiums, amphitheatres and, of course, the Olympic Games.

These preoccupations were reflected in Greek philosophy and culture. The Greek gods and goddesses were perceived not as divine beings in anthropomorphic form but rather as 'idealised representations of perfected humanity' (Dutton, 1996, p. 25). It is significant that there was only one physically flawed God, Hephaestes, the son of Zeus and Hera. Indeed, Zeus practised a sort of infanticide by banishing his son from heaven. Later Aphrodite, the goddess of love, takes pity on Hephaestes and marries him. Yet the marriage did not last as she takes an able-bodied lover, Ares, because her husband is a 'cripple'. The now familiar association between impairment, exclusion and impotency is clear. Moreover, the link between impairment as a punishment for sin also has its roots in Greek culture. For example, Sophocles' famous tale of Oedipus Rex who, after discovering he has committed incest by marrying his mother, blinds himself as retribution.

Following their conquest of Greece, the Romans absorbed and passed on the Greek legacy to the rest of the known world as their empire expanded. Moreover, ancient Rome was also a slave based economy, espoused individual citizenship rights, was highly militaristic, and had both materialistic and hedonistic values. The Romans too were enthusiastic advocates of infanticide for 'sickly' or 'weak' children drowning them in the river Tiber. Like the Greeks, they treated harshly anyone whose impairments were not visible at birth. People of short stature and deaf people were considered objects of curiosity or ridicule. In the infamous Roman games 'dwarfs' and 'blind men' fought women and animals for the amusement of the Roman people. Even the

disabled Emperor Claudius, who escaped death at birth only because he was
from the highest echelon of Roman society, was subject to abuse from both the
Roman nobility and Roman Guards prior to his ascendancy to the imperial
throne. Even his mother, Antonia, treated him with contempt and referred to
him as 'a monster of a man, not finished by nature and only half done'
(Garland, 1995, p. 41).

However, both the Greeks and Romans developed 'scientifically' based
treatments for people with acquired impairments. Aristotle, for example,
attempted to study deafness and Galen and Hypocrites tried to cure epilepsy
which they saw as a physiological rather than a metaphysical problem. The
Romans developed elaborate hydrotherapy and fitness therapies for acquired
conditions. But in each of these societies such treatments were only generally
available to the rich and powerful (Albrecht, 1992; Garland, 1995).

II. DISABILITY AND JUDEAN/CHRISTIAN RELIGIONS

Several of these traits are reflected in Judean/Christian religions – often seen
as the principal source of contemporary western moral values. Influenced by
Greek society since, at least, the time of Alexander the Great (Douglas, 1966)
the Jewish culture of the ancient world perceived impairments as un-Godly
and the consequence of wrongdoing. Much of Leviticus is devoted to a
catalogue of human imperfections which preclude the possessor from
approaching or participating in any form of religious ritual:

> 'None of your descendants throughout their generations who has a blemish may
> approach to offer the bread of his God. For no-one who has a blemish shall draw near, a
> man blind or lame, or one who has a mutilated face or a limb too long, or a man who
> has an injured hand, or a hunch back or a dwarf, or a man with a defect in his sight or
> an itching disease or scabs or crushed testicles' (Leviticus, 21. 16-20).

Biblical text is replete with references to impairment as the consequences of
wrongdoing. The Old Testament, for instance, states that if humans are
immoral then they will be blinded by God (Deuteronomy, 27-27). These
traditions are continued in the New Testament too. In the book of Matthew,
for example, Jesus cures a man with palsy after proclaiming that his sins are
forgiven (9-2).

But unlike other major religions of the period the Jewish faith prohibited
infanticide. This became a key feature of subsequent derivatives, Christianity

and Islam, as did the custom of 'caring' for the 'sick' and the 'less fortunate' either through alms giving or the provision of 'direct care' (Davis, 1989). However, the opposition to infanticide and the institutionalisation of charity is probably related to the fact that Jewish society was not a particularly wealthy society. It was predominantly a pastoral economy dependent upon the rearing of herds of cattle, goats and sheep, as well as on commercial trade. In addition, unlike their neighbours, the Jewish people were a relatively peaceful race, prone to oppression themselves rather than the oppression of others. In such a society people with impairments would almost certainly have been able to make some kind of contribution to the economy and the well-being of the community (Albrecht, 1992). Furthermore, in its infancy Christianity was a religion of the underprivileged; notably, 'slaves and women', charity, therefore, was fundamental to its appeal and, indeed, its very survival. Nonetheless, being presented as objects of charity effectively robbed disabled people of the claim to individuality and full human status. Consequently, they became the perfect vehicle for the overt sentimentality and benevolence of others – usually the priesthood, the great and the good.

III. DISABILITY AND EARLY ENGLISH HISTORY

Following the fall of Rome in the fifth century AD Western Europe was engulfed by turmoil, conflict and pillage. Throughout 'the Dark Ages' the British Isles were made up of a myriad of everchanging kingdoms and allegiances in which the only unifying force was the Christian Church. Given the violent character of this period it is likely that social responses to people with impairments were equally harsh. But by the thirteenth century, and in contrast to much of the rest of Europe, a degree of stability had been established in the British Isles. Furthermore, there is substantial documentary evidence that in England, a separate kingdom since the tenth century, all the prerequisites of a capitalist economy without factories were already firmly in place. These included a developed market economy, a geographically mobile labour force, and the commodification of land.

> 'Full private ownership had been established (and) rational accounting and the profit motive were widespread' (Macfarlane, 1979, p.196).

An indication of English society's attitude to dependence, and by implication impairment, is evident in the property transfer agreements of the period.

When surrendering property rights to their children elderly parents were often forced to ask for very specific rights in return. For

'it is clear that without legal protection in a written document they could have been ejected from the property which was no longer their own' (Macfarlane, 1979, p.141).

Until the seventeenth century, people rejected by their families and without resources relied exclusively on the haphazard and often ineffectual tradition of Christian charity for subsistence. People with 'severe' impairments were usually admitted to one of the very small medieval hospitals in which were gathered 'the poor, the sick and the bedridden'. The ethos of these establishments was ecclesiastical rather than medical (Scull, 1984).

However, during the sixteenth century the wealth and power of the English Church was greatly reduced because of a series of unsuccessful political confrontations with the Crown. There was also a steady growth in the numbers of people dependent on charity. This was the result of a growing population following depletion due to plagues, successive poor harvests, and an influx of immigrants from Ireland and Wales (Stone, 1984). Hence, the fear of 'bands of sturdy beggars' prompted local magistrates to demand an appropriate response from the central authority; the Crown (Trevelyan, 1948). To secure allegiance the Tudor monarchs made economic provision for those hitherto dependent upon the Church. The Poor Law of 1601, therefore, is the first official recognition of the need for state intervention in the lives of people with perceived impairments. But a general suspicion of people dependent on charity had already been established by the statute of 1388 which mandated local officials to discriminate between the 'deserving' and the 'undeserving' poor (Stone, 1984).

Moreover, although 'English individualism' was well entrenched by the thirteenth century the Church remained a formidable force in English and European culture. Besides offering forgiveness and a democratic afterlife in a frequently hostile world where for many life could be 'nasty, brutish and short' (Hobbes, 1983) the Christian Church asserted and retained its authority by propagating and perpetuating fear – fear of the Devil and of his influence. The biblical link between impairment, impurity and sin was central to this process. Indeed, St Augustine, the man credited with bringing Christianity to mainland Britain at the end of the sixth century AD, claimed that impairment was 'a punishment for the fall of Adam and other sins' (Ryan and Thomas, 1987, p. 87).

Disabled people provided living proof of Satan's existence and of his power over humans. Thus, visibly impaired children were seen as 'changelings' – the Devil's substitutes for human children. The Malleus Maleficarum of 1487 declared that such children were the product of the mother's involvement with sorcery and witchcraft. The religious leader and scholar accredited with the formation of the Protestant Reformation, Martin Luther (1485 – 1546), proclaimed he saw the Devil in a disabled child; he recommended killing them (Haffter, 1968).

These beliefs were also reflected in medieval literature and art. Probably the most famous example is Shakespeare's *Richard III* written in the late sixteenth century. Although Richard had no physical impairments (Reiser, 1992) Shakespeare portrays him as twisted in both body and mind. Since he cannot succeed as a lover because of his perceived physical limitations he is compelled to succeed as a villain. As in the ancient world, people with impairments were also primary targets for amusement and ridicule during the Middle Ages. Analysis of the joke books of Tudor and Stuart England shows the extent of this practice. Besides references to the other mainstays of 'popular' humour such as foreigners, women, and the clergy, every impairment 'from idiocy to insanity to diabetes and bad breath was a welcome source of amusement (Thomas, 1977, pp. 80-81). Children and adults with physical abnormalities were often put on display at village fairs (Nicholli, 1990) visits to Bedlam were a common source of amusement, and the practice of keeping 'idiots' as objects of entertainment was prevalent among the wealthy (Ryan and Thomas, 1987).

IV. DISABILITY, INDUSTRIALISATION AND SCIENTIFIC RATIONALITY

The eighteenth century witnessed a significant intensification of the commercialisation of land and agriculture, and the beginnings of industrialisation. It also precipitated the emergence of the Enlightenment and Liberal Utilitarianism. Enlightenment thinkers across Europe such as David Hume, Immanuel Kant, Jean-Jacques Rousseau, and François Voltaire developed a range of progressive ideas including a critique of established religions, an emphasis on the value of 'reason' and 'science', a commitment to social progress, and the importance of individuality. Developed in England by Jeremy Bentham and John Stuart Mill, Liberal Utilitarianism is a philosophy of secular individual and rational self-interest. In political terms, it legitimates policies favouring the majority at the expense of the few (Berlin, 1968).

Taken together these developments provided a new found legitimacy for already well-established myths and practices from earlier 'less enlightened' times. Thus, the nineteenth century is synonymous with the emergence of 'disability' in its present form. This includes the systematic individualisation and medicalisation of the body and the mind (Armstrong, 1983; Foucault, 1975), the exclusion of people with apparent impairments from the mainstream of community life into all manner of institutional settings (Scull, 1984) and, with the emergence of 'Social Darwinism', the 'Eugenics Movement', and, later, 'social hygiene' 'scientific' reification of the age old myth that, in one way or another, people with any form of physical and or intellectual imperfections pose a serious threat to western society. The 'logical' outcome of this was the proliferation of Eugenic ideals throughout the western world during the first half of the twentieth century (Jones, 1987; Kevles, 1985), and the systematic murder of thousands of disabled people in the Nazi death camps of the 1930s and 40s (Burleigh, 1995; Gallagher, 1990). It is important to remember too that Marxist Communism also has its roots firmly planted in the material and ideological developments which characterised eighteenth- and nineteenth-century Europe, and that many of its principal protagonists, both in Britain and overseas, embraced eugenic ideals as an essential corollary of the 'Utopian' hope for a better society.

However, the nineteenth-century was also significant for an upsurge of Christian charity and 'humanitarian' values among the Victorian middle and upper classes. As a consequence several charities controlled and run by non-disabled people 'for' disabled people were founded during this period. One example is the British and Foreign Association for Promoting the Education of the Blind, now known as the Royal National Institute for the Blind (RNIB), which was set up in 1863 (RNIB, 1990).

As has been well documented elsewhere, the legacy of much if not all of this remains with us today.

CONCLUSION

It is clear from the above that to appreciate fully the extent and complexity of the oppression of disabled people within contemporary society an insight into the material and social forces which shaped western culture is essential. It is essential because for most, both disabled and non-disabled, people the biggest barrier to disabled people's inclusion into mainstream economic and social activity is the attitudinal barrier. In this paper I have argued that this is little more than a reflection of western cultural values, and that this value system has its roots in the complex interplay between the economy and the culture of the ancient world of Greece and Rome, rather than the material and ideological changes which engulfed Europe and the western world in the eighteenth and nineteenth centuries.

This is not to suggest that negative attitudes are peculiar only to western culture, nor that people with apparent impairments have always been rejected within the context of everyday life in societies which appear to adhere to it. As mentioned earlier, cultural responses to people with perceived impairments are by no means universal; whilst there are several examples of cultures which accommodate the needs of so called disabled people, there are others which do not. Moreover, although infanticide for children with visible impairments has consistently characterised western cultural development, it is evident that such people have existed throughout recorded history. There are several reasons for this. Notably, human beings are not simply 'cultural dupes'. It is likely, therefore, that many parents rejected such practices and supported their disabled offspring. Also, the overwhelming majority of impairments are acquired rather than congenital; either through accident, illness or, simply, old age. Thus, ensuring that the experience of impairment was and is a common rather than an exceptional occurrence. This was certainly the case in the Graeco/Roman world where life was extremely harsh for all but the most privileged – high born, well-to-do males in perfect health.

However, in contrast to those who would problematise that which it is not necessarily problematic, some of whom are mentioned above, it is an attempt to provide a clear and understandable focus on that which can and should be changed: specifically, a value system which is rooted in a particular type of society, which is clustered around a particular view of the human condition, and which, in one way or another, oppresses all of us who are unwilling or unable to conform to its requirements.

REFERENCES

ABBERLEY, P. (1987) 'The Concept of Oppression and the Development of a Social Theory of Disability' in *Disability, Handicap and Society*, 2, 1, pp. 5 – 21.

ALBRECHT, G. L. (1992) *The Disability Business* London, Sage.

ARMSTRONG, D. (1983) *The Political Anatomy of the Body* Cambridge, Cambridge University Press.

BARNES, C. (1990) *Cabbage Syndrome: The Social Construction of Dependence* Lewes, Falmer.

BARNES, C. (1991) *Disabled People in Britain and Discrimination: A Case for Anti discrimination Legislation* Hurst and Co in Association with the British Council of Organisations of Disabled People, London.

BARNES, C. (1996) 'Theories of Disability and the Origins of the Social Oppression of Disabled People in Western Society' in BARTON, L. (ed.) (1996) *Disability and Society: Emerging Issues and Insights* London, Longman.

BARNES, C. (1996a) 'The Social Model of Disability: Myths and Misrepresentations' *Coalition* August, pp. 25-30.

BARNES, C. and MERCER, G. (1996) *Exploring the Divide: Illness and Disability* Leeds, The Disability Press.

BARTON, L. (ed.) (1996) *Disability and Society: Emerging Issues and Insights* London, Longmans.

BERLIN, I. (1956) *The Age of Enlightenment* New York, Mentor.

BEGUM, N. *et al.*, (eds.) (1994) *Reflections* London, Central Council for the Education and Training of Social Workers.

BURLEIGH, M. (1994) *Death and Deliverance: Euthanasia in Germany 1900-1945* Cambridge, Cambridge University Press.

BURY, M. (1996) 'Defining and Researching Disability; challenges and responses' in BARNES, C. and MERCER, G. (1996) *Exploring the Divide: Illness and Disability* Leeds, The Disability Press, pp. 17-38.

CAHN, M. (ed.) (1990) *Classics of Western Philosophy: 3rd Edition* Indianapolis, Cambridge.

CAMPBELL, J. and OLIVER, M. (1996) *Disability Politics: Understanding Our Past, Changing Our Future* London, Routledge.

CROW, L. (1992) 'Renewing the Social Model of Disability' *Coalition* July, pp. 5-9.

CROW, L. (1996) 'Including all of Our Lives: renewing the social model of disability' in BARNES, C. and MERCER, G. (1996) *Exploring the Divide: Illness and Disability* Leeds, The Disability Press, pp. 55-74.

DAVIS, A. (1989) *From Where I Sit: Living With Disability in an Able Bodied World* London, Triangle.

DE BEAUVOIR, S. (1976) *The Second Sex* Harmondsworth, Penguin.

DE JONG, G. (1979) 'The Movement for Independent Living: Origins, Ideology and Implications for Disability Research' in BRECHIN. A, and LIDDIARD, P. (1983) *Handicap in a Social World* Milton Keynes, Hodder and Stoughton in Association with the Open University Press, pp. 239-248.

DEVONPORT, J. (1995) 'Part M, Access and Disabled People', a seminar paper presented in the *Disability Research Unit in the School of Sociology and Social Policy*, University of Leeds, 10 February.

DOUGLAS, M. (1966) *Purity and Danger* London, Routledge and Kegan Paul.

DOYLE, B. (1995) *Disability, Discrimination and Equal Opportunities* London, Mansell.

DREIDGER, D. (1989) *The Last Civil Rights Movement* London, Hurst and Co.

DUTTON, K. (1996) *The Perfectable Body* London, Cassell.

FINKELSTEIN, V. (1980) *Attitudes and Disabled People* Geneva, World Health Organization.

FOUCAULT, M. (1975) *The Birth of the Clinic; An Archeology of Medical Perception* New York, Vantage Books.

FRENCH, S. (1993) 'Disability, Impairment or Something In-between' in SWAIN, J, et al. *Disabling Barriers: Enabling Environments* London, Sage, pp. 1726.

FRENCH, S. (ed.) (1994) *On Equal Terms: Working With Disabled People* Oxford, Butterworth Heinemann.

GALLAGHER, H. G. (1990) *By Trust Betrayed: Patients and Physicians in the Third Reich* London, Henry Holt.

GARLAND, R. R. J. (1995) *The Eye of the Beholder: Deformity and Disability in the Graeco-Roman World* London, Duckworth.

GOFFMAN, E. (1968) *Stigma: Notes on the Management of Spoiled Identity* Harmondsworth, Penguin.

GRAMSCI. A. (1971) *Selections from the Prison Notebooks* London, Lawrence and Wisehart.

GRIFFIN, S. (1984) *Women and Nature* London, The Women's Press.

HAFFTER, C. (1968) 'The Changeling: History and Psychodynamics of Attitudes to Handicapped Children in European Folklore' *Journal of the History of Behavioural Sciences* No 4, pp. 55-61.

HALES, G. (ed.) (1996) *Beyond Disability: Towards an Enabling Society* London, Sage.

HASTINGS, J. (ed.) (1918 -1921) *Encyclopaedia of Religion and Ethics* Vol. 5. Edinburgh, T. and T. Clarke.

HOBSBAWM, E. and RANGER, T. (1983) *The Invention of Tradition* London, Cambridge University Press.

HOBBES, T. (1983) 'Leviathan' in HELD, D. (ed.) *States and Societies* Oxford, Martin Robertson, pp. 68-71.

HUNT, P. 'A Critical Condition' in HUNT, P. (ed.) (1966) *Stigma: The Experience of Disability*, London, Geoffrey Chapman pp. 145-164.

KEVLES, D. J. (1985) *In the Name of Eugenics* New York, Alfred A. Knopf.

JONES, G. (1986) *Social Hygiene in the Twentieth Century* London, Croom Helm.

LONSDALE, S. (1990) *Women and Disability* Macmillan, Tavistock.

LUPTON, D. (1994) *Medicine as Culture: Illness, Disease and the Body in Western Culture* London, Sage.

MACFARLANE, I. (1979) *The Origins of English Individualism* Oxford, Basil Blackwell.

MARX, K. (1970) *Capital* Vol. 1 London, Lawrence and Wisehart

MILLER, E. J. and GWYNNE, G. V. (1972) *A Life Apart* London, Tavistock.

MORRIS, J. (1991) *Pride Against Prejudice,* London, The Women's Press.

MORRIS, J. (ed.) (1996) *Encounters with Strangers* London, The Women's Press.

MURPHY, R. (1987) *The Body Silent* New York, Henry Holt.

NICHOLLI, O. (1990) 'Menstruum quasi monstruum; monstrous births and menstrual taboo in the sixteenth century' in NUIR, E. and RUGGIERO, G. (eds.) *Sex and Gender in Historical Perspective* Baltimore, Johns Hopkins University Press.

NOG. (1996) *The Disability Discrimination Act: A Policy and Practice Guide for Local Government and Disabled People* Sheffield, Northern Officers Group.

OLIVER, M. (1983) *Social Work with Disabled People* London, Macmillan.

OLIVER, M. (1986) 'Social Policy and Disability: Some Theoretical Issues' in *Disability, Handicap and Society* Vol. 1, No. 1, pp. 5-18.

OLIVER, M. (1990) *The Politics of Disablement* London, Macmillan.

OLIVER, M. (1996) *Understanding Disability: From Theory to Practice* London, Macmillan.

PAGEL, M. (1988) *On Our Own Behalf: An Introduction to the Self Organisation of Disabled People* Manchester, GMCDP.

PARSONS, T, (1951) *The Social System* London, Routledge and Kegan Paul.

PFEIFFER, D. and YOSHIDA, K. (1994) 'Teaching Disability Studies in Canada and the USA, in *Disability and Society* Vol. 10, No. 4, pp. 475-500.

RIESER, R. (1992) 'Stereotypes of Disabled People' in RIESER, R. and MASON, M. *Disability Equality in the Classroom: A Human Rights Issue* London, Disability Equality in Education, pp. 98-104.

RISEBERO, B. (1979) *The Story of Western Architecture* London, Herbert.

RUSSELL, B. (1981) *History of Western Philosophy* London, Unwin Paperbacks.

RYAN, J and THOMAS F. (1987) *The Politics of Mental Handicap (Revised Edition)* London, Free Association Books.

SCOTT, R. A. (1969) *The Making of Blind Men* London, Sage.

SCULL, A. (1984) *Decarceration (2nd edn.)* London, Polity Press.

SHAKESPEARE, T. (1994) 'Cultural Representations of Disabled People: Dustbins for Disavowal' *Disability and Society* No. 9, Vol. 3. pp. 283-301.

STONE, E. (1996) 'Disability in China' in *Disability and Society* Vol. 11, No. 4, pp. 469-483.

STONE, D. A. (1984) *The Disabled State* Macmillan, London.

STUART, O. (1993) 'Double Oppression: An Appropriate Starting Point' in SWAIN, J. *et al.*, *Disabling Barriers: Enabling Environments* London, Sage, pp. 93-101.

SWAIN, J., FINKELSTEIN, V., FRENCH, S. and OLIVER, M. (eds.) (1993) *Disabling Barriers – Enabling Environments* Sage in Association with the Open University, London.

TALLE, A. (1995) 'A Child Is a Child; Disability and Equality among the Kenya Maasai' in INGSTAD, B. and REYNOLDS WHYTE , S. (1995) *Disability and Culture* California, University of California Press, pp. 66-72.

THOMAS, D. (1982) *The Experience of Handicap* London, Methuen.

THOMAS, K. (1977) 'The Place of Laughter in Tudor and Stuart England' *Times Literary Supplement* 21 January, pp. 77-81.

TOOLEY, M. (1983) *Abortion and Infanticide* New York, Oxford University Press.

TURNER, V. (1967) *The Forest of Symbols: Aspects of Ndembu Ritual* New York, Cornell University Press.

WEAR, A. (1992) *Medicine in Western Societies: Historical Essays* Cambridge, Cambridge University Press.

WILDE, O. (1966) *Complete Works* London, Collins.

WILLIAMS, G. (1996) 'Representing Disability, questions of phenomenology and politics' in BARNES, C. and MERCER, G. (1996) *Exploring the Divide: Illness and Disability* Leeds, The Disability Press, pp. 194-212.

WOLFENSBERGER, W. (1989) 'Human Service Policies: The Rhetoric versus the Reality' in BARTON, L. (ed.) *Disability and Dependence* Lewes, Falmer, pp. 23-42.

WOLFENSBERGER, W. (1994) 'The Growing Threat to the Lives of Handicapped People in the Context of Modernistic Values' in *Disability and Society* Vol. 9, No. 3, pp. 395-413.

ZARB, G. (ed.) (1995) *Removing Disabling Barriers* London, Policy Studies Institute.

CHAPTER 2

The Limits of Classical Social Theory in the Analysis and Transformation of Disablement —
(can this really be the end; to be stuck inside of Mobile with the Memphis blues again?)

By Paul Abberley

INTRODUCTION

In this chapter I argue that the thoroughgoing adoption of a liberative social model of disability will necessitate a break with classical sociological perspectives rooted in Enlightenment thought. These world views, in their right-wing, Durkheimian and left-wing, Marxist forms share core notions of human perfectability and labour as definitional of humanity which are incompatible with the interests of impaired people. The limits of Enlightenment radicalism, as seen in the work of Marx, are defined by the logic and values of production. The meaning of humanity becomes co-terminous with such values, and the category of 'disabled' is created negatively in relation to them. This approach forms an explanatory framework for understanding the form and nature of disablement as an historical product.

But if we remain within the social theory which gives rise to them, it also appears as inevitable. For a theory of disablement to serve the liberation of impaired people requires a break with such models of humanity and the development of philosophies which are not centred on the notion of 'homo faber'. In particular, notions of perfectability and production-oriented rationality must be transcended. The development of liberative theories of disablement involves addressing some of the major issues of 'new'social theory concerning identity and group membership, and a reconsideration of what have so far been disappointing attempts at the theorisation of the body in society.

SOCIOLOGY AND DISABLEMENT

In the last ten years sociology-based critiques of the existing situation of disabled people have proved analytically and politically most productive in a number of publications and actions based upon them. However this advance would not have been possible if it were only occurring in the minds of isolated individuals. Intimately involved in the genesis of these works is the real movement of disabled people in Britain, and the force of academic works resides to a large degree in the fact that they crystallise within them the beliefs, concerns and interests of the increasing number of disabled people who themselves see disablement as social process rather than personal tragedy.

We should, however be more precise as to which areas of sociology have been of use; it is certainly not to such an inherently conservative perspective as Functionalism that disability researchers have looked for their theoretical tools. Indeed, in the hands of a sociologist like Topliss (1982) such a perspective has been identified as part of the problem. The deficiencies of such accounts stem not from individual inadequacies but from the theoretical problematic in which they operate. The thorough critique of such perspectives involves not merely the rejection of their assertions about disabled people, but the deconstruction of their notions of disability, that is, exposing them as ideological or culturally constructed rather than as natural or a reflection of reality (Alcoff 1988).

The founding father of Functionalist sociology, Durkheim (1964), posits a fundamental distinction between non- or pre-industrial societies and industrial ones. In the former, social integration is characterised as based on the similarity of roles in the social division of labour, 'mechanical' solidarity. After industrialisation, with a growing separateness and distinction of the individual from the group as the division of labour is increasingly specialised and individuated, a good society is one with strong bonds of 'organic' solidarity. These bonds are constituted through the recognition of the role of others in the complex division of labour that makes up that society. The venue where this solidarity is to be forged is the occupational associations. Thus to be deprived of such a role is to be deprived of the possibility of full societal membership. Whilst some of his polemical writing like the essay 'Individualism and the Intellectuals' (Durkheim, 1971), written as an intervention in the Dreyfus Affair, places great stress upon the necessity for the good society to recognise diversity, there is no suggestion that this extends to the incorporation of those unable to work into full social membership.

It is then as a consequence of theoretical consistency that Topliss, operating from a functionalist perspective ultimately traceable back to the work of Durkheim, comes to advance the following argument for the inevitability of discrimination against disabled people—

'While the particular type or degree of impairment which disables a person for full participation in society may change, it is inevitable that there will always be a line, somewhat indefinite but none the less real, between the able-bodied majority and a disabled minority whose interests are given less salience in the activities of society as a whole. Similarly, the values which underpin society must be those which support the interests and activities of the majority, hence the emphasis on vigorous independence and competitive achievement, particularly in the occupational sphere, with the unfortunate spin-off that it encourages a stigmatising and negative view of the disabilities which handicap individuals in these valued aspects of life. Because of the centrality of such values in the formation of citizens of the type needed to sustain the social arrangements desired by the able-bodied majority, they will continue to be fostered by family upbringing, education and public esteem. By contrast, disablement which handicaps an individual in these areas will continue to be negatively valued, thus tending towards the imputation of general inferiority to the disabled individual, or stigmatisation.' (Topliss 1982: 111-2)

For Topliss the inevitable disadvantage of disabled people, in any possible society, stems from our general inability to meet standards of performance in work. This can be contrasted to other perspectives, like Interactionism, where some writers (Haber and Smith 1971) suggest that the core 'deficiency' of disabled people is an aesthetic one. However, aesthetic judgements may themselves be related, albeit in a complex manner, to the requirements of production, so it seems unlikely that the aesthetic explanation however attractive it may be in certain cases possesses the irreducibility that its proponents ascribe to it.

MARXISM AND DISABILITY

Given the political unacceptability of the implications of such perspectives as Functionalism and Interactionism to sociologists committed to the liberation of disabled people, one major source which we have drawn upon is Marxism. This has occurred in part because of the theoretical and political backgrounds of the sociologists involved. But equally I think because Sartre's 1963 judgement that all thinking has to operate in relation to the dominant philosophy of the age, Marxism, still holds correct. However, this utilisation has occurred at a fair distance from the fundamental economic and philosophical basics of the theory. Such notions as oppression (Abberley 1987, 1992) and hegemony (Oliver 1990, 1996), the former owing its initial credentials to Lenin's analysis of imperialism and the latter to Gramsci's work on ideology, have been found useful by some researchers and members of the disability movement. But as far as the nuts and bolts of the critique of political economy are concerned, we have largely been silent. For my part this has not been accidental, but because I have come to see profound problems in utilising a Marxian model of human beings for the liberation of disabled people.

In part this is due to the potency of Marxism as a social theory of impairment and the consequent implication that with the abolition of capitalism the material basis of disablement will disappear. The clearest and most explicit reference to impairment to be found in the Marx/Engels corpus occurs in 'The Condition of the Working Class in England', written in 1844/5.

Engels argues that the Industrial Revolution creates the proletariat in a gigantic process of concentration, polarisation and urbanisation, and with it, despite expansion of the whole economy and an increased demand for labour a 'surplus population', which Marxists were later to refer to as the 'reserve army of labour'. He was concerned to explore the conditions of life and the collective and individual behaviour that this process produced, and the greater part of the book is devoted to the description and analysis of these material conditions. His account is based on first-hand observations, informants and printed evidence, such as Commission reports and contemporary journals and periodicals. 'Cripples' are cited as evidence of injurious working practices—

> 'The Commissioners mention a crowd of cripples who appeared before them, who clearly owed their distortion to the long-working hours' (Engels 1969:180).

He cites the evidence of a number of doctors who relate particular kinds of malformation and deformity to working practices as an

> 'aspect of the physiological results of the factory system' (ibid:181)

He continues

> 'I have seldom traversed Manchester without meeting three or four of them, suffering from precisely the same distortions of the spinal columns and legs as that described...It is evident, at a glance, whence the distortions of these cripples come; they all look exactly alike' (ibid:182)

He continues for some pages to relate particular forms of impairment to factory working conditions and to condemn—

> "a state of things which permits so many deformities and mutilations for the benefit of a single class, and plunges so many industrious working-people into want and starvation by reason of injuries undergone in the service and through the fault of the bourgeoisie." (ibid:194)

He concludes his description of 'the English manufacturing proletariat' thus—

> "In all directions, whithersoever we may turn, we find want and disease permanent or temporary...slow but sure undermining, and final destruction of the human being physically as well as mentally" (ibid:238)

Engels here establishes the main form of Marxism's concern with impairment. It is exemplary of the predations of capitalism, and AS such, has propaganda value as one of the things socialism will abolish: the significance of disabled people is as historically contingent victims.

A hundred years later Hannington uses a similar analysis and sources of evidence, this time to condemn not factory-work, but the lack of it —

> "These youths ... meet problems which render them increasingly conscious of the way in which their lives have been stunted and their young hopes frustrated and of the results of the physical impairment which they have suffered through the unemployment and poverty of their parents." (Hannington 1937:78)

Doyal (1979) refines this general thesis, and documents a relationship between 'capitalism' and impairment on a wide variety of fronts, adding consumption, industrial pollution, stress and imperialism to the labour-centred concerns of Engels and Hannington.

Now I in no way wish to dispute the general accuracy and pertinence of these studies. My point is rather that for real disabled people such an analysis, linking impairment to capitalism as a very apparent symptom of its inhumanity and irrationality, is of little use. All it implies is that, with the state, impaired people would wither away in a society progressively abolishing the injurious consequences of production for profit. But there are two crucial objections to the notion of the problem of disability ending up in the dustbin of history. First, whilst socially produced impairments of the kind outlined by Doyal *et al* may decrease in number, it is inconceivable that the rate of impairment should ever be reduced to zero. Secondly, and of most significance for disabled people today, it is an issue whether such a situation, could it occur, would be desirable. As long as there is a general eugenicist consensus between left and right that impaired modes of being are undesirable, disabled people must challenge such views as, in essence, genocidal.

Whilst in practice the propagation and implementation of right-wing theories of disability are a real and ever-present problem for disabled people, the social models of disability propagated as liberative of disabled people by the Disability Movement are necessarily perspectives 'of the left' since they involve the radical overhaul of the status quo. Thus in developing our understanding of disablement and working towards its abolition, it is with perspectives which claim a critical and oppositional standpoint that we must come to grips. In particular, we need to understand the apparent failure of Marxist theory to provide concepts which we may employ to further develop a liberative social theory of disability.

I have argued above that Marxist analyses of impairment are heavily skewed towards preventation and cure. However, this emphasis seems no accidental consequence of the marginality of disabled people to Marxism's primary concern with production relations under capitalism, rather it is deeply grounded in Marxist notions of humanity. If so, it will thus apply across modes of production and historical eras. To see why this is the case, it is necessary to consider the Marxist model of humanity, in particular the role labour takes in the constitution of humanness.

For Marxism, whilst all human societies must produce their own material conditions of existence, the commodity is the form products take when this production is organised through exchange. The commodity has two aspects. First, it can satisfy some human want—it has use value: secondly, it can be exchanged for other commodities, a property Marx calls simply 'value'. Since a commodity is both a use value and a value, the labour producing it has a dual character. Any act of labour, 'productive activity of a definite kind, carried on with a definite aim'(Marx 1974 a:49) is useful labour productive of use value. This can be contrasted to pseudo-labour, (familiar to many who have undergone occupational therapy) — nothing can have value, without being an object of utility. If the thing is useless, so is the labour contained in it; the labour does not count as labour, and therefore creates no value (ibid: 48). This 'is a condition of human existence which is independent of all forms of society; it is an eternal natural necessity which mediates the metabolism between man and nature, and therefore human life itself' (ch. 1). In analysing capitalism, however, he goes on to explore that aspect of labour which endows its product with value, and this is linked to the idea of the average worker—

> "Any average magnitude ... is merely the average of a number of separate magnitudes all of one kind, but differing as to quantity. In every industry, each individual labourer, be he Peter or Paul, differs from the average labourer. These individual differences or 'errors' as they are called in mathematics, compensate one another and vanish, whenever a certain minimum number of workmen are employed together"(chl) This abstract labour, productive of value, is equivalent to socially necessary labour time—

> "the labour-time required to produce any use-value under the conditions of production normal for a given society and with the average degree of skill and intensity of labour prevalent in that society...what exclusively determines the magnitude of the value of any article is therefore the amount of labour socially necessary, or the labour-time socially necessary for its production".

Approximation to this norm serves to define the normal worker. Thus the whole project of Capital resting on the notion of abstraction from real data on wages prices profit etc. involves the construction of a norm of 'human being as worker'. Marx's and Engels' description of capitalism captures the way in which capitalism creates both disabled people and a concept of disability as the negative of the normal worker. It is labour power which workers sell to capitalists for a money-wage, and impaired labour-power that characterises and accounts for the specific character of disablement under capitalism. So, Marxism provides powerful theoretical tools for understanding the origin and nature of the oppression of disabled people. Some, pointing to the withering critiques directed against utopianism throughout the Marx-Engels corpus, suggest that we can go no further in specifying the material basis of the transcendence of disablement than to argue that the progressive reduction of the significance of labour-power along the transitional socialist road results in reduced social significance for impairment in respect of labour-power. This, combined with technological innovation which equips impaired people to take part in the production process, results in the progressive abolition of disablement.

Now whilst part of me welcomes the rigour and coherence of this line of argument, I am still concerned that it fails to provide a way of conceptualising a satisfactory future for those impaired people unable to work, around which we can potentially unite and mobilise all disabled people. This concern arises from a consideration of the way in which Marx and Marxists present human freedom, the condition supposed to develop through the transcendence of capitalism and its vestiges. Marx occasionally seems to reduce the problem of human freedom to free time, in for example the 1847 Wage-Labour and Capital (Marx 1969). On such a view there should be no problem for those unable to labour: free time would occupy the whole of life. But this position is more generally ridiculed and in the 1857/8 Grundrisse it is asserted that—

> 'Really free working is at the same time precisely the most damned seriousness, the most intense exertion'(Marx 1973:611).

In the 1875 'Critique of the Gotha Programme' Marx makes the well-known statement that

> 'in a more advanced phase of communist society...when labour is no longer just a means of keeping alive but has itself become a vital need...(we may then have) from each according to his abilities, to each according to his needs' (Marx 1974b:347).

But this implies that impaired people are still deprived, by biology if not by society. Impairment, since it places a limit upon creative sensuous practice, is necessarily alienatory, for those who accept that this term should be seen as an element of a Marxist terminological canon. This is not perhaps a problem in relation to free-time, since even in utopia people would not be expected to take part in all possible recreational and cultural activities. It does however

THE LIMITS OF CLASSICAL SOCIAL THEORY

constitute a restriction in relation to work, which is an interaction between agent and nature which results in production of social value. Whilst the distinctions between productive, reproductive and unproductive labour are crucial to the analysis of capitalism, rather than the exploration of a Marxist utopia, the ability to labour in some socially recognised sense still seems a requirement of full membership of a future good society based upon Marxist theory. Whilst children as potential workers, and elderly people, as former ones, may be seen as able to assume a status in a paradise of labour, it is hard to see how, despite all efforts by a benign social structure, an albeit small group of impaired people could achieve social integration. Following Marxist theory thus understood, some impaired lives cannot then, in any possible society, be truly social, since the individual is deprived of the possibility of those satisfactions and that social membership to which her humanity entitles her, and which only work can provide. For impaired people to be adequately provided for in the system of distribution, but excluded from the system of production, that is, on a superior form of welfare, would be unsatisfactory, since we would still be in the essentially peripheral relationship to society we occupy today. There seems to be, for Marxism, an identity of who you are with the work you do which transcends capitalism and socialism into the concrete utopia of the future to constitute a key element of humanity, and a key need of human beings in all eras. Whilst other needs can be met for impaired people, and this can perhaps be done in a non-oppressive manner, the one need that cannot be met for those unable to labour is the need to work. This appears to be true for a whole range of Marxist thinkers.

William Morris, whose News from Nowhere envisages a profound erosion of barriers between necessary labour and the rest of human life therefore attributes to work a crucial role in human happiness and identity:

'I believe that the ideal of the future does not point to the lessening of men's energy by the reduction of labour to a minimum, but rather to the reduction of pain in labour to a minimum...the true incentive to useful and happy labour is and must be pleasure in the work itself' (cited Levitas 1990: 108).

Marcuse, whilst believing that work can be more pleasant than it is today points to a deep co-incidence of analysis between Marx and Freud—

'Behind the Reality Principle lies the fundamental fact of scarcity .... whatever satisfaction is possible necessitates work, more or less painful arrangements and undertakings for the procurement of the means for satisfying needs' (Marcuse 1955: 35).

André Gorz, at the opposite pole from Morris in his advocacy of the minimisation of socially necessary labour and the maximisation of free-time, still sees purposive activity and competence as a condition of social inclusion—

> 'the abolition of work does not mean abolition of the need for effort, the desire for activity, the pleasure of creation, the need to cooperate with others and be of some use to the community'. He continues- 'the demand to 'work less' does not mean or imply the right to 'rest more'.' (Gorz 1982: 2—3).

But this is precisely the kind of right that impaired people do demand, today and for the future.

This exploration would suggest that Gouldner was correct in his judgement that—

> "Marxism never really doubted the importance of being useful. Its fundamental objection to capitalist society was to the dominating significance of exchange-value, not to use-value. It objected to the transformation of men's labor into a commodity, but it continued to emphasise the value and importance of work." (Gouldner 1971:406) It seems that Marxism, on this interpretation, along with allopathic medicine which has been so tied in to the disablement of impaired people in the modern era, can never be other than a project of the Enlightenment. It shares with other such enterprises a Rationalist adherence to aspirations of 'perfection', and cannot avoid identifying non-workers with the historically redundant bourgeoisie, one aspect of whose alienation is their failure to participate in social production.

WORK AND DISABILITY THEORY

How does this feed back into analyses of disability in society today? With less than one third of those in the relevant age-group in employment in Britain today (Martin, Meltzer and Elliot, 1988), for many disabled people the demand for access to work is seen as a crucial component of the struggle for equality. This is reflected in the focus of Government's feeble proposals to 'tackle' disabled people's oppression which focus on the workplace. Equally the British Council of Disabled People, in fighting the government's cutbacks on the Access to Work scheme has asserted 'The right to a job is a fundamental Human Right' (BCODP 1996:3). Recent work (Lunt and Thornton, 1994) has surveyed some of the issues involved in implementing employment policies in terms of a social model of disablement –but the aim itself is left unexamined. At the level of more general theory, Finkelstein has pointed out repeatedly (1980, 1993) 'that the predominant factor contributing to the disablement of different groups is the way in which people can participate in the creation of social wealth' (1993:12).

He goes on to argue that since—

'assumed levels of employability separate people into different levels of dependency....By trying to distance themselves (groups of people with particular impairments or degrees of impairment) from groups that they perceive as more disabled than themselves they can hope to maintain their claim to economic independence and an acceptable status in the community' (1993:14).

He cautions against doing this for what are essentially political reasons, that it will divide the movement, and points out that those who did this would be surrendering to the logic of the medical model, which they claim to reject. Now this appeal to unity and theoretical consistency, whilst appropriate to its context, seems to me to pass over an essential issue for disabled people—that even in a society which DID make profound and genuine attempts to integrate impaired people into the world of work, some would be excluded, by their impairment. Whatever efforts are made to integrate impaired people into the world of work some will not be capable of producing goods or services of social value, that is 'participating in the creation of social wealth'. This is so because, in any society, certain, though varying, products are of value and others are not, regardless of the effort that goes into their production. I therefore wish to contend that just because a main mechanism of our oppression is our exclusion from social production, we should be wary of drawing the conclusion that overcoming this oppression should involve our wholesale inclusion in it. As Finkelstein recognises, a society may be willing, and in certain circumstances become eager, to absorb a portion of its impaired population into the workforce, yet this can have the effect of maintaining and perhaps intensifying its exclusion of the remainder. We need to develop a theory of oppression which avoids this bifurcation, through a notion of social integration which is not dependent upon impaired people's inclusion in productive activity.

FEMINIST ANALYSES

Feminism has pointed out that Marxism is deeply marked by the maleness of its originators—and never more so than in the key role assumed by work in the constitution of human social identity. It is argued that the apparent gender-neutrality of Marxist theoretical categories is in reality a gender-bias which legitimises Marxism's excessive focus on the 'masculine sphere' of commodity production. Whilst some approaches in feminist sociology have reproduced, though from a broader perspective, the concern with work as definitional of social inclusion (Abberley 1996), others have more profoundly disputed labour-dependent conceptions of humanity.

One aspect of this involves feminist conceptions of the human body, far less abstract than classical Marxist formulations. In exploring the politics of human reproductive biology, feminism opens up other aspects of our biological lives, and thus impairment, to critical reflection. Another is that it has pointed out that the traditional policy solutions for dealing with inequality – 'get a job', and traditional technological solutions – have not resulted in a better society for women.

> 'One fact that is little understood...is that women in poverty are almost invariably productive workers, participating fully in both the paid and the unpaid work force...Society cannot continue persisting with the male model of a job automatically lifting a family out of poverty' (McKee 1982:36).

In 'Black Feminist Thought', Patricia Hill Collins quotes May Madison, a participant in a study of inner-city African Americans who has pointed out that—

> 'One very important difference between white people and black people is that white people think you ARE your work...Now, a black person has more sense than that because he knows that what I am doing doesn't have anything to do with what I want to do or what I do when I am doing for myself. Now, black people think that my work is just what I have to do to get what I want' (quoted Collins 1990: 47-8).

Whilst white male non-disabled sociologists may interpret this as evidence for the thesis of the alienated or instrumental worker, we should perhaps see it as documenting the social basis of an alternative theory of social membership and identity. This negative evaluation of the significance of 'work' and 'technology' in the present is not construed as explicable in terms of 'deformations under capitalism', but is carried forward into a critique of the viability for women of a society organised around 'work' and the 'technofix'. Such issues are, I think, of significance to the development of theories of disablement. Schweickart, amongst many! represents another strand in arguing that

> 'The domination of women and the domination of nature serve as models for each other. Thus, science and technology have a place in a feminist utopia only if they can be redefined apart from the logic of domination' (1983: 210).

This debate seems an important one for disability theory, both in terms of such detail as the desirability of care activities being performed by machines and wider issues of how far it would be correct to transform impaired people to give us access to the world. Thus amongst the 'deep' issues of the relationship between human beings and nature raised within feminism are many which echo in disability theory.

SOCIOLOGY OF THE BODY

For disabled people the much heralded advent of sociological interest in the body has been a disappointment. Sexuality, madness, textuality, sadness; all serve as diversions from the discussion of what the playful theorists of postmodernity fear to contemplate, the true negation of their sensuous savage, the disabled body.

> "The disabled body is a nightmare for the fashionable discourse of theory because that discourse has been limited by the very predilection of the dominant, ableist culture. The body is seen as a site of 'jouissance', a native ground of pleasure, the scene of an excess that defies reason, that takes dominant culture and its rigid, power laden vision of the body to task. The body of the left is an unruly body: a bad child thumbing its nose at the parent's bourgeois decorum: a rebellious daughter transgressing against the phallocentric patriarch. The nightmare of that body is one that is deformed, maimed, mutilated, broken, diseased." (Davis L 1995:5)

What we are confronted by in the literature of the body is the same as we find in the 'non-corporial' sociologies these approaches criticise: a silence on disability and impairment. And this is not a result of a lack of material. Foucault's 'Discipline and Punish' (1977) contains as one of its few illustrations a metaphorical representation of the calliper and spinal brace from 1749 captioned 'Orthopaedics or the art of preventing and correcting deformities of the body in children' (plate 10 opposite p 167). Yet this 'special' case is in the text invisible, totally subsumed and unremarked within the analysis of 'normal constraint'.

In its Anglophone version, we find a similar absence in the work of Turner. ' The Body and Society' (1984), with twenty-five separately indexed references to 'disease', fails to give a single mention to disability or any of its supposed homonyms.

Even the merely amateur psychologist may feel that so systematic an absence of the disabled body is evidence of the strong feelings of repulsion fear and disgust its prospect inspires in these theorists. Indeed I have suggested elsewhere (1993:108) that such feelings lie behind the analyses of disability provided by many psychologists themselves. But to describe such feelings should lead to the posing of the next question; what are their origins? And here I would suggest that repulsion, in terms of the theorists of the social construction of the body's own problematic, must be understood as the deeply internalised form of socially produced negative attitudes. The most deep-seated oppression, then, is the one that becomes somatised, and appears to well spontaneously from the individual's inner core. It is with such responses, also evidenced in studies of racism and homophobia, that body sociology must come to grips, if it is to develop a thoroughgoing theory, and, to me more importantly, if it is to be of potential use to disabled people. As yet, at the level of theory, it is generally so far from doing this that it represses all recognition of our existence. In one of the few cases I know of where the notion of 'reading' narrative texts and the ideas of discourse found in the work of Derrida, Lacan and Foucault have been applied to real discussions of disability, the profundity of the rejection of disabled ways of being becomes apparent. Casling describes his use of story-telling and deconstruction in a Disability Equality Workshop. He concludes—

> "In this workshop the invisible was made visible. The common experience of the non-disabled people in the stories, in all but one case assigned to the storyteller, the feelings were predicated on such constructs as 'anxiety', 'guilt', and 'anger'...The final throw of the dice came with the announcement by a group member that they had one other word written in their column of feelings attached to non-disabled people in relation to disabled people, and that was the word 'hate'...I was...reminded of the statement of Adolf Ratka that 'society hates disabled people'. I had understood this on a structural level, but here it was being cited as the apex of attitudinal discussion, as if little by little more and more difficult feelings were being made visible within the group". (Casling 1993:208.)

As I understand it, the claim made by Casling for the technique is that the process facilitates the paring away of rationalising and justificatory verbiage until what remains is the bedrock of linguistic, and thus social characterisation of disabled people. What is exposed is a core truth, the nearest we can arrive at in language to a visceral response.

SOCIAL MOVEMENTS

The theoretical perspectives I have considered above seem to me to imply an important distinction between disablement and other forms of oppression. Whilst the latter involve a utopia in which freedom can possibly be seen as coming through full integration into the world of work, for impaired people the overcoming of disablement whilst immensely liberative would still leave an uneradicated residue of disadvantage in relation to power over the material world. This in turn restricts our ability to be fully integrated into the world of work in any possible society. One implication that can be drawn from this, which finds most support in classical sociological perspectives, with their emphasis on the role of work in social membership, is that it would be undesirable to be an impaired person in such a society, and thus that the abolition of disablement also involves as far as possible the abolition of impairment.

The work-based model of social membership and identity is integrally linked to the prevention/cure orientated perspective of allopathic medicine and to the specific instrumental logic of genetic-engineering, abortion and euthanasia. Ultimately it involves a value judgement upon the undesirability of impaired modes of being. However this logic allows for the integration of perhaps a substantial proportion of any existing impaired population into the work process, but only insofar as the interface between an individual's impairment, technology and socially valued activity produced a positive outcome. Thus the abolition of an individual's disablement is ultimately dependent upon and subordinate to the logic of productivity. Recent events in China, where a genocidal eugenics law and state sponsored infanticide have been accompanied by significant equality legislation for some disabled people exemplifies this logic, which I suggest is perfectly consistent with that state's ideology.

An alternative kind of theory can be seen as offering another future insofar as it rejects work as crucially definitional of social membership and is dubious about some of the progressive imperatives implicit in modern science. But such perspectives are not mere piece-meal modifications to existing ideas of utopia. Such rejections and doubt also involve a distancing from the values of 'modern' society insofar as such a society involves the identification of persons with what they can produce in such a system. A liberative theory of disability requires the posing of values counter to the classical sociological and revolutionary consensus, the assertion of the rights of the human 'being' against the universalisation of the human 'doing'.

One mode of analysing the rejection of the instrumental rationality of the modern world is examined by Shakespeare, who explores the possibility of understanding the rise of the disability movement in terms of

'New Social Movements...most recent fixation of sociologists' (1993:257).

Whilst he considers the usefulness of a number of Social Movement theorists and finds them wanting, the work of Alain Touraine is not mentioned in his discussion. This is unfortunate, since Touraine's notion of Social Movements places particular emphasis upon the challenge that they pose to prevailing belief systems, and takes his analysis significantly beyond the empirical

From concrete explorations of the rise of Solidarity in Poland (1983a) and the French opposition to nuclear energy (1983b) Touraine concludes (1984) that far from being idiosyncratic areas of study, Social Movements constitute a central issue for contemporary sociology, since they constitute important features of its nature, in contrast to previous eras when they were essentially peripheral. For Touraine the aim of a Social Movement is not simply to react against existing inequalities, but rather to try to change the norms and values of cultural and social life.

> "The idea of a social movement...is radically different to the idea of class struggle. The latter appeals to the logic of history, whereas the former appeals to the freedom of the Subject, even if that means rejecting the pseudo-laws of history...we must open up individual and collective clearings in the forest of technologies, rules and consumer goods. The demise of the political programmes and apparatuses that have dominated the last hundred years is opening up an already crowded space for ethical principles and truly social movements" (Touraine 1995:370—371).

At the same time, Touraine is at pains to assert the effects upon actors of social structure and of history. For action to produce new elements of social structure it must work through and against pre-existing institutions and cultural forms;

> 'A social movement is at once a social conflict and a cultural project' (1995:240).

Social Movements are linked to critiques of the instrumental rationality which dominates whilst the Enlightenment values of reason, freedom, method, universalism and progress hold sway. For the Frankfurt school, Foucault and postmodernist analyses, modernity is seen as inevitably giving rise to the very oppressions it seeks to overcome. For Touraine, however, such critiques fail to recognise a 'self-critical' and 'self-destructive' aspect of modernity— that the value-based rationality embodied in the practice of Social Movements is capable of challenging, and defeating, the ascendancy of production-based instrumental rationality.

Touraine thus attempts to reintroduce the notion of action and the Social Movement, the mobilisation of convictions based in moral conviction and personal issues, against a prevailing sociological determinism. To apply this to the Disability movement, the strength of classical sociological accounts is that in seeing society as an explanatory concept as much as an object of study they allow us to identify and explore the socially produced oppression of disabled people. Their weakness lies in their notion of system as value, be that Durkheimian stasis or Marxian historicism, for neither can offer an acceptable future for disabled people.

Jenny Morris has written: the philosophy of the independent living movement is based on four assumptions:

- that all human life is of value;
- that anyone, whatever their impairment, is capable of exerting choices;
- that people who are disabled by society's reaction to physical, intellectual and sensory impairment and to emotional distress have the right to assert control over their lives;
- that disabled people have the right to full participation in society. (1993:21)

Such assumptions contain clear counter-values to prevailing productionism, posing demands without obligation to 'earn' and calling for as yet unachieved rights; they constitute a set of counter-values to prevailing social norms. As embodied in the practice of the movement, such ideas can be seen as coming to constitute a theoretical and practical alternative, in Touraine's terms, a Social Movement.

CONCLUSION

It seems to me that such theoretical perspectives as indicated above are fertile sources for sociological theories of disablement to draw upon in their future development. Politically, they unite the interests of all impaired people. Analytically, they provide ways of understanding the oppression of all disabled people as a socially-created category, not just of that subsection, however large it may be, which may potentially become part of the world of work. This is by no means to deny that the origins of our oppression, even for those with jobs, lie in our historical exclusion, as a group, from access to work, nor is it to oppose campaigns for increasing access to employment. It is however to point out that a thoroughgoing materialist analysis of disablement today must recognise that full integration of impaired people in social production can never constitute the future to which we as a movement aspire. If we must look elsewhere than to a paradise of labour for the concrete utopia that informs the development of theories of our oppression, it is not on the basis of classical analyses of social labour that our thinking will be further developed. Rather it involves a break with such analyses, and an explicit recognition that the aspirations and demands of the Disability movement involve the development and proselytisation of values and ideas which run profoundly counter to the dominant cultural problematic of both left and right. This is not a matter of choice, but of the future survival of alternative, impaired, modes of being.

I am thus arguing that we need to develop theoretical perspectives which express the standpoint of disabled people, whose interests are not necessarily served by the standpoints of other social groups, dominant or themselves oppressed, of which disabled people are also members. Such sociology involves the empowerment of disabled people because knowledge is itself an aspect of power. Disabled people have inhabited a cultural, political and intellectual world from whose making they have been excluded and in which they have been relevant only as problems. Scientific knowledge, including sociology, has been used to reinforce and justify this exclusion. New sociology of disablement needs to challenge this 'objectivity' and 'truth' and replace it with knowledge which arises from the position of the oppressed and seeks to understand that oppression. It requires an intimate involvement with the real historical movement of disabled people if it is to be of use. Equally, such developments have significance for the mainstream of social theory, in that they provide a testing ground for the adequacy of theoretical perspectives which claim to account for the experiences of all a society's members.

ACKNOWLEDGEMENT

I would like to thank all those who attended the conference at which this paper was first presented, and particularly Vic Finkelstein, for their helpful comments. The errors remain my own.

REFERENCES

ABBERLEY, P. (1987) 'The Concept of Oppression and the Development of a Social Theory of Disability *Disability Handicap and Society* vol. 2 no 1:pp 5-19.

ABBERLEY, P. (1992) 'The Concept of Oppression and the Development of a Social Theory of Oppression' in Booth, T. *et al* (eds.) *Policies for Diversity in Education* London: Routledge.

ABBERLEY, P. (1993) 'Disabled People and Normality' in Swain, J. *et al* (eds.) (1993) *Disabling Barriers – Enabling Environments* London: Sage/Open University Press

ABBERLEY, P. (1996) 'Work, Utopia and Impairment' in Barton, L. (ed.) *Disability and Society: Emerging Issues and Insights* Harlow: Longman.

ALCOFF, L. (1988) 'Cultural Feminism versus Post-structuralism: the Identity Crisis in Feminist Theory' *Signs* vol. 13 no 3:pp 405-436.

BRITISH COUNCIL OF ORGANISATIONS OF DISABLED PEOPLE (1996) Update no.14 January.

CASLING, D. (1993) 'Cobblers and Songbirds: the language and imagery of disability' *Disability and Society* vol. 8 no.2 pp 203-210.

COLLINS, P. (1990) *Black Feminist Thought* London: Harper Collins.

DAVIS, L. (1995) *Enforcing Normalcy – disability, deafness and the body* London: Verso.

DOYAL, L. (1979) *The Political Economy of Health* London: Pluto Press.

DURKHEIM, E. (1964) *The Division of Labour in Society* Illinois:Glencoe.

DURKHEIM, E. (1971) 'Individualism and the Intellectuals' (trans Lukes S. and J.) *Political Studies* XVII:pp 14-30.

ENGELS, F. (1969) *The Condition of the Working Class in England* St Albans: Granada Publishing.

FINKELSTEIN, V. (1980) *Attitudes and Disabled People: Issues For Discussion* New York: World Rehabilitation Fund.

FINKELSTEIN, V. (1993) 'The Commonalty of Disability' in Swain, J. *et al* (eds.) (1993) *Disabling Barriers – Enabling Environments* London: Sage/Open University Press.

FOUCAULT M. (1977) *Discipline and Punish* Harmondsworth: Allen Lane.

GORZ, A. (1982) *Farewell to the Working Class — An Essay on Post-industrial Socialism* London: Pluto Press.

GOULDNER A. (1971) *The Coming Crisis of Western Sociology* Brighton: Harvester Press.

HABER, L. AND SMITH, T. (1971) 'Disability and Deviance' *American Sociological Review* vol. 36 : pp 82-95

HANNINGTON W. (1937) *The Problem of the Distressed Areas* London. Gollancz Left book club.

LEVITAS, R. (1990) *The Concept of Utopia* Hemel Hempstead: Philip Allen.

LUNT, N. AND THORNTON, P. (1994) 'Disability and Employment: towards an understanding of discourse and policy' *Disability and Society* vol. 9 no 2: pp 223-238.

MCKEE, A. (1982) 'The Feminisation of Poverty' *Graduate Woman* vol 76, no 4: pp 34-6.

MARCUSE, H. (1955) *Eros and Civilization* New York: Vintage Books.

MARTIN, J., MELTZER, H. AND ELLIOT, D. (1988) Report 1 *The Prevalence of Disability among Adults*, London: H.M.S.O.

MARX, K. (1969) Wage-Labour and Capital in *Marx-Engels Selected Works* volume 1 Moscow: Progress Publishers.

MARX, K. (1973) *Grundrisse* Harmondsworth:Penguin Books.

MARX, K. (1974a) *Capital volume 1* London: Lawrence and Wishart.

MARX, K. (1974b) Critique of the Gotha Programme in *The First International and After* Political Writings volume 3 Harmondsworth:Penguin Books.

MORRIS, J. (1993) *Independent Lives – Community Care and Disabled People* London: Macmillan.

OLIVER M. (1990) *The Politics of Disablement* Basingstoke: Macmillan.

OLIVER M. (1996) *Understanding Disability: From theory to practice* Basingstoke: Macmillan.

SARTRE J-P (1963) *Search for a Method*, New York: Braziller.

SCHWEICKART, P. (1983) 'What if...Science and Technology in Feminist Utopias' in Rothschild, J. (ed.) 1983 *Machina ex Dea-Feminist Perspectives on Technology* Oxford: Pergamon.

SHAKESPEARE, T. (1993) 'Disabled People's Self-Organisation: a new social movement?' *Disability, Handicap and Society* vol. 8 no 3:pp 249-264

TOPLISS, E. (1982) *Social Responses To Handicap* Harlow: Longman.

TOURAINE, A. *et al* (1983a) *Solidarity—An analysis of a Social movement* trans. D. Denby Cambridge: Cambridge University Press.

TOURAINE, A. *et al* (1983b) *Anti-nuclear Protest: the Opposition to Nuclear Energy in France* trans. P. Fawcett Cambridge: Cambridge University Press.

TOURAINE, A. (1984) 'Social Movements: Special Area or Central Problem in Sociological Analysis?' *Thesis Eleven* no 9: pp 5-15.

TOURAINE, A. (1995) *Critique of Modernity* trans. D. Macey Oxford: Basil Blackwell.

TURNER, B (1984) *The Body and Society* Oxford: Basil Blackwell.

CHAPTER 3

From Normalisation to Where?

By Anne Louise Chappell

INTRODUCTION

This chapter will attempt to do two things. First of all, I want to acknowledge the progress that has been made with reference to challenges to the normalisation principle, as the hitherto predominant model for understanding the experiences of people with learning difficulties. Secondly, I want to take the opportunity to raise some concerns about the theoretical position of people with learning difficulties within the social model of disability. In so doing, I don't claim to have any answers. Rather, the paper is a reflection of continuing concerns about the application of the social model of disability to what has been termed the sociology of disability or disability studies. I write this paper then in the hope that the issues it raises will prompt some useful discussion. Perhaps the answers, if there are any, will come later.

THE RISE AND FALL OF NORMALISATION

My interest in disability issues was stimulated by what appeared to be, some 10 years ago, the progressive potential of the normalisation principle and its promise to improve the lives of people with learning difficulties. For those who are unfamiliar with normalisation, a simple summary is:

'The use of means which are valued in our society in order to develop and support personal behaviour experiences and characteristics which are likewise valued' (Campaign for People with a Mental Handicap, 1981, p 1)

The normalisation principle argues that people with learning difficulties are devalued by society and have stigmatised identities. A vicious circle of devalued identities reinforced by poor quality services is created. Putting into practice the normalisation principle will transform the vicious circle into a virtuous circle of high quality services which will create high quality lifestyles and enable people with learning difficulties to mix with those who have socially valued identities.

The research in which I was engaged at that time intended to use normalisation as its theoretical framework. As the research progressed, however, interviews and conversations with people with learning difficulties began to highlight a conflict between the experiences and priorities of my respondents and the goals of normalisation which claimed to articulate these experiences and priorities. At the same time, the social model of disability was emerging in the academic literature (Abberley 1987, Oliver 1990). The analysis of disability presented by the social model provided a much better fit with the experiences of the people whom I was interviewing. From here developed an attempt to critique normalisation.

At that time, it felt very difficult to raise public concerns about normalisation. There are two main reasons why this was so. The first concerns the history of normalisation. In the early 1970s, the British Government set targets for the closure of long-stay mental handicap hospitals (DHSS 1971). This marked the first clear Government commitment to community care for people with learning difficulties. It coincided with the dissemination of the North American version of normalisation within the UK. Advocates of normalisation saw this policy commitment to community care as a move in the right direction, but wanted to go much further.

In their attempts to spread the word of normalisation to service planners and providers, its advocates argued that community care was for all people with learning difficulties, regardless of the degree of impairment. Such a radical assertion went far beyond the terms of Government policy on community care. It provoked a significant degree of scepticism, if not hostility, among some service planners and providers, who feared for their jobs in the long-stay hospitals or who believed that, while people with mild learning difficulties might cope in the community, those with severe impairments always would require hospital care.

Alan Tyne, writing as long-standing supporter of normalisation has described the derision and abuse that was heaped on those who advocated hospital closure and community-based services (1987, p 80). Standing firm against this sort of hostility did not create the kind of open environment where it was permissible to question normalisation without providing ammunition for those who were opposed to community care. As Ward has noted, to question normalisation in public was to risk association with the 'forces of reaction' (1992, foreword).

The second reason concerns the content of normalisation. It is based on a powerful vision of what services should be like for devalued people. This emphasis on explicit values creates a moral blueprint for service design. Holding on to "the dream", this vision of high quality services creating a high quality life-style, has been a cornerstone of normalisation. "The dream" is conveyed to services planners and providers via intensive training programmes which can last several days. The techniques used are intended to pull on the emotions and are based on strong moral convictions, if not zeal, in some cases.

Again, this doesn't create an open, questioning environment. In addition, the emphasis placed in normalisation of the power of the subconscious (drawn from Goffman's notion of the manifest and latent functions of the long-stay institution), makes it possible to claim that those who are sceptical about normalisation have failed to acknowledge their own subconscious fears and negative values about people with learning difficulties.

Normalisation is riddled with jargon: the conservatism corollary, social role valorisation, symbolic marking, Program Analysis of Service Systems Implementation of Normalisation's Goals (PASSING). Being party to this exclusive language created a sense of belonging to a select and enlightened group.

During the 1980s, normalisation came to dominate the agenda for debates about services for people with learning difficulties. It epitomised the way forward for the design of services: anything progressive could be achieved only by adopting the normalisation principle. It had moved from being ridiculous and naïve to become the accepted wisdom. To criticise it was tantamount to heresy.

For these reasons, public criticism of normalisation was muted. The cracks in this apparent consensus began to appear at the very end of the 1980s. In the UK, these concerns came from different perspectives. The first I would term the "whole person" approach. Bayley (1991), for example, argued that the concept of culturally valued roles, so central to normalisation, was in danger of failing to support the valuable characteristics of people with learning difficulties. The emphasis was on making them conform rather than on unconditional acceptance.

Other work, for example Brown and Smith (1989) and Baxter *et al* (1990), pointed to the dangers inherent within normalisation of the unquestioning value attached to cultural norms and the determination that devalued people should aspire to them. Such an approach merely reproduces other discriminatory social norms, such as sexism and racism. These were very important arguments as they highlighted that social norms are not neutral, but are products of the society which constructs them. However, some of this work – in particular that of Brown and Smith – has advocated a rehabilitation of normalisation through debate and review. They argue that normalisation:

> 'is the best we have got to date, and should therefore be used as a starting point' (1992, pp 691-2).

My concern was to re-examine normalisation in the light of the social model of disability. I argued that normalisation was increasingly accepted by many services planners and academics who attempted to use it to improve services for people with learning difficulties. Normalisation enabled professionals, therefore, to maintain a key role in community care and adapt to new services by developing new models of practice. It continued to legitimate the authority of professionals in the move from hospital-based to community-based services. However, it is interesting to note, as Whitehead (1992) and Oliver (1994) have indicated, normalisation may have influenced many professionals, but it has not been adopted as a model for change by disabled people themselves or any organisations which are accountable to disabled people.

The functionalism of normalisation means that the power relationship between professionals and users remains intact. As normalisation reflects the concerns of professionals, it is services and not their economic and social context which are the priority. This begs the question for people with learning difficulties: what if I don't want to be in the day centre/residential home at all (however well decorated it might be), but want to live in my own flat or with friends, have a job and make my own decisions without having staff around. Community care and normalisation have generated a language about services and the people who use them but, as Oliver comments:

> 'the material fact remains, it is still professionals doing it, whatever "it" is called, to disabled people' (1994, p 7)

Normalisation's preoccupation with deviance, labelling and stigma means that people should be taught the skills to enable them to associate with those who have been ascribed a high social value. Associating with those who are likewise devalued merely creates a vicious circle of deviance, by reinforcing the stigmatised identity of the individual. Such an argument has serious implications for the nature of social relations between people with learning difficulties.

First, it demonstrates an unquestioning acceptance of the concept of stigmatised identities. There is no recognition of stigma itself as a social construct: a mark imposed by an economically, socially and politically powerful group on one which is economically, socially and politically disempowered. Secondly, normalisation concentrates on the social behaviour of the devalued person with the intention of modifying it by teaching social skills in order to facilitate relationships with socially valued (i.e. non-disabled) people. The social and material constraints on the ability of people with learning difficulties to develop friendships (notably, low income, lack of access to one's money, the way that services are organised which undermines privacy and subjects individuals to public humiliation and disciplining, the authority of staff) tend not to figure as reasons which may explain some of the problems which they face.

Normalisation encourages people with learning difficulties to mix with socially valued people, while distancing themselves from those who have stigmatised identities. Such an argument misunderstands fundamentally the nature of friendship as a voluntary relationship based on mutual respect and affection, which has at its centre shared experiences and interests. People tend to select as their friends others who are like themselves. This is not to suggest that friendships between people with learning difficulties and non-disabled people shouldn't happen; only that by discouraging people with learning difficulties from associating from other disabled people, they will be isolated from an important potential source of friendship and support. Furthermore, identifying other people with learning difficulties as the problem to be avoided (literally), undermines the possibility of collective political action, based on commonality of experience.

The first part of this chapter has recounted the history of the spread of normalisation and the development of concerns and critiques about it over the last few years. I want to look now at ways to move on from normalisation and examine the possibilities of the social model of disability for people with learning difficulties.

MOVING FORWARD FROM NORMALISATION

The critical scrutiny of normalisation and challenges to its dominance over community care debates should be regarded as positive steps. There now exists the possibility of another theoretical tool (the social model of disability) which could assist people with learning difficulties, not just in a struggle for better services (the primary concern of normalisation), but for full economic, social and political inclusion in society.

However, it is necessary to examine the implications of the social model of disability for people with learning difficulties. This section of the paper intends to raise a number of questions. Part of the impetus for wanting to address these questions comes from attending two seminars on disability. The first was in June 1992 and was intended as a forum to discuss approaches to researching disability. The second was in October 1995 and aimed to take forward some of the debates within the sociology of disability. Both these seminars were very stimulating. Yet I was struck in each by the neglect of learning difficulty within the general discussion of disability, even when in some of the discussions, it seemed to me at least, learning difficulty was of central relevance to the analyses that participants were trying to establish.

For the purposes of this chapter I will concentrate on the relationship between the social model of disability and people with learning difficulties on a theoretical level, in particular the continued marginality of learning difficulty within the sociology of disability. The disability movement comprises people with physical/sensory impairments, people with mental illness and people with learning difficulties. Clearly, this includes people with a very wide range of impairments who, traditionally, have been classified by the medical model of disability and, therefore, have defined as having little in common.

Furthermore, there is great diversity among disabled people on the basis of age, gender, ethnicity, class or sexuality. The concerns about marginality within the social model do not apply solely to people with learning difficulties, but also to disabled women or older disabled people and so on. As Morris argues in the context of the experiences of disabled women:

> 'within the disabled people's movement, (it) has tended to be tacked on as a "special interest".' (1996, p 1)

My worry about the position of learning difficulty within the social model, however, is that it is almost entirely ignored – it hasn't yet even attained the status of a "special interest". The danger is then, that some of the analyses which emerge from the sociology of disability are theoretically flawed and their explanatory power is weakened.

In the early 1990s, it seemed hopeful that learning difficulty could come to figure more prominently on the agenda of the social model of disability. The analysis of disability presented by the social model is that disability is a social construct created by a range of historically and culturally specific factors. It is the social and economic structures of a particular society which create disability through processes of prejudice, exclusion and discrimination. This explication of disability can apply equally to the experiences of people with learning difficulties or physical/sensory impairments. for example, a brief look at the history of disabled people in Britain points to certain key events which led to the emergence of the long-stay institution:

- the rise of capitalism in Western Europe
- the expansion of state activity into new areas of economic and social life and the emergence of professionals
- the growing influence of eugenicist ideas about the quality of the population

These factors all combined in the late 19th and early 20th centuries to identify disabled people as a social problem. This was the impetus to develop a system of lifetime segregation for disabled people, regardless of the nature of impairment.

As I have indicated, the social model attempts to encompass the experiences of all disabled people. In so doing, it challenges the traditional separation of disabled people from each other. To apply the social model to physical/sensory impairment, but not learning difficulty, seems to me to be akin to suggesting that the analyses of society offered by feminism are applicable only to white women, and that the neglect of the experiences of black women within much feminist writing is because patriarchy has no explanatory power for them.

Having said this, nevertheless, the question remains as to why learning difficulty is neglected within the analyses of the social model. What appeared to be the promise of the sociology of disability does not seem to have materialised. The experiences of people with learning difficulties remain as marginal as ever.

My reasons for this worrying conclusion are two-fold. First, an examination of the literature produced by writers and academics associated with the disability movement reveal that there is little usage of literature produced by writers concerned with learning difficulty to develop their arguments. The debates about disability appear to be continuing on two parallel tracks with comparatively little cross-fertilisation of ideas. There are some exceptions to this general rule. For example, in 1994, Mike Oliver presented a conference paper which used the social model to apply a materialist critique of normalisation although, to my knowledge, this paper has not been published and is not widely available. Jenny Morris's book *Encounters with Strangers: Feminism and Disability (1996)* includes a chapter about The Powerhouse, a refuge for women with learning difficulties who have experienced physical or sexual abuse. Yet these tend to be the exceptions and much literature is produced which utilises the social model, but says nothing about learning difficulty. Thus, Oliver's sketch of some of the key literature associated with the social model (Oliver, 1996) mentions no writers or debates which are specific to learning difficulty. It appears the best that people with learning difficulties can expect is an implicit inclusion in any writing about disability.

Secondly, the experiences of people with learning difficulties are generally omitted from much of the disability literature, even when those experiences are, I would argue, relevant to the arguments presented by the author. The implicit inclusion of learning difficulty mentioned above means that some of the arguments emanating from within the social model are assumed to refer to all disabled people, when in reality they do not. Such arguments clearly are very partial.

Important aspects of a debate may not be developed because they are more relevant to people with learning difficulties than those with physical/sensory impairments. For example, in 1994, I wrote that the campaign for civil rights for disabled people appeared to have little to say about the relationship between disabled people, the police and the Criminal Justice System even though equal treatment under the law is a crucial element of civil rights – a point fully recognised by feminist and anti-racist campaigners and writers (Chappell, 1994). Of specific concern to the civil rights campaign should be the powers of the 1991 Criminal Procedure (Insanity and Unfitness to Plead) Act to incarcerate defendants in special hospitals by identifying them as unfit to plead, and the many cases where people with learning difficulties have been wrongly convicted of crimes. While writers associated with the disability movement are producing important work which examines what happens to disabled people who are victims of crime (see Kennedy, 1996, Shakespeare, 1996), there is little on the discrimination against disabled people who are accused of committing crimes.

If we accept the premise that the social model of disability can and should include learning difficulty, there is a need to examine why learning difficulty remains so marginal to debates within the disability movement. There are, I think, a number of possible explanations.

FOCUSING ON THE BODY

Much of the disability literature tends to define impairment in terms of the body. There is nothing intrinsic to the word impairment which suggests physical rather than intellectual imperfection. However, the usage of the term often suggests that this is so. For example, a perusal of debates about disability and culture illustrates this, because it is images of disabled people which being examined.

Furthermore, there are occasions in the literature where "able-bodied" is used as the opposite of "disabled" (for example, French, 1993). Barnes (1996, p 43), for example, writes of the material and cultural forces 'which created the myth of "bodily perfection" or the "able-bodied" ideal'. This would be fair enough if the chapter clearly was about physical/sensory impairment, but it is entitled *Theories of disability and the origins of the oppression of disabled people in western society* (my bold italics). The use of the term "disabled people" should include people with learning difficulties, but often it does not and their experiences remain hidden.

Hevey (1993) also focuses on physical/sensory impairment in his discussion of the cultural representation of disabled people. He argues that the representation of impairment is based on gazing on the body and portraying this in cultural terms. Bodily imperfection (Oedipus and Richard III are oft-quoted examples) becomes a metaphor character defect, which entails his (usually his) eventual downfall. Thus, as Hevey argues:

> 'The history of the portrayal of disabled people is that disabled people are portrayed as flawed able-bodied people' (1993, p 118)

Such an analysis may well be applicable to people with physical/sensory impairments. However, for people with learning difficulties, it is more problematic. Here, the body is not the site of the impairment, the impairment may not be immediately apparent and nor may it be associated with any physical imperfection. Indeed, I can think of many people with learning difficulties whom I have met over the years who are, in conventional terms, extremely physically attractive. For them, impairment does not equal a failure to meet the conventional ideals of the body.

A similar problem emerges concerning the question of the sexuality of disabled people. The literature here tends to use as its starting point the conventional assumption that disabled people are asexual. This stereotype is assumed to refer to all disabled people. Yet, for people with learning difficulties, there is more than one stereotype of their sexuality. There certainly exists a view that people with learning difficulties are eternal children who never develop an adult sexuality. However, there also is a strong historical association between learning difficulty and powerful images of a very threatening and promiscuous sexuality which must be restrained.

Thus, a key factor in the segregation of people with learning difficulties in the early 20th century was their supposedly threatening sexuality. As Williams (1989) points out, not only did people with learning difficulties fail as workers, they failed as **parents**. Eugenicist concerns of this period were underpinned by fears of trade competition, the struggle for imperial expansion and the immigration of Jews from Eastern Europe. The labelling of people with Down's syndrome as "mongols" underscores the link that was made between racial and intellectual inferiority (Booth 1987).

Such concerns focused attention on people with learning difficulties and the way that their supposedly uncontrollable sexuality, promiscuity and high fertility threatened the moral fibre of society. In particular, it was people with mild or borderline learning difficulty who were seen as being especially dangerous. Their impairments were unrecognisable to the untrained person and, if unchecked, they would be able to merge into wider society and spread their pernicious immoral influence. (Discrimination against people with learning difficulties under the Criminal Justice System, which I mentioned earlier, echoes this long-standing connection between moral and mental degeneracy.)

It was for this reason, Gelb argues (1987), the American psychologist Goddard adapted the European Binet test, which attempted to classify different degrees of learning difficulty, so that it was deliberately harsh at the upper end of the scale. The express purpose of doing this was so that the test would pin-point those with a presumed mental age of 12 years who were defined as having a mild learning difficulty and retarded moral development. At the same time, pseudo-scientific studies were made of the genealogy of so-called deviant families in order to demonstrate that idiocy, moral degeneracy and criminality were all hereditary. (Interestingly, this technique of tracing the histories of deviant families has been rejuvenated in the USA in an attempt to establish the existence of the "criminal gene.") The sexuality of people with learning difficulties, therefore, appeared as socially dangerous and this was part of the impetus behind their segregation from society under the terms of the 1913 Mental Deficiency Act.

This connection between moral and mental degeneracy also operated the other way around. Contravening sexual codes of behaviour, for example, having an illegitimate child while claiming poor relief or even fraternising too closely with American soldiers during the last war (which was the reason for the incarceration in a long-stay hospital of one woman I have met) was sufficient to be classified as having a learning difficulty

This is not to suggest that all writing on disability and sexuality excludes learning difficulty. Shakespeare (1996), for example, notes the vulnerability of people with learning difficulties to sexual abuse. Obviously, this is a very serious matter which must be discussed. Nonetheless, it accords with the more general view expressed in the disability literature that disabled people are stereotyped as sexually passive and powerless and it is this which makes them vulnerable to abuse. It does not explore the possibility that some people with learning difficulties may be stereotyped as sexually predatory and dangerous (that is, stereotyped as abusers) and experience discrimination on those grounds.

THE MEANING OF IMPAIRMENT

A new area of debate which has been emerging in the disability literature seeks to examine the "reality" of the experience of impairment. Some writers and academics associated with the disability movement have indicated a concern that the definitions presented by the social model deny that impairment has any relevance. That is, there are no limitations imposed by impairment which cannot be removed by, what French refers to as, 'social and environmental manipulation' (French, 1993, p 22). This debate is sensitive because of the danger that it will be used to reassert individualistic models of disability in which impairment and disability are synonymous (Oliver 1996, Crow 1996).

My concern about this debate is its assumption that impairment is located in the body. As Crow argues, 'impairment means the experience of our bodies can be unpleasant or difficult' (1996, p 209). It is the bodily pain of impairment that is referred to and the body which must be theorised. If the view is accepted that the meaning of impairment must not be denied and that it warrants examination, then this is an important issue for people with learning difficulties too. Yet what happens to the analysis if impairment is located in the intellect? Without the inclusion of the experiences of people with learning difficulties, any analysis of the meaning of impairment will be incomplete. Moreover, the question of impairment raises issues which relate to the limitations faced by people with learning difficulties to ensure that their experiences form a central part of the agenda of the social model. Are these limitations socially-driven or impairment-driven or both? I will return to this point a little later.

THE PERSONAL IS POLITICAL

One of the most important features of the emergence of the social model has been the relevance of personal history and experience to the writing that has been produced. Writers such as Mike Oliver, Jenny Morris, Sally French, Lois Keith and Paul Abberley to name a few, have theorised their personal experiences as disabled people to develop political insights into the meaning of disability. In taking such an approach, writing about disability reflects the feminist principle that one's personal experiences do not take place in isolation from wider social, economic and political structures. The personal also must be theorised.

However, the experiences of writers and academics who have written about disability in this way is physical/sensory impairment. It is this that has tended to shape the analysis which has developed. For people with learning difficulties, the issues are more problematic. While it is possible to call to mind a number of people with physical/sensory impairments who research, write and publish (whether based inside or outside academia), I can think of none who have learning difficulties.

Why should this be? Is it simply another of the discrimination that is meted out to disabled people? Does it mean that the intellectual and academic environment should be manipulated (to use French's phrase) so that people with intellectual/developmental impairments can participate? Should we be seeking to undo the emphasis on presenting material in a theoretical way, if it precludes people with learning difficulties? What would this mean for the development of disability theory?

Or is the nature of intellectual/developmental impairment more likely to create restrictions on the ability of people with learning difficulties to gain positions (for example, as researchers) where they can present their own theorised accounts of the world in the way that people with physical/sensory impairments have been able to do? How does this fit into calls to re-examine the meaning of impairment? To paraphrase Liz Crow (1996), external disabling barriers may create social and economic disadvantage, but the subjective experience of the intellectual/developmental impairments of people with learning difficulties is part of their everyday reality.

I am not suggesting that people with learning difficulties are not capable of articulating their experiences or do not recognise prejudice and discrimination when they encounter them. It is clear that many do. However, these views and experiences have not been conveyed in the disability literature to the same extent as those of people with physical/sensory impairments. Neither have they been conveyed without the involvement of non-disabled people as "allies", "supporters" or "facilitators" (and I would identify myself as someone who has taken this approach).

The obvious danger here is that non-disabled sympathisers will assume a dominant role. For example, in some self advocacy groups attached to day centres, staff may begin as facilitators with the intention of supporting the self-advocates. Yet they end up dominating proceedings so that meetings become an opportunity for staff to justify the operation of the service and pay lip service to the principle of self-advocacy. If people with learning difficulties do require allies to enable them convey their experiences in a way which is acceptable to researchers, examiners, editors, publishers and other gatekeepers, how should the integrity of their accounts be safeguarded?

DISABILITY THEORY: AVOIDING THE ERRORS OF THE PAST

Presenting the arguments along the lines of this chapter should create a sense of *déjà vu*. Any reading of the history of second-wave feminism makes it clear that the first feminist literature which emerged in the early 1960s, with its idealist emphasis, claimed to articulate the experiences of all women. With hindsight, we can recognise that this was not the case.

The experiences of white women (*vis-à-vis* their place within the family and their relationships to the workplace and the Welfare State, for example) are quite different from the experiences of ethnic minority women. Similarly, disabled feminists (Morris 1991 and Keith 1992) and non-disabled feminists (Walmsley, 1993) have exposed the partiality of the conventional feminist wisdom on informal care, by highlighting the way that feminism has ignored the experiences of disabled women and relegated them to the status of "the other".

Is this the destiny of people with learning difficulties within the social model? Is it inevitable that their views and experiences will be ignored, marginalised and rendered largely invisible? How much more literature will be produced that begins by using the term "disabled people", but gradually lapses into the term "able-bodied people"? How much more theory will develop that fails to include and explain the experiences of people of learning difficulties?

CONCLUSION

The sociology of disability (underpinned by the social model of disability), has been one of the most significant intellectual and political developments of the last 10 years. It has transformed the meaning of disability, at a personal, intellectual and political level, for many people. As Oliver (1996) points out, this transformation is a continuing process.

So, while it is important to celebrate achievements, it is necessary also to raise concerns about the direction of some of the debates in the sociology of disability and point to new pathways for debate. Much of the content of this paper has been shaped by a sense of frustration at the continued exclusion of people with learning difficulties from the analyses of the sociology of disability. Striving to include analysis of learning difficulty in the continuing transformation of disability indeed would be an achievement worthy of celebration.

The problem of marginality requires a shared response. Part of this responsibility rests clearly with people who are committed to the social model and interested in learning difficulty. However, to strive to embrace all disabled people within the social model also is a wider collective responsibility. I end with a plea that writers in the disability movement keep the question of learning difficulty in their minds and ask themselves whether the empirical or theoretical work in which they are engaged is solely about physical/sensory impairment (if it is, this must be made clear) or is it about **disability**. If the latter, the analysis must address the question of learning difficulty.

ACKNOWLEDGEMENT

I would like to thank Mike Oliver for presenting this paper on my behalf at the *Disability and Society: Ten Years On conference*, 4th – 6th September 1996.

REFERENCES

ABBERLEY, P. (1987) The concept of oppression and the development of a social theory of disability, **Disability, Handicap and Society**, 2, 1, pp. 5-19.

BARNES, C. (1996) Theories of disability and the origins of the oppression of disabled people in western society in: L. BARTON (ed.) **Disability and Society: Emerging Issues and Insights** Harlow, Longman.

BAXTER, C., WARD, L., POONIA, K. and NADIRSHAW, Z. (1990) **Double Discrimination: Issues and Services for People with learning Difficulties from Black and Ethnic Minority Communities** London, King's Fund/Commission for Racial Equality.

BAYLEY, M. (1991) Normalisation or "social role valorization": an adequate philosophy? in: S. BALDWIN and J. HATTERSLEY (eds.) **Mental Handicap: Social Science Perspectives** London, Tavistock Routledge.

BOOTH, T. (1987) Labels and their consequences, in: D. LANE and B. STRATFORD (Eds.) **Current Approaches to Down's Syndrome** London, Cassell.

BROWN, H. and SMITH, H. (1989) Whose "ordinary life" is it anyway? **Disability, Handicap and Society**, 4, 2, pp. 105-119.

BROWN, H. and SMITH, H. (1992) Defending community care: can normalisation do the job? **British Journal of Social Work**, 22, 6, pp. 685-693.

CAMPAIGN FOR PEOPLE WITH A MENTAL HANDICAP (1981) **The Principle of Normalisation: A Foundation for Effective Services** London, CMH.

CHAPPELL, A.L. (1992) Towards a sociological critique of the normalisation principle, **Disability, Handicap and Society**, 7, 1, pp. 35-51.

CHAPPELL, A. L. (1994) Disability, discrimination and the criminal justice system, *Critical Social Policy*, 14, 3, pp. 19-33.

CROW, L. (1996) Including all of our lives: renewing the social model of disability, in: J. MORRIS (ed.) *Encounters with Strangers: Feminism and Disability* London, The Women's Press.

DEPARTMENT OF HEALTH AND SOCIAL SECURITY (1971) *Better Services for the Mentally Handicapped*, Cmnd. 4683, London, HMSO.

FRENCH, S. (1993) Disability, impairment or something in between? in : J. SWAIN, V. FINKELSTEIN, S. FRENCH and M. OLIVER (eds.) *Disabling Barriers – Enabling Environments* London, Sage.

GELB, S.A. (1987) Social deviance and the "discovery" of the moron, *Disability, Handicap and Society*, 2, 3, pp. 247-258.

HEVEY, D. (1993) The tragedy principle: strategies for change in the representation of disabled people, in: J. SWAIN, V. FINKELSTEIN, S. FRENCH and M. OLIVER (eds.) *Disabling Barriers – Enabling Environments* London, Sage.

KEITH, L. (1992) Who cares wins? Women, caring and disability, *Disability, Handicap and Society*, 7, 2, pp. 167-175.

KENNEDY, M. (1996) Sexual abuse and disabled children, in: J. MORRIS (ed.) *Encounters with Strangers: Feminism and Disability* London, The Women's Press.

MORRIS, J. (1991) *Pride Against Prejudice: Transforming Attitudes to Disability* London, The Women's Press.

MORRIS, J. (1996) Introduction, in: J. MORRIS (ed.) *Encounters with Strangers: Feminism and Disability* London, The Women's Press.

OLIVER, M. (1990) *The Politics of Disablement* Basingstoke, Macmillan.

OLIVER, M. (1994) *Capitalism, disability and ideology: a materialist critique of the normalization principle*, paper presented at the conference 25 Years of Normalization, Social Role Valorization and Social Integration: A Retrospective and Prospective View, University of Ottawa, May 10th-13th.

OLIVER, M. (1996) *Understanding Disability: From Theory to Practice* Basingstoke, Macmillan.

SHAKESPEARE, T. (1996) Power and prejudice: issues of gender, sexuality and disability, in: L. BARTON (ed.) *Disability and Society: Emerging Issues and Insights* Harlow, Longman.

THE POWERHOUSE, (1996) Power in the house: women with learning difficulties organising against abuse, in: J. MORRIS (ed.) *Encounters with Strangers: Feminism and Disability* London, The Women's Press.

TYNE, A. (1987) Shaping community services: the impact of an idea, in: N. MALIN (ed.) *Reassessing Community Care (with Particular Reference to*

Provision for People with Mental Handicap and for People with Mental Illness) London, Croom Helm.

WALMSLEY, J. (1993) Contradictions in caring: reciprocity and interdependence, *Disability, Handicap and Society*, 8, 2, pp. 129-141.

WARD, L. (1992) Foreword, in: H. BROWN and H. SMITH (eds.) *Normalisation: A Reader for the Nineties* London, Tavistock/Routledge.

WHITEHEAD, S. (1992) The social origins of normalisation, in: H. BROWN and H. SMITH (eds.) *Normalisation: A Reader for the Nineties* London, Tavistock/Routledge.

WILLIAMS, F. (1989) *Social Policy: A Critical Introduction* London, Polity Press.

CHAPTER 4

Including People with Learning Difficulties:
Theory and Practice

By Jan Walmsley

INTRODUCTION

A major development of recent years has been the inclusion of people with learning difficulties in the Disability Movement. The application of ideas associated with the social model of disability to the situation of people with learning difficulties has the potential to be an empowering and energising development.

In this chapter I use my own experiences at the Open University to chart how such ideas have inspired change, a shift to inclusion of people with learning difficulties in a particular set of activities, teaching, research and publishing in the last 10 years. In 1986 I was a member of a team which launched a course, *Mental Handicap: Patterns for Living*, about people with learning difficulties, but neither for nor with them. In 1996 a replacement for that course, *Working as Equal People*, was launched. This course was different; it was made with, by and for people with learning difficulties as well as about them. At least 25 people with learning difficulties were present at the launch, and this was neither charity or tokenism. All had contributed in some significant way to make *Equal People*.

Part of the paper, then, tells the story of how that came about, the nitty gritty practical things that made inclusion a reality, and shows some of the ways in which people with learning difficulties contributed to the final product, the course itself.

So far, so good, a positive example of theory into practice. However, I end the paper by questioning how far such strategies can take us.

THEORY AND PRACTICE

The inclusion of people with learning difficulties in ordinary, and indeed, extraordinary life has made great strides in the decade which this volume celebrates. It is the inclusion of people with learning difficulties in the rather extraordinary activities of research, writing and publishing that is the subject of this paper. In 1984 Richards could identify only five British studies in the previous twenty years where people with learning difficulties had been informants in research projects. In 1996, such a list might well run into hundreds.

I was asked to contribute to the Disability and Society 'Ten Years On' Conference on the strength of the work the Open University undertook in preparing a new pack 'Learning Disability: Working as Equal People' which was an effort to move inclusion of people with learning difficultie's onto a new plane, not only as students of the course, but as authors, contributors and critical commentators. The story of how this occurred, how we moved from making courses *for* to making them *with* people with learning difficulties encapsulates some of the shifts in practice that have occurred in the last decade, shifts which are in large part attributable to the work of self-advocacy organisations like People First, partners in making the course. So part of my task is to briefly tell that story, the practical issues which need to be addressed if inclusion is to be a reality.

But the chapter is not all descriptive. I also seek to set these developments in a broader context, of the relationship of people with learning difficulties to the wider disability movement, and of some of the particular challenges they face in being taken seriously as contributors to political and academic debate.

NORMALISATION AND THE SOCIAL MODEL OF DISABILITY

To begin, then a little bit of scene setting. The work of disabled people, including my colleague Vic Finkelstein, in developing a 'social model of disability' dates from the 1970s and 1980s (see Finkelstein 1993, Oliver 1990 for overviews of the development of the social model of disability). These academics developed an argument that disabled people, through their shared experience of social and physical barriers to full citizenship, are a distinctive minority social group, with common experiences of oppression. There followed a vigorous period of analysis, political activity and self-identification as disabled people, the force of which can perhaps be seen in the success of the campaign to get the British Disability Discrimination Act passed in 1996. This Act is flawed and limited, but it does represent an acknowledgement that disability is on the mainstream political agenda, and a public recognition that disability may be socially created, and not just a personal tragedy.

At the time Vic Finkelstein, Mike Oliver and others were thinking through the social model, a very different ideology was the dominant force in learning disability, normalisation. Unlike the work in the disability area, this 'movement' was dominated by non-disabled people. Originating in Scandinavia, the arguments were that people with learning difficulties deserved to have opportunities to enjoy normal patterns of life, the rhythms of the day and the seasons, the separation of work and play, an ordinary life, even within segregated services (Nirje, 1980, p. 33). These ideas were developed and transformed by Wolf Wolfensberger and colleagues in the North American context as a strategy to reverse institutional models of congregation and segregation, and to promote integration with 'valued' (ie non-disabled) individuals and institutions (Wolfensberger and Tullman, 1983). Normalisation, especially its North American strand, was at the time I became involved with learning disability in the mid 1980s, an incontrovertible dogma. Anyone who dared voice disagreement was labelled as dangerously ill-informed, a heretic (for a fuller discussion of the history of normalisation see Chappell in this volume). Yet normalisation was very limited in its critique of the reasons why people with learning difficulties were devalued by society, basing it on labelling theory. The argument was that because learning difficulty/mental retardation/mental handicap/etc. were negative labels, *services* (not society as in the social model) should do all they can to offer people valued social roles and positive images. It was a movement which fostered integration of people with learning difficulties into mainstream society, which aimed to disperse people and help them develop relationships with non-disabled people because they are more 'valued' as the terminology puts it, and to downplay difference, the very antithesis of the way the social model of disability critiqued social barriers and helped at least some disabled people learn to develop solidarity with one another, to revalue themselves as equal citizens, and to attribute their oppression and exclusion to social barriers, much broader than labelling.

There has been a gradual breaking down of the distinctive differences these two contrasting sets of ideas represent, partly because people with learning difficulties have 'found a voice' through self-advocacy, partly through bridge building between organisations like British Council of Disabled People and People First. There has been departure from strict normalisation principles to the extent that it is accepted practice for people with learning difficulties to appear on public platforms with a non-disabled supporter to prompt and advise them. However, the links between the disability movement and people with learning difficulties are often fragile, and most people with learning difficulties have not yet to my knowledge repudiated normalisation. The People First slogan 'label jars, not people' owes much to normalisation whose analysis is that the labelling is the cause of the oppression. Research indicates that members of self advocacy organisations are notably more likely to own the 'learning difficulty' label than other people with learning difficulties (Simons, 1992), but there is still a hesitancy in adopting the positive stance to disability which characterises the broader disability politics. One of my arguments here is that thinking in learning disability is still dominated by normalisation.

Hence I would argue that there are still differences in the ways disabled people and people with learning difficulties and their allies, analyse the situation they find themselves in and differences therefore in practice. This is a theme I will elaborate upon below, before returning to the implications for the theory of inclusion of people with learning difficulties in the disability movement.

INCLUSION IN PRACTICE

To move, then, from policy to practice, I use my own experiences in the Open University to illustrate the how of inclusion. It's a neat story, spanning just over a decade from 1985 to 1996, and the production of four different open learning courses. Coincidentally, it is also the decade which this volume celebrates.

The UK Open University, founded in 1971, was dubbed the University of the Second Chance, offering an opportunity for higher education to those many people who had been unable to qualify for university entrance through the usual route of 'A' levels (in England, Wales and Northern Ireland) or 'Highers' (Scotland). It has a completely open access policy on university entrance. Anyone who could obtain a place, and afford the modest fees was eligible to become an Open University student. In theory, this includes people with learning difficulties, though few availed themselves of the opportunity.

The OU also produces 'packs', open learning training materials for use by anyone interested enough to purchase and study them. In 1985, when I joined the OU, production of a new 'pack' was in full swing, 'Mental Handicap: Patterns for Living' made in collaboration with Mencap. In its day it was revolutionary, addressing as it did not only professionals and front line staff, but also family members and volunteers, the idea being to improve practice not only through information giving but also by bringing people from different backgrounds and in different roles together in mixed groups to study, discuss and debate. To a great extent it was successful. It sold well, and made quite an impact. It is estimated that in its ten year life at least 30,000 people made use of it.

However, revolutionary as it was in its day, its shortcomings are obvious with hindsight. It portrayed people with learning difficulties as human beings with real feelings, but did not include the 'voices' of people with learning difficulties. They were anonymous, pseudonyms were used, and they were represented through line drawings, not photographs. They were not included in the target audience, nor were they involved in any way in its production or dissemination.

Very rapidly this omission was brought to the team's attention. We might not have envisaged people with learning difficulties doing Patterns for Living, but others did. Some imaginative and dedicated students set up learning partnerships so that people with learning difficulties could do the course, some getting as far as completing the computer marked assignments and gaining a Certificate of Course Completion. Letters began to come in urging the OU to produce a course for people with learning difficulties to study. The ideas in Patterns for Living were good, but the technology was wrong, almost entirely print based, too dense, too much reading.

This led to 'Patterns for Living: Working Together' (1989) an adaptation of the original course, particularly for people with learning difficulties. The content and ideas remained unchanged, but the technology was transformed. Eight of the main case studies were recorded as audio dramas, accompanied by a cartoon style workbook, and assignments to test comprehension of the dramas. This was *for* people with learning difficulties, but it again excluded them from the production. Ordinary actors were used – no efforts were made to employ people with learning difficulties – and one criticism was that these actors relied too much on speech impairments to convey learning disability. However, in promoting the course the people who tested it were invited to speak of their responses to the course, and some were extremely effective ambassadors. The message that people with learning difficulties could lead groups of students as facilitators, either alone or in partnerships, was one that was vigorously promoted in publicity, and widely taken up.

In 1988 the Patterns for Living team began work on an undergraduate level course about learning disability, 'Mental Handicap: Changing Perspectives'. The challenge for the team was to find ways of including people with learning difficulties in a course which they were unlikely to be able to study – if the learning difficulty label means anything, surely we believed that it meant an OU degree is beyond most people so labelled (an issue I will return to below). The solution to this was to compile a book, an anthology of contributions by people with learning difficulties, entitled 'Know Me As I Am' (Atkinson and Williams, 1990). The book is the heart of the course. Students are consistently asked to refer to it, and are expected to use its content as a reference point in their written work. Thus the voices of people with learning difficulties are fully represented, though the *analysis* of what they say/write/draw was left to the course team and the students, and this is another important point.

Finally, to 'Equal People'. By 1992 the original Mental Handicap: Patterns for Living was clearly out of date. As chair, I regularly fielded letters objecting to 'Mental Handicap' in the title, there was precious little of self-advocacy, and too much about hospital life. It was time to consider its replacement. However, as such packs have to be entirely externally funded, the challenge was to persuade funders that a 'remake' was a worthwhile investment. Mencap's support was secured for the project, but how was it to be 'different'? The answer to move forward the ideas that had been around in all three courses we'd made previously:

• to develop partnerships with people with learning difficulties to make the course, as had been done with 'Know Me As I Am' in producing 'Changing Perspectives'.

- to include people with learning difficulties in the audience, alongside staff, parents, relatives, volunteers.

At the outset, the means by which either was to be done were rather vague. I describe only the partnerships to make the course here, though the inclusion of people in other roles is equally important.

PARTNERSHIPS TO MAKE THE COURSE

Initially ideas about partnership focused on an advisory group. To put this into effect I and a colleague made an appointment with People First (London Boroughs) to discuss. It is to the credit of the people we met on that day that they immediately noticed the tokenism of an advisory group. In response to the rough diagram I produced to illustrate the production process, Lloyd Page, People First volunteer, asked 'where's all the decisions made?' I pointed to the 'Course Team' at the centre. His response was 'That's where we want to be'. Indeed, that's where they ended up, though not without doubts on the part of the existing team that this was manageable or even desirable! There followed a letter from People First setting out the terms and conditions on which they would work with the OU and Mencap.

Including Lloyd Page and initially Anya Souza (later Desmond Coker-Davies) as People First representatives on the team turned out to have been an excellent decision. People First (London Boroughs) had the resources and the trained personnel to make the partnership work – efficient telephone and fax service, back-up for the representatives particularly Lois Robinson, who was the supporter throughout, a good network of contacts and on-going work on which we could draw. Questions were asked 'why London?' The answer was that it is geographically convenient for Milton Keynes, but more importantly, People First (London Boroughs) provided the organisational infrastructure with which we could engage. For example, it was possible to pay the course team members for their work without threatening benefits because the money went to the organisation, not the individuals.

On the part of the OU it was important to pay attention to the means by which our new colleagues could be helped to engage with a complex and often stressful production system. Some of the steps we took were:

- to kick off with a two-day residential planning meeting. This helped us to get to know one another, build trust, share ideas about how to proceed, all those old clichés which are nevertheless important ingredients for a successful team

- to send out material for meetings and comment in good time for Lois to support Lloyd, Anya or Desmond in making sense of what was said, at least a week in advance
- to write minutes with careful attention to language
- to prepare explanations of technicalities like schedules, assessment (including Vocational Qualifications!), ways of publishing, etc. in advance, and presenting the information at meetings
- to train colleagues who visited the Team meetings (from marketing, editing, and design) to take account of speed of delivery, sophistication of language and paperwork
- to ensure that all meetings included agenda items which everyone could make a contribution to. We called this 'Reports from everyone', and it was a good opportunity to exchange experiences and ideas which most agendas do not permit
- to include breaks to help concentration. In principle this meant we worked for a maximum of 1 hour 15 minutes at a time, though we did not always manage to keep to this when pressure of work was too great.

We had been successful enough in raising money for the course to be able to afford to pay the additional costs of extra staff, and a supporter. However, without the partnership commitment it is unlikely we would have raised the cash, so it could not be called merely fortuitous.

Apart from giving credibility to the course, People First's contributions were:

- definitions of what was important to include, particularly learning materials on bereavement and the stresses of moving house
- access to on-going projects, and people
- the group work exercises which they co-authored, based in part on People First training materials and experience
- instant feedback on what was and what was not clear language
- opportunities to test materials on the spot – for example, in the audio drama the script moved straight from the star character's sister expressing

concern that she should remember to administer her sick father's medicines to his funeral. Desmond said he thought this meant she was responsible for his death – the script was amended

- extra people to help fulfil the commitment to visit all 15 groups who tested the course in draft, groups which were geographically spread across the UK and Ireland

- because the process was less rushed than usual, I think we all found it a good team to be in. For one thing, we learnt to listen to one another, to savour what was said, rather than struggle to be heard.

Space does not allow me to go into detail about the other side of the coin, the involvement of large numbers of people with and without learning difficulties, in making video, audio, contributing to case studies and advisory groups, testing and providing feedback, featuring under their real names with photographs, not under pseudonyms and in line drawings as was the case in 1986. The course has been on sale since March 1996, and will play its part in persuading others to take inclusion seriously, and show ways in which it can be done.

So, in the decade we are considering, the OU moved from making courses *about* people with learning difficulties to making courses in partnership with them. It's indicative of the shifts in attitudes, knowledge, technology and the efforts of people with learning difficulties to get others to take them seriously.

THEORY AGAIN

So far so good, a positive story of inclusion. But it will not have escaped your notice that it is I, not Lloyd, Anya or Desmond who writes this account. Indeed, there were no speakers at the Ten Years On Conference who call themselves people with learning difficulties, and a quick scan through recent Disability and Society editions leads me to tentatively say there have been no articles written by people with learning difficulties. This must be significant. As far as the Equal People team goes, Anya and Desmond are unemployed at the time of writing, whilst Lloyd and Lois have moved onto other projects. The barriers to inclusion were only temporarily dismantled, now they are back in place.

How does this relate back to theory, and the disability movement?

I will argue from here on that there are very particular issues for people with learning difficulties in taking control of analysing their own experience, issues which are less pressing for other groups of disabled people, and which the broad disability movement must take on board if there is to be a genuine alliance, based on mutual trust and respect.

One important point is that the way people with learning difficulties contributed to 'Equal People' was based on personal experience, who they are as people with learning difficulties, and the often unique insights they have to offer from that perspective. Those skills have not been transferred to other courses as they might have been had people without learning difficulties spent two and half years contributing to an open learning project. It is important to ask whether this is due to attitudinal prejudice, lack of opportunity or to the limitations imposed by the impairment itself.

A second related point, and one made by Simone Aspis, a woman with learning disabilities, to whom I am indebted for some of the ideas aired here (Aspis, 1997), is that the contributions made by people with learning difficulties are personal – they contribute their personal experiences, their life stories, and others take on the job of interpreting them. This critique can be applied to 'Know Me As I Am', the anthology at the heart of the Changing Perspectives course referred to above, and, perhaps to a lesser extent, to the contributions made by people with learning difficulties to 'Equal People'. Again, it is appropriate to ask whether this represents a failure on the part of people like myself to enable people with learning difficulties to contribute in this way, or whether we must accept this as a result of the impairment itself.

Thirdly, the Equal People course does not tackle the politics of disability head on. It has a rights agenda, but does not set out to teach the social model of disability. I am again indebted to Aspis for this insight (personal communication 1996). She argues that it was a failure on the part of the Course Team. I am less certain than she that this is the case. My defence is that at the level at which we pitched the course, a basic training tool for people with learning difficulties, family members and untrained staff it was not appropriate. Certainly my own teaching skills are not up to that task. It was instructive to me to watch Simone expound her ideas on the limitations of self-advocacy to a mixed group of women, with and without learning disabilities. The women with learning disabilities, all of whom were active in self-advocacy and related activities, found her arguments hard to comprehend.

CO-AUTHORING AND CO-EDITING: A WAY FORWARD?

In order to overcome the many barriers to inclusion in academic and political debate, the idea of co-authoring and co-editing a book is an attractive strategy. Since completing work on 'Equal People' I and some colleagues with and without learning difficulties have formed a group, known as Women in Learning Disability (WILD) to co-write a book about women with learning difficulties to which women with learning difficulties will be editors and contributors. There is, I believe, a genuine commitment to make this more than tokenistic, and following Aspis's argument, more than the disabled women relating their 'stories' for the non-disabled women to unpick, analyse and re-package. However, there are some contradictions deeply embedded within the project, which have impeded progress.

First, there is the question of access. For most of the non-disabled women, it is important to make this a book which will be taken seriously, which will help to re-orientate policy, and shift ideas. Therefore it needs to be more than a set of training exercises, a video, or an audio led package. The peculiar conjunctions of gender and learning disability give rise to unique issues, and these are as yet poorly understood and theorised. Those of us brought up in the academic world see print as the means by which ideas are worked through, tested and clarified. The disabled women, or at least some of them, disagree. For them, the main purpose is to reach women with learning difficulties – to do this will require, not a book full of ideas expressed in complex language, but a video, or a highly illustrated set of booklets, similar to those produced by, amongst others, People First (London Boroughs) (People First, 1994a, 1994b), or indeed, 'the 'Equal People' pack (Open University, 1996). I am not sure whether these are mutually exclusive aims, but at the present state of my knowledge, I feel that they are.

Secondly, there is the issue of power, who controls the analysis. Not for the first time, I have been present as disabled women in this group re-live their disappointments, their very personal experiences of oppression, exclusion and discrimination in front of an audience. These are moving stories, yet I feel an acute sense of unease, and helplessness. It is almost like being a voyeur. The women are keen for the stories to be told, for the injustice to be recognised and the struggles acknowledged, yet I do not know how to support them in translating these experiences from the personal to the political without taking over. Nor is it yet clear how a book can represent women with learning difficulties without inviting the reader to join in as a voyeur.

Thirdly, there is, as always, the question of resources. To write a book with genuine involvement will mean lots of meetings, time, writing partnerships and struggles. What publisher will finance such a project?

And finally, even if we answer these questions, there remains a danger of creating an élite, a group of women who, admittedly, can act as role models for others, but a group which excludes many, such as people without speech, and whose members may find it as difficult to represent and reach them as do the rest of us.

It is possible to counter all these arguments – we could aim for two outcomes, one a book, the other training resources, so that all possible audiences can be reached, for example. It may be that the group has to work through issues of personal and political, to separate them so that we all become interpreters of the experiences of women with learning difficulties, with the disabled women contributing their own experiences not as raw material but as an interpretative tool. We could, perhaps, obtain resources through special fund raising, setting up as a research project rather than only as book authors. And Mike Oliver is not the only disabled academic to make the point that disabled people can and must speak for others – it is not just a matter of being representative.

THE ROLE OF ADVISERS

The discussion of the WILD project inevitably gives rise to questions about the role people without learning difficulties play as advisers, supporters, co-authors and the like. People with learning difficulties are uniquely reliant on human intermediaries to gain access to the sort of complex ideas represented by academic and political debate, and indeed, to contribute to such debate. Whilst most disabled people rely on aids, human or technical, to enable them to participate in society on equal terms, the role of advisers to people with learning difficulties is one that is more complex then, say, a British Sign Language interpreter for a deaf person. The BSL interpreter has the relatively straightforward task of translating from one language to another. The adviser has a far more complex task both of enabling a person with learning difficulties to understand ideas, and at the same time task of enabling him or her to articulate a response.

The role of advisers and supporters in the lives of people with learning difficulties is a little researched topic. Other than some practical checklists for advisers (Values into Action, 1993) there is very little written, partly because people with learning difficulties rely on such people to enable them to get into print, and standing back from that relationship to reflect upon it, and communicate it to others cannot be easy. Issues such as the degree of affection and mutual respect required to make the relationship workable, and questions about the impact of gender, age, class or ethnicity on the relationship have barely been put on the agenda. Anecdotal evidence and personal observation are all I have to draw on to in trying to make sense of a very complex relationship, and loyalty to those people with learning difficulties who have confided their personal reservations about their advisers bars me from committing much to print here. Suffice it to say, there are precious few safeguards to protect people from learning difficulties from exploitation at the hands of their advisers, and I, in common with many people who spend time with self-advocacy groups, have observed both extremely facilitative and some extremely questionable practice by advisers. It is a moot point whether the imbalance of power that is at the very root of the relationship between people with learning difficulties and their advisers can ever be remedied by better training, supervision and codes of practice. At present, none of these is in place, and the short-term funding on which most self-advocacy groups operate makes it difficult to visualise how that might happen.

CONCLUSION: UNANSWERED QUESTIONS

In the final analysis I am left with a series of questions.

What is the nature of learning disability? Is it, as normalisation theory has it, rooted in labelling?

How far can the environment be manipulated to solve the limitations learning disability imposes? Is it the nature and implications of the impairment which gave rise to the absence of speakers with learning difficulties at the Ten Years On Conference (to be replaced by people like me) or is it a failure of imagination on all our parts to enable them to contribute at the level of an academic conference, or in a volume of academic writings?

I ask whether, with all the time, technology and teaching skills in the world, it is possible for people with learning difficulties to learn the skills which will enable them to take part in such debates on equal terms?

The dice are loaded against such a development, not just because of poor opportunities for learning them, not just because we lack resources or have the wrong attitudes, but because it is ultimately a normalising agenda we are working to, an agenda which maintains that to take part in society on equal terms people with learning difficulties must heroically rise above the impairment and join in a conspiracy to deny that their intellectual limitations matter. Or maybe these limitations are not real, maybe they are socially created, and they can be undone.

Every form of disability gives rise to a particular set of restrictions on what the disabled person can do, and it is in the area of political and academic debate that people with learning difficulties will always be at a disadvantage. Even if they somehow rise above those limitations they will then run the risk of being relabelled as 'normal', as not having learning difficulties at all, a development I have witnessed in relation to individuals with particular gifts which go counter to common-sense notions of what learning disability means. Having a degree is one such example. Another is being able to think, write and publish without assistance. In a sense, there are two messages, both complementary and contradictory.

The first is that inclusion and partnership are possible. They require a will to make it work, money and time, and careful attention to detail. They require that the environment is carefully manipulated. It is work I am personally very proud to have been involved in as Chair of the Equal People course team, I'm proud of the process and proud of the product.

The second is a more mixed message. It is that including people with learning difficulties in academic and political debate will always be a struggle. Unlike other groups of disabled people with different impairments, it is unclear whether they will ever be able to engage on equal terms. It is not just a matter of time, resources, technology and positive attitudes. It is not just a learning difficulty, the sort we are too ready to say we share because we too have learning difficulties. It is where normalisation has not got all the answers. This is an area where oppression and exclusion take a distinct form for people with learning difficulties, and if they are to take their place alongside other disabled people, at gatherings like the Ten Years On Conference, for example, or in the pages of the journal, it's something that has to be addressed. This chapter is an attempt to place these questions on the agenda of people working with people with learning difficulties in this area, and of the disability movement. I look forward to a continuing debate.

ACKNOWLEDGEMENT

I am indebted to Simone Aspis of People First for the many challenges she has thrown at me, some of which are addressed in this paper. I know she will not agree with all I have said, but without her it could not have been written.

REFERENCES

ASPIS, S. (1996) Personal communication

ASPIS, S. (1997, forthcoming) 'Self Advocacy for People with Learning Difficulties: Does it have a future?' *Disability and Society*, Vol. 12, No. 4.

ATKINSON, D. AND WILLIAMS, F. (1990) *Know Me As I Am: an Anthology of Prose, Poetry and Art by People with Learning Disabilities* Sevenoaks: Hodder and Stoughton.

FINKELSTEIN, V. (1993) 'Disability: a social challenge or an administrative responsibility?' in Swain J., Finkelstein, V., French, S. and Oliver, M. (eds) *Disabling Barriers: Enabling Environments* London: Sage.

FRENCH, S. (1993) 'Disability, Impairment or something in between' in Swain J. Finkelstein, V., French, S. and Oliver, M. (eds) *Disabling Barriers: Enabling Environments* London: Sage.

NIRJE, B. (1980) 'The normalisation principle' in Flynn, R.J. and Nitsch, K.E. (eds) *Normalisation, Social Integration and Community Services* Baltimore: University Park Press.

OLIVER, M. (1990) *The Politics of Disablement* Macmillan.

OPEN UNIVERSITY (1986) *Mental Handicap: Patterns for Living* Milton Keynes: Open University.

OPEN UNIVERSITY (1989) *Patterns for Living: Working Together* Milton Keynes: Open University.

OPEN UNIVERSITY (1990) *Learning Disability: Changing Perspectives* Milton Keynes: Open University.

OPEN UNIVERSITY (1996) *Learning Disability: Working as Equal People* Milton Keynes: Open University.

PEOPLE FIRST (1994a) *Oi. it's my assessment!* London: People First.

PEOPLE FIRST (1994b) *Helping you get the services you want* London: People First.

RICHARDS, S. (1984) *Community Care of the Mentally Handicapped: Consumer Perspectives* University of Birmingham.

SIMONS, K. (1992) *Sticking up for yourself: Self-Advocacy and People with Learning Difficulties* York: Joseph Rowntree Foundation.

VALUES INTO ACTION (1993) *On One Side: The Role of Adviser in Supporting People with Learning Difficulties in Self-Advocacy Groups* London: King's Fund Centre.

WOLFENSBERGER, W. AND TULLMAN, S. (1989) 'A brief outline of the principle of normalisation' in Brechin, A. and Walmsley, J. (eds) *Making Connections: Reflecting on the Lives and Experiences of People with Learning Difficulties* Sevenoaks: Hodder and Stoughton.

CHAPTER 5

'Growing Pains' Disability Politics –

The Journey Explained and Described

By Jane Campbell

INTRODUCTION

This paper will attempt to shed some light on the complex and often quite hidden political process of the Disabled Persons Movement over the past 30 years. Although the first stirrings of political 'protest' from organisations of disabled people go as far back as the late 19th century, this chapter will concentrate on the Movement from a time when impairment boundaries were crossed and a united approach to social oppression took off.

Through our research for the book 'Disability Politics' (Campbell & Oliver, 1996) we identified the late 1960s as a watershed for disabled people's political mobilisation. Why the 1960s? We discovered through our research that it was too simplistic to suggest our liberation was 'learnt' from other civil rights movements that had been growing in number and power during the early 20th century e.g. gender, race or the US Vets challenges. I suggest that our movement's emergence took a fairly unique turn as it developed slowly through an organisational process, i.e. disabled people coming together to either form our own pressure groups or 'take over' those controlled by non-disabled paternalists. Simply by breaking away from those who spoke on our behalf and finding a space where we could beg the question, why are we excluded from society? and how can we break in?, was the key to unlock some of the fundamental principles of the Social Model of Disability that has been the unique hallmark of our struggle.

I go on to explain why the organisation the Union of the Physically Impaired Against Segregation (UPIAS) and its founders were so crucial for disabled people's personal and then collective liberation.

I then demonstrate that it has taken at least the last twenty years for the Disabled People's Movement to really 'take off', which by the early 1980s it had, not simply via the BCODP, although the majority of evidence taken for 'Disability Politics' suggests it was the vital component. There was however a great deal of activity around disability arts, independent living, and pure access campaigns (transport, inclusive education, etc.), that were not directed by BCODP but part of a broader groundswell of people aware of the oppression with tools to fight it.

As Richard Wood clearly states in 'Disability Politics',

"The definition of issues and the identity of ourselves as people distinct in society, in a unique position in society, has got to be the key success. It is our movement, nobody but disabled people own it"

A political consciousness does not in itself constitute a social movement and I will further illustrate how the awareness was transformed and built upon to the extent that we feel confident to say the disability movement has emerged but still experiences growing pains.

WHAT IS HISTORY?

Those first stirrings of disability protest that came from organisations such as the British Deaf Association or the National League of the Blind, are in much need of our contemplation and analysis. It is our deep hidden roots which will teach us more about our present struggles. However time is of the essence and alas this is not a historical thesis and our book was not a history of the movement. But it was a search into our past. A search for answers to questions that disabled people are raising more and more. Issues such as; Is there a Disability Movement? If so, what is the Disability Movement? How does it influence the shape or direction of our society? Who were/are, the movers and shakers? Does it really matter anyway?

I remember being appalled by my first History A level essay question:

> History is more or less bunk. It's tradition. We don't want tradition. We want to live in the present and the only history that is worth a tinker's damn is the history we make today.
>
> Henry Ford
> *The Tribune* 25th May 1916
> Discuss

If **'Disability Politics'** taught me anything it was that 90% of my own personal liberation and the work that flowed hence came directly from learning from others who have gone before. Grappling with their ideas; turning them around and about; using the tools to develop projects in disability equality training and infrastructures for independent living, has driven my entire working life.

Paddy Ladd, our contributor from the highly politicised deaf community admirably challenges Ford's famous quotation, when asked to consider our project:

> "the process of freeing ourselves from imposed histories is in itself a historical and dialectical process. In these new and exciting times, whatever you or I set down are merely the first steps on the road to a full and comprehensive history of not just the disability movement as a whole, but of all its constituent parts of each particular disability group."

This echoes the words of E A Freeman, that

> "History is past politics, and politics is present history."
> 1865

We need to draw on the past, constantly revisiting as we develop our thinking. The process of researching and talking to contributors, for me has been of as much value as the final writing and publishing. And I just want to spend a short time talking about that process and the value of disabled people's historical accounts.

WHAT WE DID

As with so many civil rights struggles, time, energy and effort of those involved has been in action not words. Therefore most of what we wanted was probably inside the heads of those that were involved, not in published accounts.

Hence we decided to informally interview a range of disabled people (31 in all). Not a random sample but people we identified as having shaped, in some form or another, the transformation of our understanding of disability. There are many who might well have had a higher profile, who may wonder why their contribution goes unnamed. The truth is, we had to start somewhere with the resources to hand, so we could not include everyone who has made a contribution. For us it is simply the first look at when our Movement emerged into something quite tangible. When it began crossing boundaries and filtering into parts of life, that for centuries, had denied us in every way. Hence this chapter will concentrate on the Movement from a time when impairment boundaries were crossed and a united approach to social oppression took off.

THE EMERGENCE OF THE MOVEMENT

In the late 1960s disabled people began to question as a collective, the modus operandi of a plethora of predominately impairment charities. The charities, along with the quasi medical and social service professions who also dictated the direction and pattern of our lives began to come in for more overt criticism. Why the 1960s? We discovered through our research that it was too simplistic to suggest our liberation was 'learnt' from other civil rights movements e.g. gender, race or the US Vets challenges, although they were influential to the few that had access to the ideas. John Evans and Richard Wood, felt we "had our own version", rooted in our own historical and material condition. Crafted by the combination of individual vision and rejection of old forms of organisational representation and social exclusion.

> I think what actually happened in the 60s – was an awareness that the issues were far broader, the single issues that that these single impairment groups had focused on weren't enough to satisfy the needs and aspirations of a wider range of disabled people
>
> Richard Wood

By a wider range interest group, Richard meant that we were looking beyond our impairment and those who organised around it i.e. SCOPE, Royal

National Institute for the Deaf/Royal National Institute for the Blind (RNIB), at the same time as looking beyond one barrier as the root of our exclusion. i.e. employment and physical access. This change was heralded by organisations like the National League of the Blind and Disabled and the Disablement Income Group. Although they of course helped teach us methods of political lobbying.

Simply by breaking away from those who spoke on our behalf and finding a space where we could beg the question, why are we excluded from society? and how can we break in?, was the key to unlock some of the fundamental principles of the Social Model of Disability that we hold so precious now. In Disability Politics contributors identified disabled people in the Union of the Physically Impaired Against Segregation (UPIAS) as the founders of this philosophy that relocated the burden of disability from the individual's problem to the way society was structured. The litmus paper for this shift was a short, yet profoundly powerful letter to *The Guardian* by Paul Hunt, in 1972, encouraging disabled people to join forces and vocalise their dissatisfaction with their lot in life, particularly if they were institutionalised.

Wednesday September 20th 1972

"Sir,

Severely physically handicapped people find themselves in isolated unsuitable institutions where their views are ignored and they are subject to authoritarian and often cruel regimes.

I am proposing the formation of a consumer group to put forward nationally the views of actual and potential residents of these successors to the Workhouse.

Yours faithfully,
Paul Hunt."

Many respondents to Paul's letter went on to become involved in UPIAS either through meeting or corresponding through the internal circular. These years of debate were vital for the development of our collective consciousness and 'the institution' was a good model to explain our social position and disempowerment....

"I wrote to some of those who responded to Paul's letter. I started to visit institutions to talk about what people felt about being in an institution. This is where I began to make the connections..."

Anne Rae

"Paul lived in a Cheshire Home at that time. He introduced me to the real criticisms about the institutional approach. It seemed to me that the clearest perception of what was wrong with disability was in relation to these homes."

Vic Finkelstein

Our research threw up Paul's name and work time and time again. It is clear that he was able to see the way ahead with the greatest clarity and his ability to pass that on, enthusing others to act was pivotal to the emergence of the disability movement.

"Paul knew that the future lay in raising the awareness and political aspirations of disabled people in the community. UPIAS was Hunt's tradition. It was the tradition of the residents. We regard that as our inheritance. It was perhaps the greatest gift that we could have been given."

Phillip Mason

Such a personal and then collective release inevitably sparked anger followed by political demands. UPIAS prepared the way for the future national umbrella that would attempt to unite many different interest groups, under a common goal for full inclusion and the right to self-representation.

Later the British Council of Organisations of Disabled People organised around the UPIAS Principles, 1975:

DISABILITY IS A SITUATION, CAUSED BY SOCIAL CONDITIONS, WHICH REQUIRES FOR ITS ELIMINATION THE FOLLOWING:

That no one aspect such as incomes, mobility or institutions is treated in isolation.

That disabled people should, with the advice and help of others, assume control over their own lives.

That professionals, experts and others who seek to help must be committed to promoting such control by disabled people.

CONFLICTS EMERGE

It is interesting to note that we have not deviated from this approach, although the temptation to go down a narrower incomes approach, led by the Disability Alliance and the Disablement Income Group, was powerful. Disabled people at that time were still only to willing to leave political lobbying to the able-bodied experts, within these organisations and the piecemeal legislative entitlements that were secured via the Chronically Sick and Disabled Persons' Act and the various disability and attendance allowances helped maintain that status quo. Such 'benefits' were short lived and they naturally did not meet the growing aspirations and by the mid 1980s, frustrations, of an increasing mass movement. Maggie Davis recalls:

> "DIG's lack of success in establishing a national disability income was due to it, broadly speaking, falling into the hands of the experts – many of whom were able-bodied who were good at arguing and lobbying Parliament, and because it had become remote from the grass roots membership. Membership was little more than fund-raising fodder for this élite group of well versed Parliamentary lobbyists."

Our mobilisation took a fairly unique turn as it developed slowly through an organisational process, i.e. disabled people coming together to either form our own pressure groups or 'take over' those controlled by non-disabled paternalists. Such organisations were shaped to provide practical and emotional support but most importantly to challenge the entire British charity industry that maintained our oppressed state. 'Revolution' not 'Reform', was probably our biggest strength and remains so today. For those who believed that working within established organisations FOR disabled people, to change them, were doomed to be disappointed if not abused. Peter Wade, Paul's friend and colleague, took a reformist approach and joined the Royal Association for Disability And Rehabilitation (RADAR) and the Cheshire Foundation. The years that followed according to Judith Hunt, "were very unhappy ones as he battled to bring UPIAS principles to them and met a brick wall of hostility".

Hence BCODP's tradition of organising separately and then coming to the integrated table from a position of strength has been its hallmark. It has also been the cause of many internal and external disputes. Ever since the inaugural meeting in 1981 there have been heated debates as to what some perceive as our radical if not rigid discipline. Some say it is a legacy from the strict internal discipline of UPIAS, which put activists like Micheline Mason off for a decade.

I was emotionally and intellectually battered by some UPIAS members, so some of us went off and set up the Liberation network...a woman led organisation, embodying female values. It was open to all individuals and concentrated on peer support which we conducted through meetings and a magazine 'In From The Cold'. Here we really tackled the issue of **internalised oppression**, recognised by all marginalised groups as the major 'tool' of the oppressive society.

The Liberation Network's agenda was both impressive and extensive for its time:

We challenged the conditioned hatred of ourselves and each other as disabled people; we challenged the desire to assimilate; we challenged the denial of 'hidden' disabilities; we challenged the fierce competition between us, we challenged the inability to champion, appreciate and support each other's achievements or thinking (especially when it challenged our own); we challenged the lack of information and understanding about issues of other oppressed people.

Perhaps it was too ambitious and too loose a coalition to survive the onslaught of debate and internal divisions that had to take place as we matured as a movement. Micheline also feels it was "prey to sexism" that undermined its theoretical and organisational basis. It folded, but only after "allowing a thousand flowers to bloom" for unlike UPIAS and early BCODP it provided a less rigorous, perhaps intensive forum for debate. Many active members went on to form organisations that have become vital parts of the movement – The Integration Alliance, Disability Arts and Culture, Disability Equality Training and so on.

THE EMERGENCE OF BCODP

Out of conflict comes harmony? Well not quite. Once it was agreed that the movement needed a national representative voice, we had to deal with who was in or out; our fundamental aims and objectives needed to be agreed and possibly the trickiest – the process of how we should get there.

Our interviews revealed many painful and hilarious anecdotes of conflict resolution as the movement's organisational base took shape.

> I remember the first meeting. There were those people who were for and those who were
> against including certain groups. RADAR of course was raised as being so powerful they
> had to be in. But there were too many with a strong principled approach to let that
> happen....at times that could be our downfall because we would not take a politically
> pragmatic approach – very naïve.
>
> Stephen Bradshaw

Eventually a fairly strict criteria for membership won through. No individual members, only organisations 51% controlled by disabled people. We started with 9 in a day centre in Camden – 15 years on we have 112 and have moved to a constitutional shift of taking individual membership. Our numbers if we tot up our member organisation's membership could well be in the 400,000s.

The member organisations provided the democratic bedrock of the British Council of Disabled People that became the focus of this national struggle to speak for ourselves and claim rights not charity. But does it signify an emerging movement?

Judith Hunt drew this conclusion.

> Looking at the BCODP as the major focus, I certainly feel that it's been the point at
> which the movement became very visible and took on board the social interpretation of
> disability. But it was also the outcome of what had gone before. In a sense it was the
> build-up that began to take place in the 60s that was crucial.

We suggested in 'Disability Politics', that the disability movement and the BCODP are not the same thing. Rather, it became the formal organisational focus for a range of issues including critiques of state-based and voluntary sector-based welfare, the development of independent living campaigns and projects, struggles for ADL in all its forms, peer support, challenges to negative imagery and the stereotypes which perpetuate our exclusion.

WHAT KIND OF SOCIAL MOVEMENT IS IT?

Observers of social movements suggest that the transition from emerging to emergent movement is signified when the movement becomes larger, less spontaneous, better organised, and led by formal structures rather than *ad hoc* committees and informal groups. We would suggest the BCODP only signified such an 'emergence' from the late 1980s when more formalised activities around disability arts, independent living, and pure access campaigns (transport, inclusive education, etc.), that were not necessarily directed by BCODP but part of its outer margins, took place. In this process of drawing in a broader groundswell of disabled people and participating in a mutual education exercise i.e. BCODP teaching fundamental principles yet learning wider issues of oppression and how it relates to disability, we are gaining a powerful identity. As Richard Wood clearly states:

> "The definition of issues and the identity of ourselves as people distinct in society, in a unique position in society, has got to be the key success. It is our movement, nobody but disabled people own it."

A political consciousness does not in itself constitute a social movement and an awareness of the cultures and dreams of its constituency and creating activities as a result, are what the BCODP constantly needs to engage in. This has not been an easy road to travel. Disabled people not only have to face oppression linked to impairment but many have to struggle against other forms of oppression, racism, sexism, heterosexism are probably the most obvious.

Nasa Begum expresses the dilemma that people face who experience as she calls it 'simulations oppression' within the movement:

> Many of us will identify with different bits of our identity at different times. It all has to be addressed when it presents itself. Sometimes the appalling treatment I have experienced in hospital has come from being disabled; but some is around being black and there's this sexism crap they come out with because I'm a woman.
>
> Lots of black disabled people identify disability as the main issue, they are encouraged to do so by their white peers who dominate the movement. We shouldn't be trying to separate identity. But the reality is that some of us at different stages of our lives, are going to identify with different things as at that particular point it will be more pressing perhaps. The movement must show more tolerance.

The greatest and perhaps hardest challenge to be faced are the alliances that need to be made with other oppressed groups, other civil rights activists and impairment groups within our movement who do not feel a part of the common struggle. The criticism and conflict that comes with this issue, coupled with the lack of financial and human resources to tackle it, has often led activists to immobilisation rather than activity.

However, there have been some successes. One of the largest impairment groups – people with learning difficulties, have been historically excluded from the movement's activities. In *Disability Politics* Simone Aspis, representative from People First National candidly wrote

> We face discrimination in the disability movement. People without learning difficulties use the medical model to describe our needs. We are always being asked to talk about advocacy and our impairments as though our barriers aren't disabling in the same way as people with physical impairments. We want to concentrate on our access needs in the mainstream disability movement.
>
> People without learning difficulties in the movement still fear being lumped together with us. Being put together with what society see the 'stupid, thick, mental and mad', would reinforce the stereotype that disabled people are incapable.
>
> Equality will come within the movement when people with learning difficulties are given positions of power and influence within the movement like chairperson or spokesperson.

1994 was the year that this issue was raised vehemently, in all areas of BCODP; it has been tough, some allegations were hard to hear, but as a result of nettle grasping, things have moved on. For example People First joined forces in representing throughout the passage of the Direct Payments Act.

CONCLUSION

I have concentrated on some of the organisational and political issues that have confronted those who have sought to provide a representative base for disabled people's social influence. I have been highly selective, picking out bits and pieces of the jigsaw to give a taste of our rich recent history, which explains so much of where we are today. A continued investigation and validation of our past so that disabled people new to the movement will feel clearer as to the movement's intentions for a better society, was the clearest message that came out of the research for the book. For one of the factors I came to understand was that we are a new social movement and what makes us different from other kinds of political organisation, is that as well as building an organisation and achieving political gains, we have to continue to seek to transform the consciousness of the membership.

It will be the development of the social model as the link between concrete achievements and developing consciousness, that will take us forward:

Richard Wood illustrates this well;

> There was the intensity of uncertainty of people still unsure about just how and if we were going to be able to take on board the broad range of issues that faced us. I think the thing that started to make it clearer was the total acceptance of the social model as being the core of the movement, which it soon became. It was something people could adopt and feel part of and most importantly use as a tool.

The development of the social model and its journey into the very fabric of our communities through social, political and economic infrastructures, gives the disability movement the authority to say we have emerged. Whilst we are still experiencing 'Growing Pains'! we are making a unique contribution to the world's future.

REFERENCE

CAMPBELL, J AND OLIVER, M. (1996) 'Disability Politics: Understanding Our Past, Changing Our Future', London: Routledge.

CHAPTER 6

Independent, Proud and Special:
Celebrating our Differences

By Jenny Corbett

INTRODUCTION

I find the term "independent", like the term "empowerment", to be, at best, ambiguous, and at worst, misleading. We are none of us truly independent individuals, depending as we all do on the structures which support our daily life. To be fully alive as human beings requires a complicated inter-dependency upon networks of people and systems. Independence is not about coping without help of any kind. That describes a bleak existence.

There are three key issues which I shall be exploring in this chapter. They are:

1. The need to distinguish between independence as a skills based process and independence as a mark of individuality;

2. The need to recognise the delicate and subtle relationship between independence and inter-dependence;

3. The need to respect individual differences and the ways in which the dominant culture can oppress marginalised sub-cultures.

1. WHAT DOES INDEPENDENCE MEAN?

The way in which I would define "independence" is in:

- knowing what you want and being able to express individual needs;
- having a strong sense of self which recognises personal boundaries;
- having as much control over your own life as possible.

Within so many special education programmes for disabled young adults, there is a significant emphasis upon teaching skills of empowerment and independence. Elements of such courses may well include sessions on assertiveness, self- knowledge, decision making and time management. Whilst there are clearly many techniques and practices which can be shared in these learning experiences, I would still wish to question whether "independence" is a skill which can or should be taught, without carefully contextualising it in a social and economic system.

In 1989, I wrote a paper for the then journal *Disability, Handicap & Society* called 'The Quality of Life in the "Independence Curriculum" '. This paper emerged from my research into what were then termed, "daily living skills" courses, which had become very popular in further education colleges. These courses often extended over two years full time and were designed for students with severe learning disabilities, complex physical disabilities and emotional and behavioural difficulties. The rationale for them was that a mark of true adulthood was the degree to which we all become independent in our daily lives, being able to shop, cook, budget, clean and arrange our recreational interests.

Whilst this clearly makes sense, if we construe "normalisation" as all adopting similar behaviour patterns within the society in which we find ourselves and, thus, being able to assimilate and become part of the group, it does not necessarily mean that we all experience the same level of independent living. If the daily living skills of cleaning, shopping and running a home are easy for us to manage and take up little of our time, leaving us free to do other things, that is fine. If, however, they assume such importance in our daily lives that we are left with little free time to do anything other than complete daily chores, this becomes a rather limited form of independence.

Within a society such as ours, people tend to measure their level of independence in economic terms. If they are earning a high salary, this enables them to pay others to clean and manage their household chores. They do not require the marker of independent living skills which doing all the mundane daily tasks constitutes. When young people with physical and learning disabilities are trained to manage daily living tasks for themselves, this may involve them in laborious and even painful processes, which can inhibit rather than enhance their quality of life.

My hypothesis, within that earlier paper on "The Quality of Life in the Independence Curriculum", was that the expectations being asked of disabled teenagers were higher than those asked of their non-disabled peers. Adolescence is traditionally accepted as being an experimental and irresponsible period of life. Why, then, were disabled teenagers being asked to spend so much time on the kinds of daily living tasks which their peers would avoid if possible? Having an untidy bedroom and eating unhealthy foods are surely commonplace among adolescents. For some disabled young people, on college courses in the 1980s, they were the key elements on which they were assessed as being appropriately adult.

It is important to recognise that current thinking, in, for example, books like *Whose Choice?*, edited by Judith Coupe O'Kane and Juliet Goldbart (1996), is more sensitive than in the recent past and issues of sexuality, empowerment and age-appropriateness are all explored and contextualised, acknowledging their problematic nature. The vital factor, in debating concepts like "independence" is that every person is different and will have their own form of individuality which requires a means of expression unique to them. In 1993, Sue Ralph and I wrote a joint paper for *Disability, Handicap & Society*, called "A Shared Presentation: two disabled women on video". In this, we were reflecting on two videos which we had separately made with our disabled women friends. We wanted to help them to present themselves and their daily lives as they saw things and not as others would wish to portray them.

From this experience, we learnt that what was important to them was not necessarily their ability to run their own homes without assistance – this may have been quite inappropriate in relation to the severity of their disability. What they both found most important was to be able to pursue their specific interests and to maintain their network of friendships. In other words, it was an independence of mind which seemed to create a quality of living experience. This surely applies to us all. In our choice of interests, friendships and social networks we grow and develop and enjoy the rich inter-dependence which full living offers.

2. WHY DO WE ALL NEED TO CONNECT TO OTHERS?

It seems inappropriate to talk about independence without recognising the significance of our inter-dependency. We all need to connect to others, if we are to become active citizens. There are many connections which are valuable in their different ways, be they relationships with friends, lovers, family, animals or within wider social networks. We learn about ourselves through connectedness with others. It is part of our human nature to want to give to other people, be it in the form of time, company, support, affection or co-operative efforts.

Disabled people are often the recipients rather than the providers of care. They have as much need to enjoy the pleasure of inter-dependency as others but are so often confronted with attitudes which label them as incapable carers. In a recent Channel 4 documentary, "The Story of Julia", a young woman who is deaf and blind was shown in her battle with social services to keep and bring up her baby. Her desire to be a loving mother was evident but the severity of her disability meant that the caring professionals regarded her as a potentially high-risk situation. As it was so rare for a deaf-blind mother to bring up a child, this was something of a test-case.

The young woman was extremely independent in that she expressed her views clearly and frankly, telling some of the social workers exactly what she thought of their concern. Of course, she recognised that she needed considerable practical help in order to manage her daily routines. What she wanted was a level of inter-dependency which placed her views and perceptions alongside those of the "experts", whereby she could share her own mothering tasks in the way she wanted. It was notable that this particular young woman was regarded as "difficult" and "aggressive" because she was so adamant about the degree of control she wanted over her own life. Disabled people are often expected to be compliant and dependent. Life is easier for them if they are.

In my opinion, it is far more caring to let the other person take the initiative and direct actions which can then be undertaken by non-disabled supporters than to take over control from them. However, this kind of caring requires a high level of empathy. It also calls for humility, in recognising that professional experts do not always know what is in the best interests of their clients. They are experts in types – not in individuals. Placing a high value on our inter-connectedness involves trusting that those who are trying to become more independent can only do so with support from others.

The dilemma in the "care in the community" initiative is the lack of care and the lack of community. If de-institutionalisation means, in reality, that someone is living in one room in a lodging house in the community rather than in a hospital ward in residential provision, this can hardly be seen as anything other than locational integration. For it to become a much richer form of social inclusion, this kind of bleak independence has to be supported by wider social networks and friendships. It is quite evident, in looking around our major cities, that there are many isolated individuals whose independent living involves existing on the streets, dependent upon charitable donations from passers-by. Such people can be treated as non-persons. In order to avoid the discomfort of too close an encounter with homeless individuals, fellow citizens tend to walk by hurriedly, looking straight ahead and almost pretending that they are not lying there on the pavement. People who are perceived as socially dependent are often devalued as being of less importance than those whose citizenship is defined by occupational status and social standing.

I began this chapter by stressing the importance of distinguishing between independence as a skills-based process and independence as a mark of individuality. I think that the focus upon skills for independence in the training programmes for students with physical and learning disabilities is a way of avoiding confronting the hierarchies of individual differences. The basic living skills which mark our progress into adult responsibilities might be regarded as a crude base-line for independence. It offers only the lower framework for what can become a fuller form of independent living. If we equate true independence of mind with a respect for individual differences, this requires a value system which is rarely found in our competitive society. There are definite hierarchies which delineate how and where and for whom individuality is acceptable.

3. DOES THE STATUS QUO VALUE INDIVIDUAL DIFFERENCES?

In any society, what constitutes "normality" is fluid and flexible, according to how the dominant value systems change and develop. Over the last twenty years in Britain, we have seen considerable changes in the ways in which women, people who are black, gay or disabled are regarded. We live in an increasingly pluralistic society, in which many cultural groups co-exist. This might be seen by those wishing to preserve the status quo as dangerously insecure, leading to social fragmentation and loss of the cohesion which striving for a common purpose offers. For those of us who belong to marginalised groups, the increased emphasis upon respect for individual differences provides a degree of support which was lacking in a dominant status quo from which we were missing.

In 1991, I wrote a platform piece for *Disability, Handicap & Society*, called, "So, who wants to be normal?" in which I suggested that the normality of the status quo was not something I strove to emulate. I said that I would be insulted to be labelled as "normal", which I felt seemed "to embody confinement and restraint: a pinched, arid meanness". In 1994, I went on to write a paper for *Disability & Society*, called, "A Proud Label: exploring the relationship between disability politics and gay pride", in which I compared the process of "coming out" as gay with that of "coming out" as disabled. One of the essential features of "coming out" is that of expressing both individuality and solidarity at one and the same time. It is saying, "This is who I am and I align myself with this group of people". Of course, this is to simplify what can be a most complex process.

Many disabled people do not support disability politics or seek to join groups of other disabled people but try to blend as much as possible into a varied communal environment. Similarly, many gay people have no desire to support gay politics or to mix in predominantly gay social circles. Seeking solidarity is not compulsory. It is there as an optional extra for those who find it helpful and stimulating. If "coming out" can be seen as an expression of independence of mind, it is a reflection of the individual themselves deciding that they place value on their own difference. In the recent past, it was not uncommon for many marginalised groups, including those who are disabled, black or gay, to be stigmatised as being undesirably different and to be encouraged to take on a self-deprecating role. Thus was the label of pride born: taking the bigot's labels of "cripple", "nigger" and "queer" and turning them around to become badges of strength and solidarity.

It can be seen that there is a very real struggle between the need to join forces in marginalised groups and to draw power from cohesive and collective action and the simultaneous need to express individual differences. This can be seen in the women's movement, where there are so many different experiences which struggle to find common ground. It is also evident in the black and gay movements, where there are tensions between different factions who begin to fight among themselves rather than join forces to fight for a united sense of injustice. In the disability movement, one of the more recent struggles has been between disabled women and disabled men in the debate on the relative merits of a social model of disability and a recognition of individual differences and experiences of pain.

Whilst these tensions are very uncomfortable and threaten the power of solidarity within a fragile sub-culture which needs cohesion, they can also be seen as healthy, in showing signs of individual differences and distinct needs. It seems important to me that we don't run the risk of turning marginalised groups into forces for oppression which silence awkward expressions of individualism. If views are to be heard as independent voices, their right to be different from others who are proud of their own differences must be respected and valued.

CONCLUSION

In calling this chapter, "Independent, Proud and Special: celebrating our differences", I am deliberately celebrating my own experience of difference alongside that of my friends and colleagues. In my most recent paper for this journal, "Teaching Special Needs: "Tell Me Where It Hurts"", I reflect on my own career experience and the complex reasons why I was drawn to work in special education. It is only relatively recently that I have been emotionally capable of revisiting the distressed and disturbed adolescent that I once was and helping her to feel calm and confident. In being quite unable at that time to accept, let alone celebrate, my gay identity (it was labelled by far more medical terms then), I took on the self-loathing role and gave myself a good deal of pain in the process. In now playing an active part in the disability arts group, "Survivors' Poetry: poetry workshops and performances by and for survivors of the mental health system", I am able to share and inter-connect with others who find poetry to be a valuable means of self-expression and catharsis.

I have definitely felt empowered by the love and support of other gay people. This does not mean that I want to live within an exclusively gay culture, nor to align myself with radical elements of gay politics. For me, independence of mind is about deciding who I am as a person and what my deepest needs are. I appreciate that, as an academic, I have a certain degree of access to dominant discourses. I am also able to move between varied and diverse social groups, whose value systems may be conflicting and even breed hostility. I am wary of fundamentalism, whatever form it takes. I feel that different views need to be listened to and respected, if we are really in the business of celebrating difference. Where they are clearly socially destructive opinions, they need to be heard in order to be properly challenged. I am not scared of others disliking my views and want to listen to perceptions very different from my own.

I end by asking if there is a political agenda attached to the celebration of individual differences. We need solidarity in order to build power in minority groups. As in any collective (like Trade Unions) there is a tradition of sublimating individual needs in order to foster the good of the whole. I suggest that this tends to be most necessary in the early stages of any political movement, when the oppressed need to join forces against their oppressors. It is surely a mark of maturity within a political group when they are able to allow for individual differences. It indicates a level of comfort and confidence, which acknowledges that expressions of individuality are healthy and just. There are clear differences within the disability discourses. The dominant group can be seen as those (predominantly white male) who have spinal injuries and whose voices are most often heard in academic debates. This leaves disabled women and those from other groups, like people with learning disabilities and mental health difficulties, on the edge of the dominant discourse, getting their views often marginalised. We might feel that it requires a revolution of sorts to re-locate the sites of power and change the discourse arena before it solidifies as a mirror of the hierarchies within society in general. We might, however, feel that the struggles in minority groups merely reflect the perennial inequalities in all social networks and that they are to be expected.

As a final request, I would ask you to read beyond *Disability & Society*, excellent and stimulating as it is, and to explore the many disability arts magazines which exist on the fringe, in print and in the media. They offer a true celebration of individuality and difference which communicate directly at an emotional and instinctive level, accessible to all.

REFERENCES

CHANNEL 4 TELEVISION (1996) *True Stories*, "The Story of Julia", 13th August, 1996.
COUPE O'KANE, J. & GOLDBART, J. (1996) (eds.) *Whose Choice?* London, David Fulton.

CORBETT, J. (1989) The Quality of Life in the "Independence Curriculum", *Disability Handicap & Society*, Vol. 4, No.2, pp. 145-163.

CORBETT, J. (1991) So, who wants to be normal?, *Disability, Handicap & Society*, Vol. 6, No.3, pp.259-260.

CORBETT, J., JONES, E. & RALPH, S. (1993) A Shared Presentation: two disabled women on video, *Disability, Handicap & Society*, Vol. 8, No.2, pp. 173-186.

CORBETT, J. (1994) A Proud Label: exploring the relationship between disability politics and gay pride, *Disability & Society*, Vol. 9, No.3, pp. 343-357.

CORBETT, J. (1997) Teaching Special Needs: tell me where it hurts, *Disability & Society*, Vol. 12, No. 3, pp.417-425.

CHAPTER 7

When Myths Masquerade as Science:

Disability Research from an Equality-Rights Perspective

By Marcia H. Rioux

The 10th anniversary of *Disability and Society* is important not only because the survival of a journal and all those who make it happen is, in itself, a feat worth celebrating – just getting the journal out on time and succeeding to do the number of promised volumes in a year is, in the disability literature somewhat unique. But *Disability and Society* has done much more than that. It was the first journal and remains one of only two or three periodicals around the world that challenge the fundamental assumptions of disability as it has traditionally been theorised. In the face of the transnational disability industry and the professional hegemony of medicine and therapy, this is a significant contribution. There is a lot more money to advertise "Self-Injurious

Behaviour Inhibition Systems" (SIBIS) – an aversive-therapy invention for redirecting or repatterning the behaviour of people who abuse themselves developed in the United States – than there is for a journal that takes a critical perspective on the field.

In our library and information service, we have approximately 75 journals and 100 newsletters – all related to disability. Of the journals approximately 50% highlight rehabilitation information and research; about 40% are service-oriented; and somewhere around 10% are rights-oriented journals. So the uniqueness of *Disability and Society* is not hard to see in the field. For those of us who have been working from a similar perspective and trying to develop a critical theory of disability, it has consequently provided a kind of oasis in a desert.

PERSONAL REFLECTIONS ON RESEARCH

I did not start my career in social policy, in the disability field – I started in the feminist movement doing feminist research – in the late 1960s before there really was movement. So my background was a systemic analysis of society from a gender perspective.

Starting to work in the field of disability policy in the late 1970s, I was therefore surprised to find that the "problem" (as it was always defined) was the individual and the research was focused in three main directions, all aimed at finding ways of preventing disability. The first direction was biological and medical research; the second was therapeutic intervention and the third was the production of services and service delivery. I could find very little literature about poverty, housing, unemployment, abuse, marginalisation, power imbalance, tax policy, and service monopolies. But for some of us, those are the research questions. And the contribution of *Disability and Society* in publishing work done from this perspective has made it possible for us to keep abreast of others carrying out parallel research; it has provided a forum for theory, research and methodological discussion that would have been absent otherwise.

The research agenda that is evolving from a systemic perspective of disability argues that disability has been poorly theorised. The traditional approach, dominated by the medical model, emphasises disability as an individual problem and, fails to conceptualise and develop variables to measure the wider political, social, and ethical environment and its effect on the lives of people with disabilities. Poverty, marginalisation, disempowerment, unemployment and a number of other social constraints are not analysed as critical factors in disadvantage. Disability gets defined rather as a health and social care issue and researched debated on those terms. As an alternative, research from a systemic perspective emphasises equality, empowerment, inclusion, community and diversity and develops measures for those variables.

How research and policy questions are framed is a quick barometer to the theoretical framework or paradigm from which the researcher begins. It is clear from even the most cursory examination of the journals which specialise in issues of disability that the majority of research and policy still reflects a theory of professional practice and functionalism.

In the journals we find articles with such themes as "Subgroups in autism: are there behavioural phenotypes typical of underlying medical conditions?"; "Measurement of Attention Deficit: Correspondence Between Rating Scales and Tests of Sustained and Selective Attention"; Clomipramine Treatment for Self-injurious Behaviour of Individuals with Mental Retardation: A Double Blind with Placebo; "A Comparison of Methods of Functional Assessment of Stereotypic Behaviour"; "Epidemiology of Challenging Behaviour"; "The use of Evaluation in the Development of a Staffed Residential Service for Adults with Mental Handicap"; and "Reduction of Multiple Aberrant Behaviours and Concurrent Development of Self-care Skills with Differential Reinforcement".

Research that reflects the emerging paradigm has such themes as: "Discrimination, Disability and Welfare: From Needs to Rights"; "Rights, Justice, Power: A Culture of Diversity"; "Some Ethical Issues Associated with Genetic Engineering for People with Disabilities"; and "Class and Disability: Influences on Learning Expectations".

Ways of viewing disability, of developing research questions, of interpreting research results, of justifying research methodology and of putting policies and programs in place are as much about ideology as they are about fact. It is important to recognise how significant this is to research generally and in the field of disability in particular. The roots of scientific and socio-economic justification for the allocation of research funding and for political (or state) action based on the research findings can be found in these identifiable and shifting ideological frameworks. It is therefore useful to explore the social and scientific formulations of disability which underpin research questions, methodology and findings.

Reflected in the current dominant research paradigm are two very different world views – one which is centralising and homogenising and one which stresses difference and diversity. These discrepant world views are particularly relevant when the issue is disability. The normative standard that ensues from either of these has consequences in terms both of the importance placed on either abilities or disabilities manifested by people, as well as the social contribution made by individuals.

Empirical questions are driven by these implicit normative premises, despite the claims of objectivity so readily embraced by empiricists. To some degree, then, the enterprise that researchers, have to embark on is to uncover and disclose the premises of the research. I would argue that this is important because the social, economic and political pressures are pervasive in research in this field. But I would also argue that it is a moral imperative to disclose the normative basis of the research in a field like disability where the research affects the single most identifiably marginalised class of people. Researchers must be up front about the value judgements and normative standards hidden in their empiricism. They must also, I believe engage valid arguments to justify the particular normative foundation of their research.

Rather than simply engaging in the debates about one concept versus another, I want to step back and reflect upon the perspectives which underlie the various constructions of disability. How disability is perceived, diagnosed and treated, scientifically and socially, is reflected in assumptions about the social responsibility towards people with disabilities as a group and the research agenda. The assumptions or postulates about disability I will discuss are not mutually exclusive nor have they been temporally chronological. Some disciplines, in their research, have continued to characterise disability as disease or as a personal deficit while others have adopted a framework of disability as a social and political condition. There are any number of hybrids of these two major schools of thought. Consequently, policy, programming, treatment and care and research reflect these shifting understandings of disability.

SOCIAL AND SCIENTIFIC FORMULATION OF DISABILITY

There are four identifiable social and scientific formulations of disability that are reflected in the treatment of persons with disability in law, in policy, in

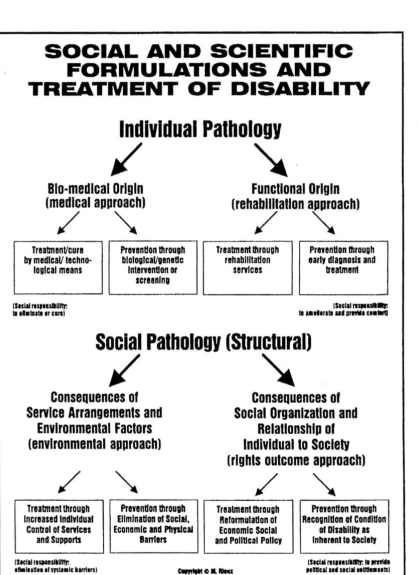

SOCIAL AND SCIENTIFIC FORMULATIONS AND TREATMENT OF DISABILITY

Individual Pathology

Bio-medical Origin (medical approach)

Functional Origin (rehabilitation approach)

| Treatment/cure by medical/ technological means | Prevention through biological/genetic intervention or screening | Treatment through rehabilitation services | Prevention through early diagnosis and treatment |

(Social responsibility: to eliminate or cure)

(Social responsibility: to ameliorate and provide comfort)

Social Pathology (Structural)

Consequences of Service Arrangements and Environmental Factors (environmental approach)

Consequences of Social Organization and Relationship of Individual to Society (rights outcome approach)

| Treatment through Increased Individual Control of Services and Supports | Prevention through Elimination of Social, Economic and Physical Barriers | Treatment through Reformulation of Economic Social and Political Policy | Prevention through Recognition of Condition of Disability as Inherent to Society |

(Social responsibility: elimination of systemic barriers)

Copyright © M. Rioux

(Social responsibility: to provide political and social entitlements) programs and in rights instruments and in research agendas. Two of them emanate from theories of disability as a consequence of individual pathology and two from disability as a consequence of social pathology.

These approaches have implications for both the formulation of research questions and the methodology used in research.

FORMULATIONS THAT FOCUS ON DISABILITY AS RESIDING IN THE INDIVIDUAL (INDIVIDUAL PATHOLOGY)

Within the context of disability as an individual pathology two broad approaches can be identified – the bio-medical approach and the functional approach. These formulations have a number of common characteristics:

- they approach disability as a field of professional expertise
- they use a positivist research paradigm
- they emphasise primary prevention including biological and environmental conditions
- they characterise disability as incapacity in relation to non-disabled persons: comparative incapacity
- disability is viewed as anomaly and social burden, including costs
- the inclusion of people with disabilities is seen as a private rather than a public responsibility
- the unit of analysis is the individual
- the point of intervention is the individual condition

THE BIO-MEDICAL APPROACH

The bio-medical approach to disability research has been a powerful influence in determining disability policy, practice, and research. Throughout the nineteenth and early twentieth century, infectious disease was the major cause of illness and death.

The advent of the "germ theory" of illness and disease facilitated the capacity to more correctly diagnose symptoms and led to the pre-eminence of biological science as the basis for diagnosing disability, influencing treatments and guiding access to disability benefits.

From the perspective of molecular biology and the attendant bio-medical approach, it has been assumed that disability is caused by a mental or physical condition that can be prevented or ameliorated through medical, biological or genetic intervention. In such a characterisation of disability, the condition itself becomes the focus of research attention. The aim of the researcher is to decrease the prevalence of the condition in the general population. Treatment and prevention occur by means of biological intervention and critical care, including surgery, drug therapy, pre-natal screening and genetic intervention. Commonly, then, the individual or the foetus is viewed as sick, injured or afflicted and research is directed to the cure.

With the rise of institutional facilities and public benefits, medical science became established as the mechanism for gatekeeping those who are legitimately to be considered disabled. Assessments became a scientifically justified activity extending to various aspects of an individual's range of disability such as educational, training and work capabilities; fine motor skills and hand-eye co-ordination; the need for financial benefits and mobility aids and devices; as well as access to rehabilitation.

The bio-medical approach with a focus on altering the biological condition, places less emphasis on the role that society plays in limiting and enabling people.

THE FUNCTIONAL APPROACH

The second of the two approaches of disability as an individual pathology is the functional approach. Like the bio-medical model, the underlying presumption is that the deficit stems from an individual condition or pathology. However, from this approach the way of treating the functional incapacity is through amelioration and enabling strategies.

From the functional approach, the problems experienced by people with disabilities are interpreted as a result of a functional incapacity resulting from an individual impairment. To treat this functional incapacity, services are made available to enable the individual to become as socially functional as possible. For example, the goal of rehabilitation is to increase an individual's range of skills and abilities to function more independently and to become a productive member of society. The success of programs is measured by how closely people who use services can approximate the lives of "normal" people, and to what extent they can achieve the skills of non-disabled persons.

Services developed from a functional approach (for example, physiotherapy, occupational therapy, nursing and health visiting) have gone beyond therapeutic programs associated with the bio-medical model to include life skills, pre-vocational training, functional assessments, counselling and job training, as well as skills for independent living.

Behaviour modification and developmental programming are also offshoots of the functional approach to disability. Behaviour modification uses a variety of reinforcement techniques to elicit individual behaviours that have been deemed socially desirable or useful. The approach is also used to eliminate behaviours deemed inappropriate or ineffective for adjusting to the demands of everyday living. Developmental programming research targets knowledge and skills that people usually acquire as they mature, identifies where and why individuals may be falling short of those benchmarks, and intervenes to assist individuals to maximise their developmental potential.

In placing the focus on the individual, a functional approach to disability research loses sight of environmental and situational factors that may limit individuals from achieving their ambitions. In targeting the individual for change, professionals and researchers using a functional approach run the risk of legitimising assumptions about the person's "best interests" that may not always coincide with what the person wants for him or herself.

FORMULATIONS THAT FOCUS ON THE SOCIO-POLITICAL NATURE OF DISABILITY (SOCIAL PATHOLOGY)

As well as the two formulations of disability based on individual pathology, there are two identifiable formulations based on social pathology. Both start from a perspective that assumes that disability is **not** inherent to the individual. Rather they assume that the disability is inherent to the social structure. The identifiable pathology is that there is something wrong with the society that we have to fix rather than something wrong with the individual (WHO, 1980).

These approaches have a number of shared characteristics:

• they assume that disability is not inherent to the individual independent of the social structure

• they give priority to political, social and built environments

• they recognise disability as difference rather than as an anomaly

• disability is viewed as the interaction of individual to society

• inclusion of people with disabilities is seen as a public responsibility

• the unit of analysis is the social system

• the point of intervention: social, environmental and economic systems

THE ENVIRONMENTAL APPROACH

Advances in knowledge based on an understanding of disability as a social pathology have shown that personal abilities and limitations are the result not only of factors residing in the individual, but of the interaction between individuals and their environments. Increasingly, researchers are demonstrating that the failure of ordinary environments to accommodate people's differences results in disability.

From an environmental perspective on disability, the research focus is placed on the way environments are arranged. For example, research has shown that the absence of ramps into an office building creates an employment handicap for someone who relies on a wheelchair for mobility. The lack of an ergonomically adapted work space, it has been demonstrated, makes it impossible for a person with limited upper body movement to perform job tasks. Similarly, many research studies have shown that the lack of proactive hiring and employment retention policies create disadvantages for individuals who require time away from work because of the fatigue and other conditions caused by impairment. An educational service disadvantages persons with a speech impairment where it fails to provide the opportunity to learn an alternative method of communication (e.g. through bliss symbolics or sign language instruction).

Increasingly, research is showing that the impact of disability can be lessened as environments are adapted to enable participation. Building codes, principles of barrier-free design, adapted curricula, targeted policy and funding commitments are being shown in policy research to be useful tools to this end. Research shows that these tools enable modifications and supports to be made in home, school, work, and leisure environments, and increase the participation of people with disabilities in society and limiting the disadvantages they otherwise would face.

THE RIGHTS-OUTCOME APPROACH

Another formulation of disability is based on the notion that disability has social causes and is a consequence of how society is organised and the relationship of the individual to society at large (Roth, 1983) (Beresford, 1994) (Rioux, 1994) (Rioux, 1994) (Roeher Institute, 1996) (ICIDH, 1991) (Oliver, 1990). Research from a rights-outcome approach looks beyond particular environments to focus on broad systemic factors that keep certain people from participating as equals in society.

This research approach finds wide variations in cognitive, sensory and motor ability are inherent to the human condition. It draws from a variety of disciplines (e.g., anthropology, sociology, economics, law) in methodology and conceptualisation, but it frames disability issues through the lens of human rights principles. It assumes that public policy and programs should aim to reduce civic inequalities, to address social and economic disadvantage and also assumes that various supports, (e.g., personal services, aids and devices) will be needed by some people in order to gain access to, participate in and exercise self-determination as equals in society.

Research from a rights-outcome approach constructs an analysis of how society marginalises people with disabilities and can be adjusted to respond more effectively to their presence and needs. This approach focuses on the disabling aspects of society, on supporting human diversity, and on empowering disadvantaged individuals. It makes the exercise of human rights by persons the dependent variable in the research questions and social structure the independent variable.

SOCIAL OBLIGATION OF RESEARCH

The social obligation of research in this approach to disability is on how to reduce civic inequalities, that is, the degree to which social and economic disadvantage have been addressed through providing supports and aids and devices that enable social and economic integration, self-determination and legal and social rights. It is distinct from the social obligation of research grounded in individual pathology, where within the bio-medical approach the goal is to eliminate or cure disability and the functional approach that has as its social obligation to ameliorate and provide comfort.

FORMULATIONS AND IDEOLOGY

Research from these social and scientific formulations of disability ascribe different attributes in terms of cause, prevention and social responsibility of the researcher and of society towards persons with disabilities.

Spurious research can, consequently, be legitimated because of the social obligation attached to the ideological framework of the researcher. It may be possible thereby, for example, to legitimate exclusionary practices by the research.

These formulations also provide a mechanism to identify the way in which scientific ideology has provided the justification for particular treatment modalities, social programs, laws, and policies. Because of the difference in world view and in fundamental assumptions about disability, each of these approaches will likely lead researchers to have a different view of what is best with respect to disability and how to frame the research questions. Consequently, the formulation of disability leads to different ways of measuring and evaluating what is accomplished, and policy and program formulation.

These four approaches to research in disability can be evaluated on the basis of the degree of myopia of the disciplinary limits from which they approach disability. Arguably there is nothing wrong with any one of them in their own right, rather it is the harm they cause by claiming the field of disability as the exclusive domain of one particular discipline. There are few other examples where a marginalised group has been subjected to this degree of scientific hegemony. The tradition of the ethical and scientific responsibility of the researcher and the parameters of what constitutes "good research" needs to be made explicit, both in terms of context and procedural methodology. Disability researchers could therefore be usefully evaluated on the degree to which empowerment and reciprocity are central to their research questions, to their methodology and to the sharing of their findings. There is a difference in design, sample and outcome if the question is studied from these different perspectives. Often researchers who use a systemic approach in studying disability are accused of naïveté in understanding the degree of physical and intellectual impairment that some people have – in particular in evaluation research.

There is, however, no reason to deny the need to address physical or intellectual conditions while still understanding that ways are needed to move beyond that as the sole or most important criterion of support. To go further, there are identifiable cases where while research will show success in treating the individual impairment the treatment could arguably be considered a failure – for example, where the provision of services are at the expense of rights. This has major implications in terms of policy, and in particular in terms of policy that provides funding for services or supports provided within segregated settings, or which confer a lesser status on persons with disabilities. Terms such as "uneducable" or "unemployable" or "trainable" which claim scientific validity often entitle people to significant services and state support but they can only be held to be successful in the clinical context in which those distinctions are constructed and enforced. But we must ask, enforced at what cost?

Let me give you an example – the use of aversive therapies on people with clinically defined undesirable behaviours is claimed to be "successful" in reducing an unwanted set of socially problematic behaviours. The important factors in scientific measures of success are how many times an undesirable behaviour occurs, given that certain stimuli are introduced or removed (e.g., electric prods, time-out rooms, ammonia sprays, and so on).

If, however, we opt for another measure of success, we are brought face to face with some limitations that must regulate service and support and evaluation criteria. In this instance, "scientifc" success implies an outcome and ways of achieving it that are in keeping with the human dignity and well-being not only of each individual, but necessarily of society as a whole. The kinds of measures of success are embedded in such research questions as: What are society's obligations to ensure that forms of "care" other than the use of behavioural management are made available in meaningful ways to individuals who have a disability and who need service and support in ways that enable them to exercise their rights? To what extent is technology substituted for the changes necessary to enable a citizen to integrate into the social and economic structures?; To what extent are efficient and cost-effective technologies developed and deployed at the expense of rights?

Research evaluation of supports and services that is formulated within an understanding that disability is an individual pathology differs in the indicators it uses from evaluation research that understands disability as a social pathology. What are some of those differences?

INDICATORS BASED ON INDIVIDUAL PATHOLOGY	INDICATORS BASED ON SOCIAL PATHOLOGY

• diminishing of maladaptive behaviours
• increase of daily-living skills
  • toilet training
  • self-feeding
  • social skills
  • communication
• motor skills development
• provision for adequate staffing & support
• extent to which safety & security are enforced
• the administration of medications
• extent to which there is a reduction in deviation from valued & normal social roles
• use of physiotherapy
• the quality of professional intervention
	• capacity of community and social systems to adapt to individual interests
	• acceptance of individual by communities
	• individual choice and economic control of decisions about support and service
	  • hiring staff
	  • deciding where to live
	• adaptability of job workplace and labour market to account for individual diversity
	• extent to which community and government take on the agenda of disability as political agenda

Likewise in research in disability there might be scepticism of the conventional research which was designed to study the non-disabled population. It is not enough simply to add disability as a category to existing studies. Recent research on abuse and violence uncovered an entirely different set of conditions faced by people with disabilities (Roeher Institute, 1994).

People with disabilities have spawned a research industry that, in the main, has failed to address the fundamental issues of their disenfranchisement. We have barely begun in most countries to deal with the intangible barriers – poverty and prejudice; segregation; and subservience. The research agenda, now, should be how people with disabilities can get a fair footing on the economic ladder, how to fight the kind of discrimination for which there is no recourse enshrined in law, and where to direct the battle for disability equality. To hear in the last few years of the 20th century people appealing to (scientifically discredited) IQ tests as a basis for classifying people; to hear that therapy and services will resolve the systemic exclusion and isolation of people with disabilities; to hear the inherently eugenic arguments of the genetic scientists with the underlying assumption that society must be rid of disability is disturbing. That these can go on, unchallenged, speaks to the disregard with which people with disabilities are held; it speaks to a failure of rigour in scientific work, and it speaks to a profound misconception of the relationship between ethics and science. The light in this tunnel is sometimes dim but there is a steady increase in disability pride activism. I hang my hopes on that, to build a solid civil rights movement in disability throughout the world, one that can guide the research community to the questions worth asking.

REFERENCES

BERESFORD, P. C. J. (1994). "Disabled People, Service Users, User Involvement and Representation." *Disability & Society,* Vol. 9, No. 3, pp. 315-325.

ICIDH, C. S. F. (1991). "The Handicap Creation Process." *ICIDH International Network* 4(1-2).

OLIVER, M. (1990). *The Politics of Disablement*. Basingstoke, Macmillan.

RIOUX, M. (1994). "Towards a Concept of Equality of Well-Being: Overcoming the Social and Legal Construction of Inequality." *Canadian Journal of Law and Jurisprudence* VII(1):pp. 127-147.

RIOUX, M. H. AND BACH, M. (EDS) (1994). *Disability is not Measles: New Research Paradigms in Disability.* North York, Ont., The Roeher Institute.

ROEHER INSTITUTE (1994). Harm's way: The many faces of violence and abuse against persons with disabilities. North York.

ROEHER INSTITUTE (1996). *Disability, Community and Society.* North York (Ont.), The Roeher Institute.

ROTH, W. (1983). "Handicap as a Social Construct." *Society* 20(3).

PART TWO

CHAPTER 8

Personal Trouble or Public Issue?

Towards a model of policy for people with physical and mental disabilities

Anne Borsay

(First Published 1986)

INTRODUCTION

During the past 30 years, services for people with physical and mental disabilities or impairments have been increasingly thrust in a community direction, as policymakers have come to recognise the financial and the human costs of institutional care. But being essentially a reaction to incarceration, community strategies have grown up in an *ad hoc* fashion, without a coherent framework to guide policy development. As Richard Titmuss observed way back in 1961, community care occurred outside the hospital; it 'conjured up a sense of warmth and . . . kindness'; it appeared to be economical, and that was enough for good intentions to be 'transmuted, by the touch of a phrase, into hard-won reality' (Titmuss, 1976). Such a policy vacuum cannot be satisfactorily filled until the position which disabled people occupy in modern Britain has been tackled. Therefore, in this paper, we first undertake a sociological exploration of physical and mental impairment and then, on the basis of that analysis, propose two models which help to untangle the confusion which for so long has bedevilled community social services.

THE INDIVIDUALISTIC PERSPECTIVE

Broadly speaking, two sociological conceptions of disability compete for attention. One is individualistic and the other is social, along the lines of C. Wright Mills' classic distinction between 'personal troubles' and 'public issues'. Writing in the 1950s, Mills maintained that:

> Troubles occur within the character of the individual and within the range of his immediate relations with others; they have to do with his self and with those limited areas of social life of which he is directly and personally aware. Accordingly, the statement and resolution of troubles properly lie within the individual as a biographical entity and within the scope of his immediate milieu—the social setting that is directly open to his personal experience and to some extent his wilful activity. Issues have to do with matters that transcend these local environments of the individual and the range of his inner life. They have to do with the organisation of many such milieux into the institutions of a historical society as a whole, with the ways in which various milieux overlap and interpenetrate to form the larger structure of social and historical life. (Mills, 1970)

What happens if this theoretical taxonomy is applied to physical and mental impairment? When disability is interpreted as a 'personal trouble', sharp distinctions are drawn between different types of impairment and their causes are sought exclusively within the individual: thus, mental and physical handicaps are construed as mere biological deficiencies; mental illness is explained with reference to personal genetics, biochemistry or psychology; and ageing is viewed as an unavoidable physiological process. Not only is causation conceived of in an individualistic way, and without reference to the shared economic, social and political dependencies which give these groups many common needs. Additionally, the assumption is made that deviation from 'normal' behaviour is necessarily a tragic loss or misfortune, particularly where the 'sufferer' is young. Parallels are commonly drawn with death and, like the bereaved, the recently impaired are said to pass through a stage of mourning and to undergo a series of traumatic emotions: shock, denial, anger and depression, before attaining some degree of equilibrium and perhaps finding substitute social roles. With the elderly, there is a heavy sense of inevitability; physical and mental decay is envisaged as a natural part of ageing and the old may be advised to achieve successful adjustment by withdrawing or disengaging from society, to become preoccupied with personal concerns (Cumming *et al.*, 1972; Fitzgerald, 1974; Forsythe, 1979; Oliver, 1981; M. Oliver, 1983; Oliver, 1986). But regardless of age, the individual is expected to cope with disability by adapting himself to society; society is not expected to adapt to him.

Despite its widespread appeal, the individualistic approach has a number of flaws. Even within its own narrow boundaries, personal characteristics crucial to the psychology of disabled people are overlooked; for impairment is assumed automatically to trigger off a single reaction which restricts functioning in all spheres and lowers morale—irrespective of personality, age, sex, type of disability, work and the financial situation, social relationships and previous life-style (Eisdorfor & Cohen, 1980; Greenblum, 1984; Harris & Cole, 1980; Harrison, 1983; Thomas, 1982; Ward, 1979). Most telling, however, is the omission of societal factors because without the socio-economic and political context provided by the 'public issue' or social perspective, we are ill-equipped to comprehend both the causes of disability and the social policies which it has provoked.

THE SOCIAL AETIOLOGY OF DISABILITY

Whereas the individualistic interpretation ascribes disability to intrinsic mental or physical shortcomings, its social alternative recognises a role in causation for extrinsic factors of a 'structural' and an 'interpretative' kind. These social factors may directly cause or help to cause impairment, but they are also responsible for processes which aggravate the effects of functional limitation and so further encumber disabled people (Walker, 1980a). Let us deal with the direct causes first of all, beginning with the structural ones.

There is an unhappy tendency in the social sciences to ally the structural perspective with the methodological stance of positivism, thereby implying that individual action is determined by the social system and that the 'social world' is 'accessible to understanding and explanation by . . . use of the research strategies of the natural sciences' (Cuff & Payne, 1979). However, the term 'structural' does not have to be adopted in a strict, deterministic manner; it can also simply stress the possible impact of economic, social and political institutions without suggesting any necessary curtailment of freedom of action, or indeed the personal autonomy which many disabled people believe that they are able to achieve in spite of their dependencies (Shearer, 1981, 1982; Sutherland, 1981). With the individualistic perspective, any such sensitivity to the structure of society is missing and, consequently, impairment is regarded as a regrettable chance event which randomly afflicts certain individuals. But, in fact, societal factors of various sorts precipitate mental and physical incapacity, and economic organisation is especially culpable. Not only do industrial practices cause pollution and workplace injuries and diseases. Private enterprise may also eschew the firm regulation of defective or harmful goods, drugs and services, and capitalism requires a competitive structure of relationships which may damage mental health (Cochrane, 1983; M.I.N.D., 1979) and give rise to social inequalities which cause the disabilities of poverty associated with low socio-economic class. At the same time, the state itself may increase impairment by intervening in the public interest when there is a risk to some individuals, as vaccine damage illustrates. Obviously, personal biology and psychology on occasions mingle with these factors, but any admission of social causation makes an explanation of disability incomplete unless it takes cognizance of the environmental dimension (Walker, 1980a).

Whatever this balance between direct individual and social causes, social processes also contribute to the aetiology of impairment. For interpretative social scientists, these are the only relevant considerations; the idea of any input from the individual is dismissed out of hand and disability is seen solely as an artificial creation of society, which would vanish almost overnight if social organisation and social attitudes were transformed. Although comprising a diverse collection of opinions, authors of this ilk are united in their rejection of positivism and anxious to emphasise the meanings which individuals attach to social situations in which they engage (Ingleby, 1981). Thus, the critical issue is how physical and mental impairment is perceived by parties to a social encounter. Perhaps the best example of this interpretative tradition is anti-psychiatry, an area of some controversy in mental health which has generated lively debate. Anti-psychiatry points to the centrality of the social audience in defining a person as mentally ill (Pearson, 1975). To quote the famous American psychiatrist, Thomas Szasz:

> In medical practice, when we speak of physical disturbances, we mean either signs (for example, a fever) or symptoms (for example, pain). We speak of mental symptoms, on the other hand, when we refer to a patient's communications about himself, others, and the world about him. He might state that he is Napoleon or that he is being persecuted by the Communists. These would be considered mental symptoms only if the observer believed that the patient was not Napoleon or that he was not being persecuted by the Communists. This makes it apparent that the statement that 'X is a mental symptom' involves rendering a judgement. The judgement entails, moreover, a covert comparison or matching of the patient's ideas, concepts, or beliefs with those of the observer and the society in which they live. The notion of mental symptom is therefore inextricably tied to the social (including ethical) context in which it is made in much the same way as the notion of bodily symptom is tied to an anatomical and genetic context. (Szasz, 1960)

Since decisions about mental illness are so moral and subjective, Szasz argues that the positivist methods of medicine—a perfectly appropriate response to physical disease—are totally wrong in mental health; anti-psychiatry then goes on to accuse most psychiatrists of labelling certain emotions and behaviour as pathological, not due to some inherent and objective quality, but because they offend arbitrary social rules and norms (Becker, 1963; Manning and Oliver, 1985).

Anti-psychiatry, in the main a criticism of medical hegemony in mental health, has usually been content to berate the application of positivist techniques to 'psychological problems', while tacitly accepting their pertinence to physical conditions (Sedgwick, 1982). However, sociologists and doctors have become ever more aware that responses to physical symptoms, pathways to treatment and the adoption of a sick role are affected by characteristics like age, sex and social class (see, for example, Goldberg and Huxley, 1980; Miles, 1978; Tuckett, 1976; Tuckett and Kaufert, 1978). Thus, the uncompromising use of medical concepts in all spheres of health care is losing credibility and some authorities now deny any distinction between physical and mental conditions. Sedgwick, for instance, claims that:

> the medical enterprise is from its inception value-loaded because we have chosen to consider as 'illnesses' or 'diseases' those natural circumstances which precipitate... death (or failure to function according to certain values). (Sedgwick, 1982)

Sedgwick's thesis is called in question by the fact that physical and mental conditions carry different social meanings. Nevertheless, the justified attack on conventional medicine has encouraged an interpretative perspective on physical impairment as well, and Victor Finkelstein has taken the short step from physical illness to suggest that physical handicap too is nothing more than an artificial social construct. Finkelstein draws a sharp division between impairment and disability. Quoting from a paper by the Union of the Physically Impaired Against Segregation, he defines

> *Impairment* as lacking part or all of a limb, or having a defective limb, organ or mechanism of the body; and *disability* as the disadvantage of restriction of activity caused by contemporary social organisation which takes no or little account of people who have physical impairments.

Disability is, therefore, a 'special' form of discrimination, or social 'oppression' (Finkelstein, 1980); it is imposed by a society which expects all its members to conform to the yardstick of able-bodied normality, and builds physical and social environments which penalise any 'misfits'.

SOCIETAL STRUCTURE AND DISABILITY

Although important, interpretative thinking is incomplete as a social construction of handicap unless, like recent work by M. Oliver (1983, 1984) and D. Stone (1985), it attempts to address the economic, social and political structures which underpin our value systems and so help to stigmatise disabled people. Some of the best structural accounts of impairment emerge from the literature on ageing which has accumulated on both sides of the Atlantic. In Britain, Townsend blames

> the tradition of functionalism in sociology, as well as the more descriptive and empirical traditions of social work and social administration (for encouraging) the kind of theory of ageing which attributes the causation of problems to the difficulties of individual adjustment to ageing, retirement or physical decrescence, while acquiescing in the development of the state, the economy, and inequality.

Townsend declares forcefully that, contrary to the individualistic position, it is society which 'creates the framework of institutions and rules within which the general problems of the elderly ... are manufactured' (Townsend, 1981). His comments apply equally to younger people with physical and mental impairments. Therefore, a sociology of disability must give proper consideration to economic, social and political status.

ECONOMIC STATUS

The economy is a pivotal feature of modern Britain and economic rationality is a central goal. Consequently, society is organised to achieve maximum 'efficiency, productivity and material progress' (Shearer, 1981) and the personal qualities commensurate with these objectives are hallowed—good health, independence, resourcefulness, enthusiasm, energy, ambition, resilience (Harris and Cole, 1980; Topliss, 1982). In the competitive environment of the labour market which expresses these values, disabled people are disadvantaged for at least three reasons. First, the growth of credentialism may undermine the prospects of those who, due to age or an interrupted and inadequate education, have failed to amass qualifications which mirror their abilities. Secondly, while mechanisation and technical change may open up new opportunities for younger disabled people, innovation devalues the experience of older employees and their expiring working life makes them unpopular candidates for retraining. Finally, despite evidence to the contrary, employers often consider all disabled people an unreliable, high risk group unable to reach normal productivity levels and hence unsuitable both for initial recruitment and promotion. The net effect of these trends is that many of working age with physical and mental impairments are located at the bottom of the income ladder, or out of work and dependent upon social security benefits like the majority of the disabled who are elderly (Buckle, 1971; Davoud and Kettle, 1980; Estes *et al*, 1982; Hendricks and McAllister, 1983; Jordan, 1979; Kettle, 1979; Locker, 1983; Maclean and Jeffreys, 1974; Oliver, 1982; M. Oliver, 1983; Taylor and Ford, 1983; Townsend, 1979, 1981; Walker, 1980a, 1981, 1982a,c; Wansbrough and Cooper, 1980; Ward, 1979).

SOCIAL STATUS

Work not only has financial repercussions; there are also s   -offs for social and political status. Ageing is asociated with contracting social relationships; and as old people start to play fewer roles and fill more time with home-centred activities, their links with the community are severed (M. Abrams, 1980; Cumming *et al*., 1972; Tunstall, 1966; Wenger, 1984). The younger disabled may also experience impoverished social interaction, and for similar reasons. Loss of mobility and negative community attitudes may make socialising difficult; poverty, stemming from retirement, unemployment or poor wages, may cramp leisure pursuits; and without a job to regulate life-activity and serve as a foundation for intercourse, it may be hard to put together social networks (Goffman, 1968; Harris and Cole, 1980; Locker, 1983; Locker et al., 1979; Miles, 1981; Weir, 1981a,b). Townsend argues that the high esteem of the aged within the family helps to compensate for their low 'public status' (Townsend, 1981). Geographical mobility, however, has splintered multi-generational families and many relatives are now too distant to be convivial with elderly or younger disabled kin on a regular basis (Rosser and Harris, 1965; Wenger, 1984). Moreover, in a highly fluid society, where knowledge is quickly outdated, the elderly who do remain near relations lose their worth as counsellors and advisers (Rosow, 1974); and at all ages, dependencies which breach the conventions of family life—for example, husband financially beholden to wife, or frail parent reliant upon adult offspring—may sully relationships and leave the disabled person with tasks insufficient to offset the humiliation from loss of function (Bergmann et al., 1984; Dartington et al., 1981; Dowd and La Rossa, 1982; J. Oliver, 1983; M. Oliver, 1983). But, above all, non-economic family roles in a capitalist society rarely carry the prestige of paid employment. Therefore, although these activities, many in the field of child care, may satisfy elderly women whose lives have always revolved around domestic affairs, they may be second best for the individual of either sex who has been economically active outside the home.

POLITICAL STATUS

Just as economic factors influence social relationships, so they also affect the political status of disabled people. Marx pushed this logic to its outer limits, claiming that the capitalist mode of production so determined 'the rest of the social structure' that 'political and administrative intervention' was unable to 'decisively shape the reality of the economic order' (Mishra, 1977). However, it is possible to accept some elbow-room for political institutions, while still conceding that economic and political status are intimately intertwined. In our industrial society, any adult not performing work-linked economic and social roles is a thorn in the flesh of economic rationality and may even be feared as a menace to political stability. There is no one way of handling this trouble spot, but with physical and mental impairment the sick role is deployed to minimise the effects of dependency. When subjected to this status, 'ill' disabled people are, according to their degree of incapacity, excused various duties and absolved of responsibility for their situation, in return for agreeing that their condition is undesirable and co-operating with 'appropriate' help (De Jong, 1981; Miles, 1981). Any reduction of this process to crude social control is simplistic; there is no conspiracy to divest deviance of its political significance and hence defuse a 'threat or potential threat to the existing . . . conditions of society' (Treacher and Baruch, 1981; Manning and Oliver, 1985). Nevertheless, application of the sick role to disabled people does devalue their input to political debate by conveying the mistaken impression that, being indisposed, they are either unable to speak for themselves or have nothing worthwhile to say (Shearer, 1981). Thus, political status is corroded by an apparently humanitarian action.

Consumer engagement in the welfare state is further undercut by the British system of representative democracy which endorses participation by the elector singly and indirectly, rather than more pugnacious forms of political activity. In the absence of direct and effective user participation, disabled people have to champion their interests through pressure groups and the electoral system. Since the mid-1960s, organisations from within the disabled power movement (the Union of the Physically Impaired Against Segregation, the Liberation Network of People with Disabilities, the British Council of Organisations of Disabled People, Disabled People's International) have been fighting to raise the political consciousness of their constituencies (Dartington et al., 1981; Oliver, 1984; Sutherland, 1981). They have met with some success but, unfortunately, there are inherent obstacles to much further progress both in this area of pressure group politics and electorally. A major problem is dogged adherence to economic rationality, which reproaches those who are not fully productive and discourages them from organising around a negatively perceived condition. However, the incoherence of the impaired as a political group also reduces their impact. Splintering along class lines is one cause; handicapped members of the upper and middle classes, with wealth and investment incomes, higher salaries or better superannuation schemes, have a very different experience of impairment to people who must rely exclusively on state social services. But other tensions within the disabled population are important too. The traditional medical approach to handicap, for example, has created artificial fissures between disease categories which obscure common social needs; and as the majority of disabled people are elderly, the distinction between handicap and old age is likewise divisive. In turn, this age profile has implications for the nature of political participation because, although the elderly are growing in numerical terms, they mostly confine themselves to voting at elections and are less likely than younger age bands to take part in more aggressive activities—signing petitions, demonstrating, and founding pressure groups. Satisfaction with the status quo born of past deprivation may be one reason for this passivity; and the 'new' elderly, and younger disabled people may be more ready to complain. But whatever the intensity of their grievances, the impaired of all ages encounter practical difficulties when attempting to voice political opinions. Poverty and poor health may sap their energy; immobility and inaccessible public buildings may constrain them; and they may have little confidence in their powers of verbal or written communication. The upshot is that citizens with physical and mental disabilities are relatively powerless to shape the formulation and administration of policies which play a fundamental part in their lives (Borsay, 1986) [1].

THE SOCIAL POLICY RESPONSE

In dismantling the individualistic perspective and assembling an alternative social one, we have so far dealt with the social causes of disability, considering the direct connections between socio-economic organisation and the incidence of impairment, interpretative views of the social construction of disability, and the ramifications of societal structure for economic, social and political status. Within the context of this paper, however, it is not adequate to posit that disability is socially manufactured, by whatever means. To examine more fully the pock-marks in community care, we must now tease out the implications of our sociological analysis for policy development.

Since the conception or explanation which is given to a problem 'contains an implicit prescription for policy' (Townsend, 1979), it is possible to outline an individualistic and a social model of community social services for disabled people. At present, the individualistic perspective has a stranglehold, and provisions exhibit many of the characteristics summarised for this model in the Table below. Thus, all community care is rudimentary and under-financed. The state leaves families to cope with disability almost unaided. Services—for example, education and purpose-built accommodation—may segregate their recipients from the rest of the community and defy co-ordination. Mechanisms for direct consumer participation are variable in their success. The distribution of benefits neither significantly reduces material inequalities in income and housing, nor achieves equity in health care, education and the other social services. There are few attempts to prevent the economic and social causes of disability. And, last but not least, half-hearted employment initiatives, such as the discredited three per cent quota of disabled workers for companies with more than 20 employees, fail to tackle the labour market discrimination which lies at the heart of ambivalence towards impairment in an advanced industrial society.

TABLE I. Policy responses under the individualistic and social models

	Individualistic Model	Social (structural) Model
Public expenditure	Lower	Higher
State intervention	Reluctant	Enthusiastic
Family and community support	Minimum	Maximum
Service organisation	Segregated	Integrated
	Disjointed	Co-ordinated
	More unequal/inequitable	Less unequal/inequitable
	Producer-dominated	Consumer-sensitive

In sharp contrast, the social models are more conscious of 'the larger structure of social and historical life'. In the past, the interpretative version has not been very relevant to policy discussions. Either writers have by-passed reform within the existing social system and preferred to imagine the disappearance of disability in some future 'brave new world' (Leonard, 1975; Ramon, 1982); or, alternatively, they have lapsed into naïvité when confronting 'the larger complexes of society', as opposed to 'small-scale structures and relationships'. Thomas Szasz, for instance, shows great faith in the private contract between psychiatrist and client, without appreciating that many most in need of help 'are hardly in a position to compete in the therapy-purchasing market' (Sedgwick, 1982). More recently, groups of disabled people have started to arrange services for themselves, sometimes employing assistants and sometimes on a self-help basis. However, many of those involved are from younger age groups whose impairments (e.g. spinal injury) are typically static. Others may not have the energy or resources to forge innovatory patterns of care. Nor may then they be able to offer help, particularly in the early stages of disability; and so mutual aid organisations move towards 'voluntary assistance from longer term members to newer ones' (Richardson and Goodman, 1983). Therefore, while accepting the personal significance of such initiatives, they are unlikely to satisfy the needs of the majority of disabled people with the degenerative conditions of later life. It follows that there is more mileage for policy analysis in the structural than in the interpretative version of the social model.

Since the structural approach recognises the societal causes of many disabilities, an ideal package of economic and social policies, ambitious and wide-ranging, is prescribed. The state would intervene energetically in the organisation of employment to reduce physical and mental damage to workers. Goods of all descriptions would be tested stringently and banned when they were a threat to health and safety. Vigorous attempts would be made to maximise job opportunities for elderly and younger disabled people who wished to work. Generous income maintenance programmes would prevent poverty due to impairment. And to meet housing, health, education and welfare needs, the state would evolve a comprehensive, integrated and co-ordinated collection of services which were equitably allocated in all localities, geared to family and community resources, and politically accountable to their users. Yet if the social model recommends these strategies to combat the faults of individualistic policies, it also reveals that the prospects for successful implementation are slim because the same societal forces which manufacture disability also mitigate against a structural response. Cost is the initial stumbling block. Throughout the twentieth century, public expenditure has consumed an increasing proportion of the gross national product (GNP) and the expansion of social services spending on social security, welfare, health, education and housing has been especially marked. Thus, between 1910 and 1975, during which time total state expenditure grew from 12.7% to 57.9% of GNP (at factor cost), social services expenditure increased sevenfold, from 4.2% to 28.8% (again, at factor cost). When the national product was itself on an upward trend, the level of public spending was less of an issue; profits and real wages grew over time and provided 'the material base for reformism and the welfare state'. As the GNP started to falter, however, government expenditure came under heavy fire and the present intensive assault, dating from the mid-1970s, is conducted in the conviction that our economic difficulties will be ameliorated by better housekeeping. Economists now clash over the details of a strategy for recovery, but neo-Keynesians and monetarists alike agree that public spending, if uncontrolled, is 'a major cause of the . . . economic crisis and must be cut' (Gough, 1979). Therefore, the global cost of a structural policy response to disability is inhibiting (Oliver, 1984), particularly given the ideological commitment after 1979 to replace statutory services with the family and the private and voluntary sectors.

But even if the economy was buoyant enough to fuel an extended welfare state, all-embracing policies towards disability would still be frustrated because of the primacy which is given to economic over social goals. In contemporary Britain, the work ethic is considered essential to economic survival; it is believed that talent and effort must be materially rewarded and an income differential between the economically active and economically inactive preserved, in order that citizens have an incentive to find and keep employment. Consequently, national insurance contributions and taxation are pegged at relatively low levels, and hence a strict threshold imposed on all public expenditure but especially that directed towards social ends (George and Wilding, 1984). Ironically, however, the emergence of human needs is often closely interwoven with the economic development of industrial societies, and recourse to statutory services by disabled people is no exception. Since the Second World War, the economy has demanded a more geographically mobile workforce and increasing numbers of married women have been attracted back to paid employment. As a result, relatives and friends may no longer live in close enough proximity to help disabled people; neighbourhood networks, generated in some localities by decades of shared residence, may be less supportive (P. Abrams, 1980); and women, the traditional and still the most numerous carers, no longer have so much time to spare (Briggs, 1983; Charlesworth et al., 1984; Equal Opportunities Commission, 1980; Green et al., 1979; Jones and Vetter, 1985). These changes are not inevitably destructive; mobility and female employment may enhance living standards and open up opportunities for individuals previously fettered by tight-knit family and community life. Nevertheless, new needs do appear which demand greater statutory support for disabled people and this structural policy is a costly one, with little economic return. Unlike expenditure on education or curative medicine, community care cannot be put forward as a means to improved productive capacity (Sleeman, 1979); nor, in a period of high unemployment, is the release of valuable labour a defence, particularly when many carers are women with few occupational skills who seek part-time work as secondary earners. Therefore, community care for disabled people cannot be pursued through the economic justifications which hold most sway in a capitalist society.

Social services to substitute for relatives and neighbours also contravene the principle of *laissez-faire*, which with its emphasis on self-help reiterates the competitive individualism of the market-place. In the context of families and local communities, state 'interference' is said to imperil the sanctity of the home and the neighbourhood, and to undermine the natural sense of mutual obligation found in each. But the commitment to *laissez-faire* overflows into political institutions too, making central administrations first loathe to weaken the (theoretical) autonomy of local government by instructing the authorities responsible for many community services to innovate or extend their activities; and, second, loathe to intervene in industry—to insist on strict workplace safety standards; to humanise employment conditions; to regulate the production of dangerous goods; to attack discrimination against disabled workers. In other words, a spirit of free enterprise persists and although governments have moved to eliminate the worst vagaries of local democracy and the worst abuses of industrial organisation, attitudes to further statutory intervention are often ambiguous, in all the main political parties. Conscious of the liberty of the citizen, as a producer, consumer and local elector, the state may be hesitant to hedge in his freedom of action, even if the cost of acquiescence is inadequate community services, more disability and less job opportunities for impaired workers.

As well as disclosing opposition to the extension of community policies for disabled people, the structural model also indicates that defects in the social services will be resistant to change. At the heart of this conservatism lie the professional groups who implement social policies and mediate between the welfare state and its clients. Pure humanitarianism is not the sole inspiration of these practitioners, despite the reveries of some functionalists; but nor are they the mere lackeys of economic and political élites. Rather, believing in the ideals of care embraced by their ethical codes, they use the power, which stems from an ability to stymie government policy through non-co-operation, to enter into a partnership with the state based on a shared, if fluctuating and unbalanced, commitment to the welfare ethic. Nevertheless, there are inherent contradictions; for as repayment for the privileges of professional status—autonomy, community sanction, the respect of politicians and civil servants—social services personnel are prepared to apply the sick role to disabled people and work in agencies which reinforce this status through segregation, the unequal/inequitable distribution of resources and the denial of opportunities for genuine consumer participation in decision-making (Wilding, 1982).

Segregated social services owe their origins to the individualistic policy model, which focuses on accommodating disabled people within the structures of 'normal' society instead of showing flexibility in the face of human diversity. Thus, there is a tendency to reduce those who cannot act out the usual gamut of economic and social roles to the trait which stops their proper participation in society; to assume that their differences rule out the possibility of an ordinary life in all spheres; and then to use this 'deviance' to justify separate or segregated provisions which treat special needs (Purkis and Hodson, 1982; Study Group of the 1978 Co-ordinated Research Fellowship Programme, 1980). Professional groups, well to the forefront in identifying these special needs, have from time to time managed to orchestrate policy initiatives; and in the short term, disabled people have gained by the introduction of segregated facilities to replace harsh institutional regimes or gross community neglect. As specialists, however, professionals tend 'to diagnose a problem in relation to what they themselves can offer' and so the welfare state has been carved principally by their pattern of occupational skills (Walker, 1982b). The resulting division of labour bears little resemblance to consumer needs; for example, the vested interests of teachers has hampered transfer of disabled children from special education, which isolates them from their peers and depresses academic attainment, to standard classrooms giving a better chance of equal opportunities. In addition, competing professional ideologies and fierce rivalry stifle both the co-ordination of help to individuals and the reform of services to bring them more into line with disabled people's requirements— not just in the segregated sector but throughout the welfare state (Bytheway and James, 1978; Pascoe and Thompson, 1979; Robinson, 1978). In the longer term, therefore, the separatism and insularity encouraged by professional influence has produced disjointed social services which may be out of step with consumer needs.

Segregation is essentially an extreme form of inequality which isolates and excludes minorities (Webb, 1980), but inequality itself is not confined to special services; integrated policies potentially open to all citizens are also affected. The social security system, for instance, awards to those injured at war or in employment levels of benefit significantly higher than the invalidity schemes, retirement pension or supplementary benefit; and by so articulating the worth of service to society, propagates a hierarchy among state dependants within the disabled population (Shearer, 1981; Topliss, 1982; Oliver, 1984). But even at the top of the pecking order, payments do not always lift their recipients from poverty; and onto this foundation of financial inequality are piled housing and the other material deprivations which arise from low income. Bearing in mind the universal nature of monetary and accommodation needs, equality is a suitable criterion against which to measure policy. However, where needs are not common to us all, thinking in terms of equality serves 'merely to underwrite existing inequalities' (Jones *et al.*, 1978) and, therefore, equitable access to assistance commensurate with personal and social circumstances becomes the appropriate test (Shearer, 1981). The equitable distribution of resources is just as elusive to health care, education and the personal social services as equality is to social security and housing. In both cases, the reason is the alliance of the welfare state to the values of a capitalist economy and in particular to the work ethic. However, where equity is at issue, professional discretion, exercised at the margins in housing and social security decisions, is elevated in importance. Although the professions are not blatant agents of social control, the perspectives which guide their operation do embody a therapeutic model of practice—a 'problem-treatment-cure' approach which with adults concentrates on a return to 'normal' economic and social roles and with children aims for a healthy and socially competent labour force for the future. This emphasis on rehabilitation is devastating for disabled people, where not dramatic change but modest improvement, or perhaps the prevention of further deterioration, is perceived as the most likely effect of intervention. To begin with, services designed for children and the working population may be peripheral to the needs of individuals with long-term dependencies. But even when help is relevant, the assumption that professional skills are superfluous may encourage the automatic allocation of disability referrals to less prestigious occupational groups, or a second-class service from professionals whose training has instilled the superiority of therapeutic work and devalued association with patients or clients of limited economic potential. It is this allegiance between social services personnel and the state which underpins the inequitable treatment of disabled people (Borsay, 1986) [1].

Paradoxically, shortcomings in the social services obstruct the path to user accountability. In the first place, imperiously supplying assistance and attaching the label, 'illness', to citizens with physical and mental impairments foster a false image and sense of dependence (Purkis and Hodson, 1982) which, when combined with representative democracy's espousal of indirect participation, helps to dismiss them as incapable. However, segregation, inequality and inequity also take their toll; for by discriminating negatively on the basis of disability, they not only reinforce the sick role but also deter campaigning by communicating that impairment is a stigma, to be hidden not brandished. If consumers are written off as incompetent and passivity is promoted, professional control of the welfare state is exonerated and any attempts at more direct participation—Community Health Councils, patients' committees, tenants' associations—are likely to be cosmetic. But this is not surprising. The imperfections of community care stem primarily from tensions which surround dependency in an advanced industrial society; and until these dissonances are resolved, disabled people will continue to suffer from denuded political status.

CONCLUSION

It has been the aim of this paper to develop a model of community care disciplined by a sociological appraisal of physical and mental impairment. To this end, two conflicting interpretations of disability have been compared, one individualistic and the other social. Under the individualistic perspective, disability is presented as a 'personal trouble' and the victim is expected to come to terms with his plight, assisted by relatives and close acquaintances. Under the social perspective, conversely, disability is acknowledged as a 'public issue' and emphasis is placed on the role of society in its manufacture— by directly causing physical and mental impairment; by applying pejorative labelling processes; by operating economic, social and political institutions which are deaf to the needs of disabled people. Naturally, different policies are derived from these two interpretations. In line with its conception of disability, the individualistic policy response is unhappy to sanction extensive government spending and intervention; it acquiesces in the strain imposed upon families and neighbourhoods; and accepts social services which are segregated and disjointed, unequally or inequitably distributed, and dominated by professionals. From its grounding in the structure of society, the social model prescribes diametrically opposed policies: heavy public expenditure and state intervention; maximum support for carers; and integrated, co-ordinated social services, allocated according to principles of equality or equity and tuned in to consumer needs. But at the same time, this model also demonstrates clearly the problems of moving from individualistic policies, typical of much current provision, to a more socially orientated programme of community care. Of course, welfare goals are not invariably incompatible with the economic rationality which is a hallmark of industrial Britain; for, historically, as Robert Pinker observes:

> The political interest in maintaining social order and consensus, the growing awareness that what was good for social welfare was also good for the economy, and the relevance of social policy to military efficiency and patriotic unity have . . . contributed greatly to the extension of the welfare state. (Pinker, 1974)

At the same time, however, the cost of increasing any social service quickly becomes prohibitive; and where the beneficiaries hail from largely non-productive minority groups, endemic impediments to change become even more intractable. Better community care threatens work incentives through bigger tax and national insurance bills, without the fillip of an economic return; high profile government—to help relatives, friends and neighbours, to expand and overhaul health and local authority services, to prevent disability—threaten the cherished independence of families and communities, local political institutions and employers; the pursuit of integration, equality/equity and consumer participation threaten the autonomy of the professions and their symbiotic relationship with the state. Given these barriers to change, the social model carries a doubly pessimistic message: yes, reform of community care is pressing but the resistance will be formidable.

NOTE

[1] I am grateful to the editor of the Occasional Papers on Social Administration, in which series this book appears, for permission to use the above paragraph.

REFERENCES

ABRAMS, M. (1980) *Beyond Three-Score and Ten* (Mitcham, Age Concern Publications).
ABRAMS, P. (1980) Social change, social networks and neighbourhood care, *Social Work Service*, pp.12-23.
BECKER, H. (1963) *Outsiders* (New York, Free Press).
BERGMANN, K., MANCHEE, V. & WOODS, R.T. (1984) Effect of Family Relationships on Psychogeriatric Patients, *Journal of the Royal Society of Medicine*, 77, pp. 840-844.

BORSAY, A. (1986) *Disabled People in the Community* (London, Bedford Square Press).

BRIGGS, A. (1983) *Who Cares?* (Chatham, Association of Carers).

BUCKLE, J. (1971) *Work and Housing of Impaired Persons in Great Britain* (London, HMSO).

BYTHEWAY, B. & JAMES, L. (1978) Reaching across the wild borders, *Health and Social Service Journal*, pp. 936-938.

CHARLESWORTH, A., WILKIN, D. & DURIE, A. (1984) *Carers and Services* (Manchester, Equal Opportunities Commission).

COCHRANE, R. (1983) *The Social Creation of Mental Illness* (Harlow, Longman).

CUFF, E.C. & PAYNE, G.C.F. (Eds) (1979) *Perspectives in Sociology* (London, Allen & Unwin).

CUMMING, E., DEAN, L.R., NEWELL, D.S. & MCCAFFREY, I. (1972) *Human Ageing* (London, Penguin).

DARTINGTON, T., MILLER, E. & GWYNNE, G. (1981) *A Life Together* (London, Tavistock).

DAVOUD, N. & KETTLE, M. (1980) *Multiple Sclerosis and its Effects upon Employment* (London, Multiple Sclerosis Society).

DE JONG, G. (1981) The movement for independent living: origins, ideology and implications for disability research, in: A. BRECHIN, P. LIDDIARD & J. SWAIN (Eds) *Handicap in a Social World* (Sevenoaks, Hodder & Stoughton).

DOWD, J.J. & LaRossa, R. (1982) Primary group contact and elderly morale: an exchange/power analysis, *Sociology and Social Research*, 66, pp. 184-197.

EISDORFOR, C. & COHEN, D. (1980) The issue of biological and psychological deficits, in: E. F. BORGATTA & N. G. MCCLUSKEY (Eds) *Ageing and Society* (Beverly Hills, Sage).

EQUAL OPPORTUNITIES COMMISSION (1980) *The Experience of Caring for Elderly and Handicapped Dependants* (Manchester, Equal Opportunities Commission).

ESTES, C.L., SWAN, J.H. & GERARD, L.E. (1982) Dominant and competing paradigms in gerontology: towards a political economy of ageing, *Ageing and Society*, 2, pp. 151-164.

FINKELSTEIN, V. (1980) *Attitudes and Disabled People* (New York, World Rehabilitation Fund).

FITZGERALD, R.G. (1974) Reactions to blindness: an exploratory study of adults with recent loss of sight, in: D. M. BOSWELL & J. M. WINGROVE (Eds) *The Handicapped Person in the Community* (London, Tavistock).

FORSYTHE, E. (1979) *Living with Multiple Sclerosis* (London, Faber).

GEORGE, V. & WILDING, P. (1984) *The Impact of Social Policy* (London, Routledge & Kegan Paul).

GOFFMAN, E. (1968) *Stigma* (London, Penguin).

GOLDBERG, D. & HUXLEY, P. (1980) *Mental Illness in the Community* (London, Tavistock).

GOUGH, I. (1979) *The Political Economy of the Welfare State* (Basingstoke, Macmillan).

GREEN, S., CREESE, A. & KAUFERT, J. (1979) Social support and government policy on services for the elderly, *Social Policy and Administration,* 13, pp. 210-218.

GREENBLUM, J. (1984) Age and capacity devaluation: a replication, *Social Science and Medicine,* 19, pp. 181-1187.

HARRIS, D.K. & COLE, W.E. (1980) *Sociology of Ageing* (New York, Houghton Mifflin).

HARRISON, J. (1983) Women and ageing: experience and implications, *Ageing and Society,* 3, pp. 209-235.

HENDRICKS, J. & McALLISTER, C.E. (1983) An alternative perspective on retirement: a dual economic approach, *Ageing and Society,* 3, pp. 279-299.

INGLEBY, D. (1981) Understanding 'mental illness', in: D. INGLEBY (Ed.) *Critical Psychiatry* (London, Penguin).

JONES, D.A. & VETTER, N.J. (1985) Formal and informal support received by carers of elderly dependants, *British Medical Journal,* 291, pp. 643-645.

JONES, K., BROWN, J. & BRADSHAW, J. (1978) *Issues in Social Policy* (London, Routledge & Kegan Paul).

JORDAN, D. (1979) *A New Employment Programme Wanted for Disabled People* (London, Disability Alliance).

KETTLE, M. (1979) *Disabled People and their Employment* (Banstead, Association of Disabled Professionals).

LEONARD, P. (1975) Towards a paradigm for radical practice, in: R. BAILEY & M. BRAKE (Eds) *Radical Social Work* (London, Edward Arnold).

LOCKER, D. (1983) *Disability and Disadvantage* (London, Tavistock).

LOCKER, D., RAO, B. & WEDDELL, J.M. (1979) Public acceptance of community care for the mentally handicapped, Apex, 7.

MACLEAN, M. & JEFFREYS, M. (1974) Disability and deprivation, in: D. WEDDERBURN (Ed.) *Poverty, Inequality and Class Structure* (London, Cambridge University Press).

MANNING, N. & OLIVER, M. (1985) Madness, epilepsy and medicine, in: N. MANNING (Ed.) *Social Problems and Welfare Ideology* (Aldershot, Gower).

MILES, A. (1978) *The social content of health*, in: P. BREARLEY, J. GIBBONS, A. MILES, E. TOPLISS & G. WOOD, The Social Context of Health Care (Oxford, Blackwell/Martin Robertson).

MILES, A. (1981) *The Mentally Ill in Contemporary Society* (Oxford, Martin Robertson).

M.I.N.D. (1979) *Prevention in Mental Health* (London, National Association for Mental Health).

MISHRA, R. (1977) *Society and Social Policy* (Basingstoke, Macmillan).

OLIVER, C. (1982) *Older Workers and Unemployment* (London, Unemployment Alliance).

OLIVER, J. (1983) The caring wife, in: J. FINCH & D. GROVES (Eds) *A Labour of Love* (London, Routledge & Kegan Paul).

OLIVER, M. (1981) Disability, adjustment and family life: some theoretical considerations, in: A. BRECHIN, P. LIDDIARD & J. SWAIN (Eds) *Handicap in a Social World* (Sevenoaks, Hodder & Stoughton).

OLIVER, M. (1983) *Social Work with Disabled People* (Basingstoke, Macmillan).

OLIVER, M. (1984) The politics of disability, *Critical Social Policy*, No. 11, pp. 21-32.

OLIVER, M. (1986) Social policy and disability: some theoretical issues, *Disability, Handicap and Society*, 1, pp. 5-17.

PASCOE, N. & THOMPSON, Q. (1979) Co-operation and conflict: an examination of the interface between housing and social services departments, *Housing Review*, 28, pp. 71-74.

PEARSON, G. (1975) *The Deviant Imagination* (London, Macmillan).

PINKER, R. (1974) Social policy and social justice, Journal of Social Policy, 3, pp. 1-19.

PURKIS, A. & HODSON, P. (1982) *Housing and Community Care* (London, Bedford Square Press).

RAMON, S. (1982) The logic of pragmatism in mental health policy, *Critical Social Policy*, 2, pp. 38-54.

RICHARDSON, A. & GOODMAN, M. (1983) *Self-help and Social Care* (London, Policy Studies Institute).

ROBINSON, T. (1978) *In Worlds Apart* (London, Bedford Square Press).

ROSOW, I. (1974) *Socialisation to Old Age* (Berkeley, University of California Press).

ROSSER, C. & HARRIS, C. (1965) *The Family and Social Change* (London, Routledge & Kegan Paul).

SEDGWICK, P. (1982) *Psycho Politics* (London, Pluto Press).

SHEARER, A. (1981) *Disability: whose handicap?* (Oxford, Blackwell).

SHEARER, A. (1982) *Living Independently* (London, Centre for Environment for the Handicapped/ King Edward's Hospital Fund for London).

SLEEMAN, J.F. (1979) *Resources for the Welfare State* (Harlow, Longman).

STONE, D. (1985) *The Disabled State* (Basingstoke, Macmillan).

STUDY GROUP OF THE 1978 CO-ORDINATED RESEARCH FELLOWSHIPS PROGRAMME (1980) *New Forms in the Structures and Organisation of Social Services, Including Multidisciplinary Centres and Systems to Encourage Client Participation* (Strasbourg, Council of Europe).

SUTHERLAND, A. (1981) *Disabled We Stand* (London, Souvenir Press).

SZASZ, T. (1960) The myth of mental illness, *American Psychologist*, 15, pp. 113-118.

TAYLOR, R. & FORD, G. (1983) Inequalities in old age: an examination of age, sex and class differences in a sample of community elderly, *Ageing and Society*, 3, pp. 183-208.

THOMAS, D. (1982) *The Experience of Handicap* (London, Methuen).

TITMUSS, R.M. (1976) *Commitment to Welfare* (London, Allen & Unwin).

TOPLISS, E. (1982) *Social Responses to Handicap* (Harlow, Longman).

TOWNSEND, P. (1979) *Poverty in the United Kingdom* (London, Penguin).

TOWNSEND, P. (1981) The structured dependency of the elderly: a creation of social policy in the twentieth century, *Ageing and Society*, 1, pp. 5-28.

TREACHER, A. & BARUCH, G. (1981) Towards a critical history of the psychiatric profession, in: D. INGLEBY (Ed.) *Critical Psychiatry* (London, Penguin).

TUCRETT, D. (Ed.) (1976) *An Introduction to Medical Sociology* (London, Tavistock).

TUCKETT, D. & KAUFERT, J.M. (Eds) (1978) *Basic Readings in Medical Sociology* (London, Tavistock).

TUNSTALL, J. (1966) *Old and Alone* (London, Routledge & Kegan Paul).

WALKER, A. (1980a) The social origins of impairment, disability and handicap, *Medicine in Society*, 6, pp. 18-26.

WALKER, A. (1980b), The social creation of poverty and dependency in old age, *Journal of Social Policy*, 9.

WALKER, A. (1981) Towards a political economy of old age, *Ageing and Society*, 1, pp. 73-94.

WALKER, A. (1982a) *Unqualified and Underemployed* (Basingstoke, Macmillan).

WALKER, A. (1982b) Social need, social services and mental illness, in: *Housing Management, Social Work and Mental Illness* (London, King's Fund Centre).

WALKER, A. (1982c) Dependency and old age, *Social Policy and Administration*, 16, pp. 115-135.

WANSBROUGH, N. & COOPER, P. (1980) *Open Employment After Mental Illness* (London, Tavistock).

WARD, R.A. (1979) *The Ageing Experience* (New York, Lippincott).

WEBB, A. (1980) The personal social services, in: N. BOSANQUET & P. TOWNSEND (Eds) *Labour and Inequality* (London, Heinemann Educational).

WEIR, S. (1981a) Our image of the disabled and how ready we are to help, *New Society*, 1 January.

WEIR, S. (1981b) Has International Year helped disabled people? *New Society*, 24/31 December.

WENGER, G.C. (1984) *The Supportive Network* (London, Allen & Unwin).

WILDING, P. (1982) *Professional Power and Social Welfare* (London, Routledge & Kegan Paul).

WRIGHT MILLS, C. (1970) *The Sociological Imagination* (London, Penguin)

CHAPTER 9

The Politics of Special Educational Needs

Len Barton

(First published 1986)

TAKING SIDES

In what has now become a classic article entitled: 'Whose side are you on?', Howard Becker argues that in their research, sociologists can never avoid taking sides [1]. For those of us who are now devoting our attention to the issues of disability and handicap, it is essential that we make our own value-positions clear.

My reasons for working in this area are threefold. First, because as a result of my own school experience I know what it is to be a constant failure. I left school without a single academic qualification. My memories are quite vivid of some of those numerous occasions within school, when I experienced public degradation ceremonies in which I was explicitly told that I was 'thick', 'stupid', or 'a hopeless problem child'. The realities of a secondary modern school, with large classes, poor buildings, few resources and a high staff turnover, also combined to establish a sense of inferiority or second-class citizenship. I therefore feel a very strong affinity towards those pupils who are now described as 'children with special educational needs' which in the vast majority of cases, is a euphemism for failure. Secondly, from my own experience of working with young people, many of whom were categorised as 'severely' mentally handicapped, I became aware of the significance of social factors in the construction of handicap. Despite good intentions and a great deal of effort, the contradictory nature of the work context, the assessment procedures used, combined to restrict the nature of our knowledge to a rather surface and mechanical level of appreciation. We did not know them as people, in a deeply profound sense, but rather, saw their disabilities as the all-enveloping factor. Because we did not really understand them, we often underestimated them. From my understanding of work within special education today, this is still a key issue that needs to be addressed. Finally, my motivation for working in this field of study is influenced by a belief that we can develop a more adequate understanding of the nature of society by examining the ways in which disadvantaged groups are dealt with. The importance of this perspective is illustrated in a recent analysis by Booth (1985a) of children with Down's syndrome. He maintains that:

> ...the extent to which their physiognomy, or physical impairment, or incompetence is a handicap *depends* on the way they are treated, the attitudes shown towards them, the provision made for them and the opportunities they are permitted. (p. 22, my emphasis.)

As a sociologist, I feel that sociology has a contribution to make towards a more adequate understanding of some of these issues by, for example, illuminating taken-for-granted assumptions, the disjuncture between rhetoric and practice, the influence of economic and political forces on definitions and decisions and the way labels are constructed and responded to in given social contexts.

Sociologists are interested in the social construction of categories, how they are created, ascribed, received and changed. Part of this interest is directed towards attempting to identify the relationship(s) between specific types of categories and the dominant ideologies of the wider social order. Within our own society, various categories have been used to describe the handicapped. These include: 'mad', 'lunatic', 'insane', 'idiot', 'feeble-minded' and 'severely sub-normal'. An adequate analysis of the generation of these categories, the purposes they served and the assumptions they involve, must include a consideration of the interplay of historical, political and institutional forces [2].

SOCIOLOGY AND SPECIAL EDUCATION

Sociologists maintain that the educational system is one of the most important means by which societies reproduce themselves. From this perspective, school is viewed as a socialising agency. It is involved in the shaping of identities, in the distribution of particular forms of knowledge and skills, as well as the transmission of dominant values and beliefs. School contributes to the creation of differential forms of consciousness and outcomes, which themselves sustain fundamental divisions in the wider society (Hall, 1977; Apple, 1980; Weis, 1986).

This is a complex, uneven and contradictory process, in which schools are both constrained and constrain. Whilst earlier sociological interest focused on the centrality of class-relations, more recent work attempts to examine the interplay of class, gender and race (Davies, 1985; Weis, 1985). Critical of the over-determinism of much previous analyses, this research is concerned with the dynamic relationship between structural forces and lived-culture. Thus, it is not a question of mechanical imposition but rather, as Apple (1985) so forcefully reminds us,

> . . . that rather than being places where culture and ideologies are imposed on students, schools are the *sites* where these things are produced. And like the workplace, they are produced in ways that are filled with contradiction and by a process that is itself based on contestation and struggle. (p. 26)

The sociological imagination is thus concerned with bringing 'news' about the nature of constraint and control (Bernstein, 1975). It is interested in demystifying the social world, and attempting to establish connections between, for example, institutional procedures and the daily practices of given participants in particular situations.

Sociological interest in the field of education has covered a range of issues including the following.

> The relationship between schooling and social inequality.
> The description and analysis of the social organisation of schools.
> The analysis of the assumptions on which the organisation and content of the school curriculum is based.
> Gender and the reproduction of sexual divisions.
> The school as a social process, including how participants within school construct, manage and change their everyday worlds.
> The material basis and ideological support for the control of minority groups (Bernstein, 1975; Karabel and Halsey, 1977; Robinson, 1981; Walker and Barton, 1983, 1986).

However, until recently within the United Kingdom, very little sociological interest has been shown in the field of special education. A number of reasons have been proposed for this neglect. For example, Tomlinson (1982) argues that sociologists have concentrated on demonstrating the nature and extent of inequalities of selection by 'brightness' in education, and failed to examine the increasing removal of pupils from normal schools on the grounds of 'defect, dullness, handicap or special need'. Quicke (1986) maintains, as a result of analysing school-based ethnographies published within the past decade, that the concerns of sociologists were usually with pupils who were described as 'disruptive', 'troublesome', or 'difficult' children. Attention was therefore not given to those pupils in remedial departments, or those who were seen as 'slow learners'. Thus Quicke argues:

> Deviancy for these researchers does not seem to include the *majority* who would fall into the special needs category of 'learning difficulty'. (My emphasis, p. 83.)

The lack of sociological interest may also have been as a result of the excessive emphasis on individualism that characterises much of the thinking and practice in the field of special education.

Given this situation, we have at an earlier point in our involvement identified several areas of concern for sociologists and more recently have offered a further series of ideas on this topic (Barton & Tomlinson, 1981, 1984). Sociological analysis is often critical of existing practices and institutional arrangements (Lane, 1981). Critical analysis is viewed as an essential prerequisite for change and, as such, can have a disquieting and unsettling effect on existing authority relations. Croll & Moses (1985) have recently criticised the application of a particular sociological analysis to the area of special education. Part of their argument is that sociologists working from within structuralist frameworks always attribute the worst possible motives to professional judgement and practice and that these sociological accounts fail to do justice to the very real needs that these particular children experience.

It is important to offer a number of observations about this form of criticism. Those who present such sociological critiques do not deny the existence of exciting innovations and good practice within the field of special education. Indeed, there are many teachers achieving great things against enormous odds. It is important to encourage more of these developments. Also, by offering a critique of professionals and their vested interests, it is quite misleading to argue that all their motives are being seen in the worst possible manner. Rather, it is maintained that 'well-meaning,' individual intentions, constrained by organisational and structural demands, often result in unexpected consequences (Bart, 1984). Finally, the sociological analysis should not be taken to mean that we do not recognise that many pupils have real difficulties in school. We accept this, but as Carrier (1986) argues, we want to treat:

> . . . as questionable and worthy of investigation the ways they are identified as having one or another condition, the ways in which we explain the nature of their condition and its consequences, and the ways in which the condition is a reflection of educational practices and the forces which influence them. (p. 5)

What sociologists have argued is that the view that concern for the handicapped has developed as a result of progress, enlightenment and humanitarian interests, is totally unacceptable. The experience of this particular disadvantaged group has generally been one of exploitation, exclusion, dehumanisation and regulation. In an excellent analysis of the development in the treatment of insanity in nineteenth century England, Scull (1982) contends that:

> . . . it remains the case that to present the outcome of reform as a triumphant and unproblematic expression of humanitarian concern is to adopt a perspective which is *hopelessly biased and inaccurate*: one which relies, of necessity, on a systematic neglect and distortion of the available evidence. (p. 15, my emphasis)

The establishment of the then-known asylums, was partly due to a desire to protect society from contamination and possible threat to the established order [3]. Added to this was the growing distinction that was developed, as a result of the rise of capitalism, between the able and non-able bodied, the productive and non-productive elements within society.

Asylums were institutions for the less-than-human groups within society, those who had no legal rights and who were viewed as having no powers of decision-making. They were believed to be sick and suffering from a disease. The treatment they required needed to be provided by doctors. Thus we have the emergence and dominance of the medical profession in the definition, diagnosis and treatment of the handicapped.

One cannot underestimate the influence of this particular professional group in organising and decisively moving insanity into the medical arena. Part of their success was due to their claims to scientific expertise with, as

Scull (1982) argues:

> ...its emphasis on order, rationality and self-control; goals which could only be reached in an institutional setting. (p. 44)

So, in terms of a society needing to control a deviant section of its population and provide a particular form of institutional management and legitimation, the role of the medical profession has been very significant indeed.

Two particular outcomes of this involvement need to be noted. Through the impact of medication, the problem was firmly diagnosed as being within the individual's physiological structure. Also, the existence of such a powerful group of experts, who were viewed as definers of need, resulted in an increased demand for their services. The effectiveness of their influence can be seen in that it was only in 1970 that the education of severely handicapped children became the official responsibility of the Department of Education and Science. It was previously under the control of the Department of Health and Social Services.

We have argued elsewhere (Barton and Tomlinson, 1981), that the history of education and special education in particular, can be understood in terms of the outcome of a struggle between powerful groups. Part of the conflict is over the maintenance of vested interests and the desire on the part of the professionals involved, to strengthen their hold over how 'priorities' and 'problems' are defined and 'solutions' provided.

This raises questions of power-relations between professionals and clients, as well as between professionals themselves. The existence of disagreement between professionals over what constitutes the needs of a particular child, is often overlooked by much of the literature. However, in a discussion of 'needs' and 'needs assessment', their meaning and use across a range of services, Baldwin (1986) argues, that they have been used *differently* by various professionals. An important issue therefore arises, that of understanding in whose interests needs assessments are conducted? Professionals tend to define and create needs which involves client relationships—fundamentally characterised by *dependency*. He maintains that this particular confusion over consensus of understanding has serious significance for those 'clients' who are not able to express their ideas, or more importantly, are viewed as being incapable of such thought processes.

Another powerful group involved in this process are the educational psychologists. Cyril Burt [4] was appointed as the first official educational psychologist in Britain, by London County Council in 1913. He has been one of the most influential figures behind the shaping of policy and practice in the field of education and in particular in the development of psychometry or mental testing (Simon, 1985). Recent analyses has tried to offer some explanations for the growing influence of this particular professional group. Their suggestions include; the gradual implementation of the 1944 Education Act and the special provision for particular handicapped pupils; the 1968 Summerfield Committee established to investigate the employment of psychologists in the educational service; the increased popularity of psychology as a subject in universities and higher education coupled with the establishment of training courses for educational psychologists and finally, the growing belief that the education of mentally handicapped children should depend primarily on educational considerations, not on medical diagnosis (Thomas, 1985; Quicke, 1984).

Whilst the role of the educational psychologist now includes not only assessment and placement but also an advisory element, particularly to teachers, there is little evidence to question the belief that the use of psychometrics is decreasing in their daily work. A relatively uncontroversial approach to questions of assessing a child's level, stage, need or skills with respect to emotional or cognitive functioning are still prominent features of their philosophy and practice and as Quicke (1984) goes on to argue:

> The allegedly 'neutral', 'objective' and value-free concepts and measuring instruments of the educational psychologist have served a vital function for the system by bringing a semblance of order and rationality to a potentially chaotic and contentious area. It is no exaggeration that the development of special education, in the broadest sense of the term, was not only assisted by but in a large part made possible by, the educational psychologist's technology. (pp. 123,124)

With the introduction and growing implementation of the 1981 Education Act, the role of the educational psychologist in the identification, assessment and provision for pupils who are believed to be in need of some form of special education has greatly increased.

A particular psychological approach that is having an increasing impact on special education programmes both in the United States and England, is that of behaviourism [5]. Discussing the nature of this view of education, Shapiro (1980) notes that:

> Its goals are highly circumscribed, minutely fragmented and quantifiable. Such an approach generally excludes a concern with imaginative, creative or divergent thinking.

. . Education becomes a process in which the student attempts to come as close as possible to the outcomes already anticipated by a teacher. (p. 221)

Increasingly, this perspective is resulting in the creation of more curricular materials that are total instructional packages. Apart from the question of the deskilling and re-skilling of teachers involved in this form of practice (Bart, 1984), the emphasis again is on *individualising* the problem.

CHANGING THE LABEL

During the 1960s and early 70s, increasing government attention was given to the question of young blacks in our society. They began to be described as a special group or 'special problem' in that they were alleged to be suffering from personal or cultural inadequacies. Exacerbating this concern was the question of increasing black youth unemployment and the belief that, as a result of alienation and frustration, they would become a danger and increasingly politicised (Rex, 1970; Humphry, 1972; Rex and Tomlinson, 1979; CCCS, 1982).

The ideology of 'special needs' was used to both legitimate State intervention and as Solomos (1986) argues,

> Just as in educational ideologies the notion of 'compensatory education' relied on the notion that those who failed educationally needed remedial help, so the special needs ideology saw minority groups as having failed because of personal or cultural inadequacies. (p. 136)

This emphasis upon 'need' within the field of special education began to be expressed during the 1960s. Needs in any society are related to values—to power. Decisions about people's needs involves value-judgements.

It is essential to recognise as Tomlinson (1985) has recently argued, that an ideology of 'special needs' not only obscures contradictions and conflicts, but can also serve to support various policies and practices of the wider social order. Also, the rhetoric may be humanitarian but the practice can be mainly one of control. The concept of 'special needs' already has a history of being used to support a deficit model of various disadvantaged groups.

THE WARNOCK REPORT

One of the most influential documents since the 1944 Education Act has been the Report of the Committee of Enquiry into the Education of Handicapped

Children and Young People, better known as the Warnock Report. It has been influential in terms of informing the nature of the 1981 Education Act and stimulating a great deal of debate. Questions raised go beyond the concerns of a small group of children, to the sort of educational provision we believe to be important for all children.

In November 1975, Margaret Thatcher, then Secretary of State for Education and Science, appointed a Committee with the following terms of reference:

> To review educational provision in England, Scotland and Wales for children and young people handicapped by disabilities of body or mind, taking account of the medical aspects of their needs, together with arrangements to prepare them for entry into employment; to consider the most effective use of resources for these purposes; and to make recommendations (Warnock Report, 1978, p. 1).

Two of the key recommendations of the Report include:

(1) The abolition of the then existing ten statutory categories of handicap and replacing them with the notion of 'special educational needs'. Part of the rationale for this was the belief that:

Categorisation perpetuates the sharp distinction between two groups of children—the handicapped and the non-handicapped. (p. 43) Furthermore, categorisation focuses attention on only a small proportion of all those children who are likely to require some form of special educational provision. We therefore recommend that statutory categorisation of handicapped pupils should be abolished. (p. 43)

(2) A further recommendation was that the concept 'special educational needs' should apply to a much larger number of pupils within mainstream schools than had been previously regarded as in need of special education. The Report states that:

We refer to the group of children—up to one in five—who are likely to require some form of special educational provision at some time during their school career as 'children with special educational needs'. (p. 41)

Thus, the Report raises issues and makes recommendations that are not only applicable to those involved in the segregated sector of special school provision, but are for teachers in *all* schools. Secondly, it is concerned with encouraging a more positive attitude towards these pupils. Finally, the Report uses the concept of 'special educational needs as a means of legitimating the expansion of provision (Fish, 1985; Tomlinson, 1985).

However, the Report is not without its critics. Sociologists have been critical of the strong medical/psychological emphasis underpinning the Report. Also, they have argued that the notion of 'special educational needs' is largely a tool of administrative convenience which will lead to the increased bureaucratisation of the system and the power of professional judgements.. Finally, they have criticised the Report for its failure to seriously address questions of the organisational structure of schools, the impact on the curriculum, teacher expectations and pedagogy, in terms of their contribution towards the creation of handicap (Lewis and Vulliamy, 1981; Tomlinson, 1982; Ford *et al.*, 1982, Oliver, 1984b). One of the most powerful and insightful criticisms of the Report and policy issues in the field of special education has been provided by an American, David Kirp (1983). In a comparison of British and United States legislation and policy, he maintains that in the British situation, the membership of the Warnock Committee tells you a great deal about the power of civil servants in determining the composition of such a group and the nature of the final outcome. Kirp claims that members were chosen to represent particular professional viewpoints: medical, psychological and teaching in particular. He notes that only one of the Committee's 26 members was a parent of a handicapped person and that there was no member of the black community, no lawyer and no handicapped person on the Committee. According to Kirp, it should come as no surprise that the Report fails to give serious consideration to system issues and encourages a reliance on professional judgement. Its basic message is 'trust professionals'. The approach to policy and the handicapped in Britain generally, including the Warnock Report, is characterised by a model of welfare that:

> . . . does not recognise conflict; it is silent concerning politics, and actually antagonistic toward law. It contemplates professionals and administrators working on behalf of an ever-expanding clientele toward an agreed-upon common good. (p. 106)

A great deal of the literature dealing with topics relating to special education is still of a very non-critical nature.

THE 1981 EDUCATION ACT

For some people this Act has been received as a clear indication of progress and a vindication of a great deal of the efforts of the Warnock Committee.

The new definitions, though expressed in sexist language, are:

(1) For the purposes of this Act a child has 'special educational needs' if he has a learning difficulty which calls for special educational provision to be made for him. (p. 1)

(2) . . . a child has a 'learning difficulty' if:
(a) he has a significantly greater difficulty in learning than the majority of children of his age; or
(b) he has a disability which either prevents or hinders him from making use of educational facilities of a kind generally provided in schools, within the area of the local authority concerned, for children of his age. (p. 1)

One astute commentator has noted that within these brief definitions, learning difficulties are alleged to be the property of pupils, a deviation from a population norm and relative to the provision within a local education authority (Booth, 1985b).

A number of contradictions have been identified within the Warnock Report and the 1981 Act:

(1) There is an assumption that they have introduced a totally new approach to special education, but we have no precise specification of the nature of this approach (Booth, 1985b).

(2) New opportunities for partnership with parents are being encouraged. At the same time they are now faced with a bewildering array of bureaucratic procedures.

(3) Emphasis is being given to maximising the opportunity of a certain group of children to be educated normally but we are now seeing the emergence of a new breed of person, the statemented child [6] (Jones, 1985).

However, perhaps the most important lesson, that we can draw from these developments, is that what we call 'special' is fundamentally determined by the nature of normal or mainstream education. It is this particular issue I now wish to briefly consider.

THE NATURE OF SCHOOLING

Policy and practice within education is fundamentally based upon a rationale in which economic priorities are central. In the past five years particularly, there has been an unprecedented intervention on the part of government in the field of education. The nature and control of the curriculum, the establishment of a new examination system, the role of the ManPower Services Commission [7] the control of local authority spending on education, the nature of governing bodies within schools, the organisation and future evaluation of teacher-education, all testify to this trend.

Pressures for accountability have been legitimated by allegations, in both the academic and popular press, of declining standards in schools, increasing discipline problems, inadequate time being devoted to the basic subjects and 'wrong' teaching methods.

Demands for greater control and monitoring of standards within school are now finding their expression in calls for a specific form of assessment and evaluation of teachers. Indeed, legislation precisely concerned with this issue has been considered in Parliament (Barton and Walker, 1984; Lawn, 1985; Grace, 1985).

The government's position has been expressed through many official documents, but a recent article by Sir Keith Joseph, the former Secretary of State for Education, sums up their concerns most clearly. In a discussion of the achievements and intentions of government, he says:

> Now we have turned our attention to standards, the aims and indeed the content of education and to the curriculum itself. The government's aim is to raise standards in all our schools. (1985)

Also, in a recent document presented to Parliament entitled *'Better Schools'* (1985), the principal aims of the Government for schools are set out. It is quite clear how standards are to be primarily achieved:

> For most pupils, the period of compulsory education culminates in assessment through public examinations. The Government believes that this should continue to be so. Examination results are one important means of assessing achievement; examinations, properly designed, are a stimulus to good performance, and parents and employers, as well as many pupils, rightly value them. (p. 29)

The pursuit of academic excellence through examinations is unquestionably still the dominant feature of our educational system.

Schools are thus involved in differentiating pupil from pupil on the basis of a narrow definition of ability. They find it difficult to offer equal status to other aspects of development. Knowledge within school is appropriated by the means of individual competition. Schools segregate pupils on the basis of age and they are characterised by an affiliation to, and presentation of, certain forms of knowledge. This knowledge as Young (1971) has argued is hierarchically ordered, with value being placed on abstract, individual and examinable knowledge.

This process of selection or differentiation has a number of features. First, as this type of schooling demands that the majority of pupils fail, an essential outcome of this evaluation is as Bates (1984) notes:

> Rather than a means of furthering the *educational* purposes of individual development and emancipation, educational evaluation has become, like class, a mechanism of exclusion (p. 128)

Thus, in terms of both the quality and duration of educational opportunity, many pupils are denied access. Secondly, by giving priority to certain forms of knowledge, schools tend to devalue other types of knowledge, particularly those of black and white working class pupils. Lastly, this process of differentiation helps as Connell *et al.* (1982) maintain

> . . . to generate a social dichotomy, stereotyping, and hostility between the 'brains' and the 'dumbos', those who can 'use their heads' and those who are 'good with their hands'... (p. 195)

Within this system of evaluation particular categories take on a crucial and specific importance. They include such notions as 'bright', 'able', 'intelligent', 'highly motivated' and 'average', 'slow', 'thick', 'difficult' and 'lazy'. The teacher's position in mediating these labels and the messages they contain to pupils, must not be underestimated.

The school is an agency of social control and through constant attendance, children are subject to numerous social and cultural lessons. These include the establishment of cultural differences, what constitutes 'normality', 'competence', 'disaffection' and 'deviance'. Through the powerful mechanisms of ritual and routine, this complex process becomes the natural, taken-for-granted aspect of schooling. Of course, as we noted earlier, pupils are not passive in this process, but mediate these messages in different ways, and at times, actively work back on the system. They struggle to realise different priorities and are motivated by other concerns than those of educators. Yet paradoxically given the nature of the dominant hierarchy within schools, their very actions can be seen to be part of a response that is to be expected from 'this type of child', and can be the means of reinforcing the need for more remediation.

In summary, I am arguing that developments in special education cannot be divorced from those in the mainstream. Schooling is fundamentally influenced by selection and the comprehensive ideal of ameliorating social class divisions has not been realised. Schooling cannot be viewed as socially disinterested or culturally neutral (Wexler, 1981). Schooling is profoundly social, yet its emphasis on individualism can lead to a fallacy in which questions relating to social functions are ignored (Hargreaves, 1982). The powerful influence of examinations and the ideologies associated with them, have historically been a legitimation for the existence of a segregated section of special educational provision. They are special in the sense that both institutions and pupils fail to live up to the standards established by normal or mainstream schooling. Thus pupils who are identified as lacking ability, difficult to teach, need to be given an alternative form of experience. Special education has been a safety valve for the mainstream system.

It is important therefore to set the debate about special education within the context of the wider issue of education generally. If we go back to the notion of the Warnock Report, that one in five children will be in need of some special educational provision, then this, for some a modest estimate, will inevitably mean an expansion of services. It is likely that many more children from white and black working class backgrounds will be identified as having special educational needs. By recognising this and considering it in relation to growing youth unemployment, Tomlinson (1985) has recently argued that the expansion of special education is a political response to a critical dilemma facing the educational system and society generally. This is the need to control more and more disenchanted youth.

In a recent two-year study of young people in Wolverhampton directed by Paul Willis (1985) the Report suggests that the young unemployed are being thrust into a 'new social condition'. These young people are experiencing an extended period of relative poverty and dependency on the family and an increasingly mean and coercive state. This new condition not only includes wagelessness and dependency, but also, for example, 'alienation, depression and pessimism about future prospects'. Whilst acknowledging that there will be particular and distinct combinations of these characteristics according to race and gender, Willis (1986) is quite adamant that this is essentially a working-class experience. These young people, he maintains, have been sentenced to "the personal neurosis of individual worry for a structural problem over which they have no control". (p. 112)

These unemployed youths will increasingly be viewed as a special problem and post-school programmes catering for special needs, will become more and more essential. The Manpower Services Commission will be actively involved in providing such requirements. These programmes will act as a buffer-zone between the State, young people, and the realities of the labour market. Many of those pupils identified as having special educational needs will become the unemployed of tomorrow.

FUTURE DIRECTIONS

It is essential that careful consideration is given to questions of teacher awareness and the relationship between the personal and the political. Teachers involved in special education need to be acutely aware of the nature of the inequalities outlined above within society. They need to examine the implications of a system of education that is fundamentally concerned with selection and differentiation. [7].

Whilst the demands of teaching may encourage a focus on pragmatic concerns, questions relating to class, race and gender must not be neglected. Indeed, from the perspective of this paper, these are extremely relevant and urgent issues. In a recent paper on Inservice Training Progress in Special Education, Booth (1985b) illustrates their significance by noting that in Britain:

> Virtually all pupils sent to schools for pupils with moderate learning difficulties or day maladjusted provisions are working class. (p. 11)

In the United States this is also true of many of those pupils who are involved in programmes for those with 'learning disabilities' (Ysseldyke *et al.*, 1982; Sigmon, 1985). He also notes that:

> The disproportionate number of black pupils in disruptive units or recommended for E.S.N. (M) [8] provision remains a cause of argument and conflict. (p. 11)

In the United States there is an over-inclusion of black pupils in classes for the mentally retarded (Collins and Gamblin, 1983).

> All categories of special school have a majority of boys and the preponderance in maladjusted schools is overwhelming (Booth, 1985, p. 11).
> In the first three years of the Open University course 'Special Needs in Education', 78% of students were women. (p. 11)

Adequate explanations for these occurrences will only be found when we relate them to wider complex social, economic and political factors. This should include considering them in relation to mainstream or normal education and how they are both a response and contribution to the social inequalities, stereotypes and discriminating ideologies and practices of a divided society. One encouraging sign is the publication of the Fish Report entitled 'Educational Opportunities for All?' which is the outcome of an independent review committee chaired by John Fish. It was concerned with the availability of provision to meet special educational needs within the Inner London Education Authority. This document is unique, in that it raises the question of the rights of children and young people with learning difficulties within the context of anti-racist and anti-sexist policies. Priority is given to developing equal opportunities for all pupils within a truly comprehensive system.

In attempting to argue for the importance of a perspective that recognises the contribution of social factors towards the creation of handicap, criticism has been offered of some of the dominant assumptions and ideologies relating to this topic. Thus, it is worthy of note that the number of childen labelled as having special educational needs increases in proportion to the available provisions. The nature of those needs, assessment and placement of particular cases are as much to do with the question of available resources than anything to do with inborn traits of the people involved. Economic considerations have always been a paramount factor in the development of Special Education.

Also, understanding how pupils with special needs experience the world must involve an examination of the *context* within which their interaction takes place. Thus, the physical features of a school, the ethos, the hidden and official curriculum and the teacher's expectation must be seen as powerful forces in the process of creating deviance and problems for pupils within school. As Ford *et al.* (1982) maintain:

> The range of processes which have an effect upon the pupil's career is enormous: the style of pastoral care, the availability of remedial provision, the content of the curriculum, the existence of a parent-teacher association and the creation of playgroups are only five very diverse examples of factors which might have a bearing upon the pupil's chances of being labelled and referred for a problem behaviour. (p. 169)

Many of those existing arrangements within schools catering for pupils with learning difficulties, such as withdrawal groups for remedial help, specific curriculum for less able pupils and special units, have been severely criticised. Confirming the observation of previous analysis, Galloway (1985) notes that the common elements in these approaches do not give mainstream teachers opportunity or encouragement to consider how the school contributes to the pupil's difficulties in the first place.

One of the effects of scientific interest in handicapped people has been to view them in terms of clinical and behavioural symptoms. Much of the life we have provided for them is unsatisfying and unrewarding. What we desperately need is a new vision or, as Martin Luther King would say, 'a dream'. We need to work for what Wexler (1981) has called, a liberating perspective, one which provides an alternative cultural basis for meaning and personal identity. Individual dissatisfaction is, as Wexler notes:

> Only an initial condition for the realisation of existing alternative social possibilities. (p. 259)

An important step in this process will be both in our theoretical work and in our practice to shift concentration on the differentiation of children and to identify what they have in common (Simon, 1985). Collective identity and struggle will be an essential feature of an effective demand for social justice and equality. Encouragement can be taken from the recent analyses of disabled people themselves who both recognise the inadequacy of existing theory and are attempting to develop a more effective foundation for radical change [9]. Some of their work is beginning to be expressed within the sociology of education (Oliver, 1984a, b, 1986; Abberley, 1985).

Those of us who are attempting to contribute to the struggle for change can learn much from contemporary feminist thought and practice. One crucial lesson is the importance of connecting the *personal* with the *political*, so that what has been seen in mainly *individual* terms, can be viewed as a social predicament and thus a political issue (Eisenstein, 1984). This perspective assumes that what people feel and experience in their lives matters. By sharing these experiences members of subordinate groups can begin to realise that they are not alone. Through this means they can begin to develop a greater sense of their worth and agency.

The task is an immense one—of moving from powerlessness and oppression to self and collective actualisation. It is important to let *people* speak for themselves. As McDonald (1980) writes,

> To be imprisoned inside one's own body is dreadful. To be confined in an institution for the profoundly retarded does not crush you in the same way; it just removes all hope.... Never seeing normal children, we were not sure what they were like. Where did we fall short? In your ugly body it was totally impossible that there could be a mind. Vital signs

showed that your title was 'human'; but that did not entitle you to live like normal children. You were totally outside the boundary which delineated the human race. (p. 8)

As educators we need to ask: What sort of a society is it that generates and legitimates the policies and practices involved in treating people in this way? In making their private thoughts public, handicapped people provide essential substance for public campaigns and the basis of political alliances and endeavour [10].

ACKNOWLEDGEMENTS

I am indebted to a group of teachers on an in-service course, who I have had the privilege of working with during the past two terms. They have helped me clarify my thinking and have raised serious issues, some of which I have still not resolved. Some of their concerns I have attempted to address in this paper. I am also grateful to John Quicke for his constructive criticism of an earlier version of this paper and to two referees of the Journal.

NOTES

[1] In a paper of this nature it is impossible to discuss some of the complex issues involved in this question. Within the sociology of education as a result of feminist concerns and an upsurge of interest in ethnography, questions relating to the perspective of the researcher, the relationship with respondents, the purpose(s) of the analysis have taken on important significance.

In a recent analysis of the development of approaches in the sociology and politics of education, Whitty in a discussion of the contributions made by sociologists who are committed to a radical perspective says (1986):

Certainly, there is no obvious reason to suppose that a concern to interrogate situations with a view to informing radical practice creates any less of an incentive to be empirically rigorous than producing knowledge for its own sake or to further one's own career. (p. 84)

[2] This is a very under-developed area. We have little material that provides us with an historical understanding of these issues in relation to the emergence and expansion of special educational provision.

[3] A predominant view at one period, was the belief that not only had handicapped people been conceived in promiscuity but that they would breed similar children and degenerate that quality of the genetic stock. Thus we had the significance of the Eugenics movement in this country (Woodhouse, 1982).

[4] It would seem that even the revelations of the fraudulent nature of his research have done little to question his authority (Gillie, 1978; Simon, 1985). Very little serious consideration has been given to the issue within psychological or educational journals.

[5] One recognises that this term covers a number of approaches (Ainscow & Tweddle, 1979; Wheldall et al., 1984). Nevertheless there are indications of a strong behavioural approach to teaching children with special educational needs. This is particularly so with regard to those who have severe learning difficulties.

[6]   The 1981 act now specifies clearly the sorts of advice a local education authority must obtain when determining a child's special educational needs. Advice must be taken from the child's teacher, school medical officer and an educational psychologist as well as other professionals if it is felt necessary. Once a full assessment has been carried out the local education authority can issue a 'statement' which determines the special education provision which is necessary for the child. A draft of the statement must be issued to the parents and their views sought. The authority may then decide to amend the original statement. Further appeals can be made by the parents with the ultimate appeal being to the Secretary of State for Education and Science.

[7]   The Manpower Services Commission is a body responsible for schemes concerned with providing young people with a more relerant training than what schools have allegedly been able to do. It is an extremely powerful body whose responsibility is not to the Department of Education and Science nor to the local authority (see M.S.C., 1981).

[8]   E.S.N. (M) was the former category used for educationally subnormal children who had moderate learning difficulties.

[9]   Critical of existing functionalists and Weberian perspectives on special education and disability, they use the concept 'oppression' both as a means of expressing their experiences and as a way of developing links between disadvantaged groups. We are at an early stage in the development of their ideas but there does seem ground for optimism here.

[10] The United States, for example, has a growing body of people involved in the Self-Advocacy Movement. In this country we are just beginning to see similar developments taking place.

REFERENCES

ABBERLEY, P. (1985) *Policing Cripples: social theory and physical handicap* (Bristol, Bristol Polytechnic Library).

AINSCOW, M. & TWEDDLE, D. (1979) *Preventing Classroom Failure: an objectives approach* (Chichester, Wiley).

APPLE, M. (1980) Analysing determinations: understanding and evaluating the production of social outcomes in schools, *Curriculum Inquiry,* 10, pp. 55-76.

APPLE, M. (1985) *Education and Power* (London, Ark Publications).

BALDWIN, S. (1986) Problems with needs, *Disability, Handicap and Society,* 1, pp. 139-145.

BART, D. S. (1984) The differential diagnosis of special education: managing social pathology as individual disability, in L. BARTON & S. TOMLINSON (Eds) *Special Education and Social Interests* (Beckenham, Croom Helm).

BARTON, L. & TOMLINSON, S. (Eds) (1981) *Special education: policy, practices and social issues* (London, Harper & Row).

BARTON, L. TOMLINSON, S. (Eds) (1984) *Special Education and Social Interests* (Beckenham, Croom Helm).

BARTON, L. & WALKER, S. (Eds) (1984) *Social Crisis and Educational Research* (Beckenham, Croom Helm).

BATES, R. (1984) Educational versus managerial evaluation in schools, in: P. BROADFOOT, (Ed.) *Selection, Certification and Control* (Lewes, Falmer Press).
BECKER, H. (1967) Whose side are we on? *Social Problems*, 14, pp. 239-247.
BERNSTEIN, B. (1975) *Class, Codes and Control*, ch. 7 (London, Routledge & Kegan Paul).
BOOTH, T. (1985a) Labels and their consequences, in: D. LANE & B. STRATFORD (Eds) *Current Approaches to Down's syndrome* (New York, Holt, Rinehart & Winston).
BOOTH, T. (1985b) Training and progress in special education, in: J. SAYER & N. JONES (Eds) *Teacher Training and Special Educational Needs* (Beckenham, Croom Helm).
CCCS (1982) *The Empire Strikes Back: race and racism in 1970's Britain* (London, Hutchinson).
CARRIER, J. (1986) *Learning disability: social class and the construction of inequaliy in American education* (forthcoming).
COLLINS R. & CAMBLIN, L. (1983) The politics and science of learning disability classification: implications for black children, *Contempòrary Education*, 54, pp. 113-118.
CONNEL, R., et al. (1982) *Making the Difference: schools, families and social division* (London, Allen & Unwin).
CROLL, R. & MOSES, O. (1985) *One in Five* (London, Routledge & Kegan Paul).
CROSSLEY, R. & McDoNALD, A. (1980) *Annie's Coming Out* (London, Penguin).
D.E.S. (1978) *Report of the Committee of Enquiry into the Education of Handicapped Children and Young People* (Warnock Report) (London, HMSO).
D.E.S. (1985) *Better Schools* (London, HMSO).
DAVIES, L. (1985) *Pupil Power: deviance and gender in school* (Lewes, Falmer Press).
EISENSTEIN, H. (1984) *Contemporary Feminist Thought* (London, Unwin Paperbacks).
FORD, J., MONGON, D. & WHELAN, M. (1982) *Special Education and Social Control: invisible disasters* (London, Routledge & Kegan Paul).
FISH, J. (1985) *Special Education: the way ahead* (Milton Keynes, Open University Press).
GALLOWAY, D. (1985) Meeting special educational needs in the ordinary school or creating them? *Maladjustment and Therapeutic Education*, 3, pp. 3-10.
GILLIE, O. (1978) Sir Cyril Burt and the great I.Q. fraud, *New Statesman*, 24 November, pp. 688-694.

GRACE, G. (1985) Judging teachers: the social and political contexts of teacher evaluation, in: L. BARTON & S. WALKER (Eds) *Education and Social Change* (Beckenham, Croom Helm).

HALL, S. (1977) Education and the crisis in the urban school, in: J. RAYNOR & E. HARRIS (Eds) *Schooling in the City* (London, Ward Lock).

HARGREAVES, D. (1982) *Challenge to the Comprehensive School* (London, Routledge & Kegan Paul).

HIUMPHRY, D. (1972) *Police Power and Black People* (London, Panther).

I.L.E.A. (1985) *Educational Opportunities for All?* (Fish Report) (London, ILEA).

JONES, N. (1985) The silent agenda of special education in: J. SAYER & N. JONES (Eds) *Teacher Training and Special Educational Needs* (Beckenham, Croom Helm).

JOSEPH, K. (1985) Education for a new Society, *The Tablet,* No. 45, pp. 569-571.

KARABEL, J. & HALSEY, A.H. (Eds) (1977) *Power and Ideology in Education* (Oxford, Oxford University Press).

KIRP, D. (1983) Professionalisation as a policy choice: British special education in comparative perspectives, in: J. CHAMBERS & W. HARTMAN (Eds) *Special Education Policies: their history, implementation and finance* (Temple University Press).

LAWN, M. (1985) Teachers' hard lessons, *Marxism Today,* December, pp. 29-32.

LEWIS, I. & VULLIAMY, G. (1981) The social context of educational practice: the case of special education, in: L. BARTON & S. TOMLINSON (Eds), op. cit.

M.S.C. (1981) *A New Training Initiative* (London, M.S.C.).

OLIVER, M. (1984a) The politics of disability, *Critical Social Policy,* 11, pp. 21-32.

OLIVER, M. (1984b) The integration and segregation debate: some sociological considerations, *British Journal of Sociology of Education,* 6, pp. 75-92.

OLIVER, M. (1986) Social policy and disability: some theoretical issues, *Disability, Handicap and Society,* 1, pp. 5-17.

QUICKE, J. (1984) The role of the educational psychologist in the post-Warnock era, in L. BARTON & S. TOMLINSON (Eds) *Special Education and Social Interests* (Beckenham, Croom Helm).

QUICKE, J. (1986) A case of paradigmatic mentality? A reply to Mike Oliver, *British Journal of Sociology of Education,* 7, pp. 81-86.

REX, J. (1970). *Race Relations in Sociological Theory* (London, Routledge & Kegan Paul).

REX, J. & TOMLINSON, S. (1979) *Colonial Immigrants in a British City: a class analysis* (London, Routledge & Kegan Paul).

ROBINSON, P. (1981) *Perspectives in the Sociology of Education* (London, Routledge & Kegan Paul).

SAYER, J. & JONES, N. (Eds) (1985) *Teacher Training and Special Educational Needs* (Beckenham, Croom Helm).

SCULL, A.T. (1982) *Museums of Madness* (London, Penguin).

SHAPIRO, H. (1980) Society, ideology and the reform of special education, *Educational Theory*, 30, p. 211-223.

SIGMON, S.B. (1985) Foundations of education and learning disabilities: toward a new understanding, *Research Communications in Psychology, Psychiatry and Behaviour*, 10, pp. 71-97.

SIMON, B. (1985) *Does Education Matter?* (London, Lawrence & Wishart).

SOLOMOS, J. (1986) The social and political contexts of black youth unemployment: a decade of policy developments and the limits of reform, in: S. WALKER & L. BARTON (Eds) *Youth, Unemployment and Schooling* (Oxford, Oxford University Press).

THOMAS, J. (1985) Psychologists, psychiatrists and special educational needs, *The Exceptional Child*, 32, pp. 69-80.

TOMLINSON, S. (1981) The social construction of the E.S.N. (M) child, in: L. BARTON & S. TOMLINSON (Eds), op. cit.

TOMLINSON, S. (1982) *The Sociology of Special Education* (Beckenham, Croom Helm).

TOMLINSON, S. (1985) The expansion of special education, *Oxford Review of Education*, 11, pp. 157-165.

WALKER, S. & BARTON, L. (Eds) (1983) *Gender, Class and Education* (Lewes, Falmer Press).

WALKER, S. & BARTON, L. (Eds) (1986) *Youth, Unemployment and Schooling* (London, Open University Press).

WEIS, L. (1985) *Between Two Worlds: black students in an urban community college* (London, Routledge & Kegan Paul).

WEIS, L. (1986) Thirty years old and I'm allowed to be late: the politics of time at an urban community school, *British Journal of Sociology of Education*, 7, pp. 241-263.

WEXLER, P. (1981) Body and soul: sources of social change and strategies of education, *British Journal of Sociology of Education*, 2, pp. 247-264.

WHELDALL, K. & MERRETT, F. (1984) *Positive Teaching the behavioural approach* (London, Allen & Unwin).

WHITTY, G. (1986) Review article—recent American and Australian approaches to the sociology and politics of education, *Educational Theory*, 36, pp. 81-85.

Part of this paper was presented at the Comparative Education Conference, Toronto, March 1986.

CHAPTER 10

The Concept of Oppression and the Development of a Social Theory of Disability

Paul Abberley

(First published 1987)

I would like to preface this article with some short autobiographical notes, not because I think these are ultimately relevant to the adequacy or otherwise of the ideas put forward, but rather because an understanding of the context in which the material was produced may make clearer the reasons behind certain concerns and emphases.

At the age of five I contracted poliomyelitis in the last major epidemic of the disease to occur in this country. I spent six weeks in an iron lung, eight months in a hospital bed, and by the age of seven had regained sufficient mobility to attend a state primary school. Some 25 years later, working as a lecturer in sociology, I began to receive requests from some of my colleagues to talk to their students about 'disability'. My first response was one of annoyance and resentment, since I had spent most of my life, as many 'successful' disabled people do, attempting as far as possible to deny and ignore what is in fact a very obvious collection of impairments. But beyond this, I felt that, as a sociologist, I had nothing to say about disability, since the small amount of academic material I was familiar with struck me as both inadequate as an explanation of my own experiences and quite foreign to what I considered 'good sociology'.

Further investigation, during a year's study leave at the University of Warwick, convinced me that, with a few notable exceptions, the sociology of disability is both theoretically backward and a hindrance rather than a help to disabled people. In particular it has ignored the implications of significant advances made in the last 15 years in the study of sexual and racial inequality, and reproduces in the study of disability parallel deficiencies to those found in what is now seen by many as racist and sexist sociology. Another aspect of 'good sociology' that I feel is generally absent is any significant recognition of the historical specificity of the experience of disability. In my own case, had I been born a few years earlier, before the development of respiratory support systems, I would have died; a few years later and the advent of effective vaccination techniques would have made my contraction of the disease improbable. In view of this, and similar related considerations, I came to understand my own disabilities in terms of a unique conjunction of factors, a view which I now try to apply to disabled people in general. It is on the basis of such ideas about myself as a disabled person that the following work has been produced.

A number of writers (Oliver, 1986) have employed the term 'oppression' in the analysis of disability. However, the meaning attached to this term is ill-specified. Oliver, for example, in an earlier draft of his paper, though not in the published version, where any attempt to give precise meaning is absent, uses it interchangeably with exploitation, and it is not defined but rather seen as an 'obvious' but difficult to substantiate characteristic of 'social relations under capitalism'. While this is clearly an advance on the 'personal tragedy theory of disability' criticised in the same article, for the notion of oppression to be a useful one the term must be more clearly specified, both in general and in relation to disability in particular.

To draw an analogy between disabled people and groups to whom the term oppression has been applied is by no means a new occurrence. In the literature of disability a number of studies comment, but no more than comment, on the similarity between disabled/normal interactions and those encountered in studies of race relations. Barker for example remarked as long ago as 1948: "the physically disabled person is in a position not unlike the Negro, the Jew and other underprivileged racial and religious minorities," (Barker, 1948, p. 31) while Handel in 1960 observed that his report "sounded as though we were considering a problem of race relations instead of disability" (Handel, 1960, p. 363). Again Chesler in 1965 claims to have found that individuals manifesting high ethnocentrism, or high rejection of outgroups, also expressed rejection of the physically disabled (Chesler, 1965, pp. 877-882).

A recent study in the *Journal of Maxillo-facial Surgery*, reported in *New Society* in June 1985, claims that on the basis of a photograph study "children don't start reacting badly to abnormal looks until they are at least 11 years old" and that consequently "discrimination against funny-looking people is not some innate result of evolutionary forces, it is socially learned" (*New Society*, 1985). There is a striking parallel here to Davey's book length study of racism and its acquisition (Davey, 1983). Interestingly, amongst the studies reported in this volume is one (Richardson and Green, 1971) where it was found in a sample of white children in London schools that visible physical handicap was a greater deterrent to friendship than blackness. In Davey's discussion this is regarded as an 'encouraging' finding! (op. cit., 113). But despite observations and insights of this kind, the sociological literature of disability has carried such ideas no further.

Indeed, the oft-quoted Davis asserts: "Because the visibly handicapped do not comprise a distinct minority group or subculture, the imputations of generalized deviance that they elicit from many normals are more nearly genuine interactional emergents than the conventionalized sequelae to intergroup stereotyping, as for example, might obtain between a Negro and white" (Davis 1961:122). Yet there is no argument *per se* for this position. Rather Davis gives an illustrated Interactionist account, made 'special' by its emphasis on 'coping' behaviour, and concludes by emphasising a similarity to and continuity with 'normal' interaction. The focus of Davis's analysis upon personal interactions and the denial of any generalised group membership, reduces the issue of disability to a 'deviance' progressively dissolved in repeated interactions with particular individuals, only to be re-encountered on each new acquaintance.

It is clear then that if the notion of oppression is to be of use in the analysis of disability in society, and most importantly of use to disabled people in understanding and transforming their own situation, we must clarify and develop what is meant by the term.

THE CONCEPT OF OPPRESSION

Given the complexity of theoretical issues surrounding theories of oppression, (Barrett, 1981; Jaggar, 1983; Brittan and Maynard, 1984) at this stage it is possible to say only in broad outline how a theory of oppression could inform our understanding of the situation of disabled people in Britain today. To argue that we need to analyse the position of disabled people as a form of oppression is not to make the claim that we can arrive at a monolithic theory of oppression into which we can fit women, black people, disabled people or gay people depending on which particular oppressed group is under discussion at the time. A crucial feature of oppression and the way it operates is its specificity, of form, content and location; so to analyse the oppression of disabled people in part involves pointing to the essential differences between their lives and those of other sections of society, including those who are, in other ways, oppressed. It is also important to note that probably more than half of disabled people in Britain today suffer the additional burden of racial and/or sexual oppression (Campling, 1981; Confederation of Indian Organizations (U.K.), 1986).

To claim that disabled people are oppressed involves, however, arguing a number of other points. At an empirical level, it is to argue that on significant dimensions disabled people can be regarded as a group whose members are in an inferior position to other members of society because they are disabled people. It is also to argue that these disadvantages are dialectically related to an ideology or group of ideologies which justify and perpetuate this situation. Beyond this it is to make the claim that such disadvantages and their supporting ideologies are neither natural nor inevitable. Finally it involves the identification of some beneficiary of this state of affairs.

The term oppression, while regularly encountered in discussion of racial and sexual disadvantage and of the 'national question', does not appear in encylopedias of social science, nor in the generally useful *Dictionary of Marxist*

Thought (Bottomore, 1983). *Collins English Dictionary* gives four meanings for the word oppress:

(1) to subjugate by cruelty, force, etc.;
(2) to lie heavy on (the mind, imagination, etc.);
(3) to afflict or torment;
(4) an obsolete word for overwhelm.

In talking of racial or sexual oppression we are clearly not employing any one of these definitions, although aspects of all four meanings are contained within the term, whose use has developed in relation, and complementary, to classical Marxist class analysis. Class analysis *per se* has emerged as an unsatisfactory tool for the analysis of racial and sexual disadvantage, which is experienced in addition to, or perhaps more accurately through, people's class experiences. It is to such sets of experiences that the concept of oppression is addressed.

> Oppression and exploitation are not equivalent concepts.... Exploitation speaks to the economic reality of capitalist class relations for men and women, whereas oppression refers to women and minorities defined within patriarchal, racist and capitalist relations. Exploitation is what happens to men and women workers in the labour force; woman's oppression occurs from the relations that define her existence in the patriarchal sexual hierarchy—as mother, domestic labourer and consumer. Racial oppression locates her within the racist division of society alongside her exploitation and sexual oppression. Oppression is inclusive of exploitation but reflects a more complex reality. Power—or the converse, oppression—derives from sex, race and class, and this is manifested through both the material and ideological dimensions of patriarchy, racism and capitalism. Oppression reflects the hierarchical relations of the sexual and racial division of society. (Eisenstein, 1979: 22-3)

For this author oppression is not an alternative explanatory device to exploitation, rather it is addressed to a different order of phenomena, those connected with a person's gender or race experiences rather than their class experiences. Oppression is complementary to exploitation, extending the range of Marxist analysis to cover areas the latter concept cannot reach.

In developing theories of sexual and racial oppression it has been necessary for theoreticians of the women's and anti-racist movements to settle accounts with biology, which in both cases has been employed to explain and to justify social disadvantage. For a theory of disability as oppression however an important difference arises when we consider the issue of impairment. While in the cases of sexual and racial oppression, biological difference serves only as a qualificatory condition of a wholly ideological oppression, for disabled people the biological difference, albeit as I shall argue itself a consequence of social practices, is itself a part of the oppression. It is crucial that a theory of disability as oppression comes to grips with this 'real' inferiority, since it forms a bedrock upon which justificatory oppressive theories are based and, psychologically, an immense impediment to the development of political consciousness amongst disabled people. Such a development is systematically blocked through the naturalisation of impairment.

Further, the evaluative connotations are cognitively as well as effectively contained in terms which themselves imply deficiency, in contrast to 'woman' and 'black'. This is not to suggest that perceptions can be changed by changing words but to point to the deeply entrenched rejection of 'impairment' as a viable form of life and to the 'commonsense', 'natural' and 'unconscious' nature of ideologies of impairment, disability and handicap. This rejection of the authenticity of impaired life forms is exhibited both in the obvious form of what Dartington, Miller and Gwynne (1981) call the "less than whole person" view, and its inverse, the "really normal" ideology, which finds its expression in everyday life in the exceptionalism of 'but I don't think of you as disabled', denying a key aspect of a disabled person's identity in what is intended as a compliment. Compare this phrase to 'played like a white man' and 'she thinks like a man'.

What is required is essentially an attitude of ambivalence towards impairment, that is "co-existence in one person of love and hate towards the same object" Concise Oxford Dictionary (1964). Impairment must be identified as a bad thing, insofar as it is an undesirable consequence of a distorted social development, at the same time as it is held to be a positive attribute of the individual who is impaired. An analogy may be drawn here with the feminist treatment of so-called 'women's troubles'. The key distinction that must be made is between the prevention of impairment, on the one hand, and attitudes to and treatment of people who are already impaired on the other.

A pertinent recent example of the necessity for such a distinction is displayed in the boycotting of the 1985 Manchester International Conference on Education of the Deaf by the British Deaf Association and the National Union of the Deaf. "The objection is that the main discussion will be the development of electrode implants, which have the potential to restore 'hearing' even to the totally deaf, provided that they once could hear" (The Guardian 5 8 85). The education chairman of the National Deaf Children's Society said that deaf children could lead a full life using other forms of communication such as sign language. "They shouldn't get the idea that the thing is to be more like a hearing person at any cost" he said (ibid.). While the boycotters' attitude to impairment is one of ambivalence, as defined above, and thus of respect for disabled people, the members of the medical profession who determined the agenda clearly expressed their own rejection of the disabled state by determining that a dubious 'rectification' procedure, to which they raised only *technical* objections, should be the main business of a conference which occurs once every five years.

Yet if the inferiority embodied in impairment is understood as purely or primarily biological in origin, the suggested analogy with racial and sexual oppression appears to be an inherently dubious one, since the core of such theories is that disadvantage is ultimately a social and not a biological product. A theory of disability as oppression then must offer what is essentially a social theory of impairment.

IMPAIRMENT AS A SOCIAL PRODUCT

The general tendency within medicine has been to attribute most impairments which are not identified as the consequence of acute illness and infection to 'normal' wear and tear on the human body. Causation, on this view, is ascribed either to 'germs' or to 'life'. Any 'social' involvement is presented as secondary or peripheral to the major identified patterns of 'natural' causation. But an alternative account of the origin of impairments is at least as viable.

To take the major cause of impairment in Britain, some five million people are thought to suffer from osteo-arthritis, and some one million from rheumatoid arthritis (British League Against Rheumatism, 1977). While often regarded as 'simply' a degenerative process, "a number of rheumatic problems are known to arise in connection with various occupations. Unfortunately economic factors have usually not allowed this knowledge to be fully exploited. Primary prevention would call for changes in methods of working and in the job environment, and these are often costly" (Arthritis & Rheumatism Council (n.d.: 11)). Thus an alternative view of this major cause of impairment would locate explanation not at the 'natural' or 'individual' level, but in the socio-economic context of its occurrence, of which 'physical degeneration' is by no means an independent variable. To extend this argument further, the pace and direction of the development of preventative and ameliorative techniques are themselves the product of socio-economic factors, which are in turn effected by what are fundamentally political decisions. Thus at both these levels social aspects of impairment causation may be discerned.

Whilst most incapacity resulting from injury sustained at work is categorised as of relatively short duration, about a third results in permanent or possibly permanent damage (Pearson, 1978). In addition to accidents, some 16,000 people a year contract an industrial disease as prescribed under the 1975 Social Security Act, the main categories being infective dermatitis (10,000), traumatic inflamation of the tendon (3400) and beat knee (1000). However, the comparison of such statistics, based on DHSS records which exclude certain diseases known to be caused or exacerbated by industrial injury, to a personal injury survey, led Pearson to conclude:

> There were substantial numbers of illnesses where there appeared to the sufferer to be a probable link between the illness and conditions of work, possibly amounting to five times the number of prescribed diseases recorded by the DHSS (Pearson, 1978, Vol. 2:66)

Nichols (1986) echoes this sentiment, as have other writers who argue that official figures on work-based impairments constitute merely the tip of the iceberg (Kinnersley, 1973; Thunhurst, 1982; Navarro, 1982), and argues further that since 1978 the rate of disabling injuries and deaths in manufacturing industry has increased.

Mirroring impairment caused by the process of production is that attributable to the willing or unwilling consumption of its products. While perhaps the most notorious example in Britain is the drug Thalidomide, other products of the pharmaceutical industry are, or should be, similarly implicated. Of the 70,000 personal injuries attributed by Pearson to defective products or services (about 2½% of all injuries) around half involved prescribed drugs.

At the World Mental Health Congress in Brighton in July 1985, Dr David Hill, Senior Psychologist at Walton Hospital, Chesterfield, argued that 25 million patients throughout the world had suffered irreversible brain damage as the result of the administration of powerful tranquillisers such as Largactil (*The Guardian*). His critics made no attempt to rebut this contention, but simply averred that there was no alternative.

At a world level, the deleterious health effects of prescribed drugs is chillingly documented (Muller, 1982). While, in the 'developed' world, at least, vaccination has reduced to a trickle the number of cases of many diseases, vaccine-related damage has itself caused impairment, in those who have paid the individual cost of general health improvement. The development of

ation techniques has also had the paradoxical effect in some ...vantaging those who have already been impaired by a disease. For example:

> The end of the recurrent epidemics of polio meant that the disease, and therefore its victims, lost their high profile. There was a reduction in new research on the disease, its process, and its management. This meant that knowledge about the epidemiology and pathology of polio has been essentially stalled at the level of medical knowledge in the mid-1950s.... Part of the context of any particular disability is its topicality in the medical or in the public eye. Like cancer today, polio once attracted attention beyond its actual level of threat to the population; however, once immunization removed that threat, polio became a 'non-issue'. (Kaufert & Kaufert, 1984: 616)

It should be noted that any removal of the threat of polio is only a local one. Contrary to general medical belief in the 1940s and 1950s, polio is by no means a 'disease of civilisation'; recurrent outbreaks are still endemic in much of the world, where vaccination has been seen as unnecessary or where methods of administration have been ineffective.

It is estimated that the world population of disabled people is around 500 million, over two-thirds of whom live in developing countries, and that one in ten of the world's children is physically or mentally disabled. Some authorities argue that up to 50% of world disablement is either preventable or significantly rehabilitable at a cost of a few pounds per head (Shirley, 1983). For example around 6000 children go blind each year in Tamil Nadu due to easily remediable vitamin A deficiency. Yet Dr Michael Irwin, UNICEF co-ordinator for the International Year of Disabled People said, "only 1 or 2% of the disabled children in the Third World are reached by any rehabilitation" (*The Guardian*, 1981). Another major contributory factor in the aetiology of impairment is nutrition; yet it is universally recognised that world food supplies exceed world need, and that malnutrition today is a consequence of political decisions, not 'acts of God'. As far as the majority of the world's disabled people are concerned, impairment is very clearly primarily the consequence of social and political factors, not an unavoidable 'fact of nature'.

Returning to the developed world, advances in medicine have had the effect of increasing the survival rate of previously 'non-viable' individuals, producing an increased proportion of severely and multiply impaired young people—the improved survival rates of people suffering from Down's syndrome and spina bifida are cases in point. The generally unquantified effects of environmental pollution, and the impairing effects of the consumption of foodstuffs, tobacco and alcohol on individuals and their future offspring must also be noted, although here I will deal with these aspects no further.

Impairment may result from so-called hereditary factors or injury incurred at or soon after birth. Data from the National Child Development Study showed an incidence of serious defects which were congenital or had arisen shortly after birth as 30.8 per thousand live births. By seven years old the incidence was 19.6 per thousand, about half resulting in disablement. A further nine children had very poor sight, and three per thousand poor hearing (Davie et al., 1972). The example of Phenylketonuria (P.K.U.) reveals the complex interconnection between congenital and social factors in the production of impairment. This hereditary inability to metabolise the amino-acid phenylalanine may today be detected and, through dietary control, mental retardation be prevented. Prior to the development of methods of detection and treatment, it may have appeared eminently reasonable to characterise the disorder as a congenital one; it would now appear equally correct to characterise it as socially determined, in that only individuals born in environments in which tests for the presence of the P.K.U. phenotype are not conducted, and where there is no available treatment, will suffer the subsequent impairment. It would thus seem impossible to adequately draw a dividing line between genetic and environmental, and thus ultimately social, factors. Rather, the designation of genetic factors as primarily causative is itself a judgement determined by knowledge, interest and intention, in other words, a political judgement.

It is possible at this point to clarify the nature of the claim that *impairment* is to be understood as social in origin, and to distinguish it from the more usual sociological generalisations about the social origins of *handicap*. The latter position, at least in its more worked out forms, presents handicap as totally the product of social meanings, in other words as reducible to 'attitudes'. It implies that a change in attitudes could abolish disability. Claims about the social origin of impairment, however, are directed at the explication of the social origin of what are material and biological phenomena, and should be understood not as dissolving these material elements into attitudes or ideas, but rather as pointing to the inextricable and essential social elements in what constitutes a material base for ideological phenomena. Thus such a view does not deny the significance of germs, genes and trauma, but rather points out that their effects are only ever apparent in a real social and historical context, whose nature is determined by a complex interaction of material and nonmaterial factors. For example, while the link between tobacco consumption and lung cancer, bronchitis and ischaemic heart disease is demonstrably a material one, the occurrence and incidence of tobacco consumption is to be understood primarily in terms of social factors, as is the level and kind of ameliorative provision available.

At a political level, focusing upon kinds and rates of impairment, posing as they do in an explicit and graphic form the contradictions between the potentially beneficial nature of medical science and its restrictions and deformations in the capitalist mode of production, can be seen as forming a materialist basis for a theory of disability as oppression. It is the general failure of the Left to make such connections between capitalism and impairment which accounts for the fact that "no group on the 'revolutionary Left' . . . takes disablement seriously" (Sutherland, 1981: 17). But Sutherland takes the discussion no further in his reliance on the 'naturalistic' view that "disablement is not merely the physical state of a small minority of people. It is the normal condition of humanity" (ibid., 18) since such a view separates some abstract 'human condition' from the social and historical conditions of its production. It cannot answer the question, why, if disablement is the 'normal condition of humanity' are only some members of the human race accorded the label 'disabled'?

COMMON FEATURES OF DISADVANTAGE

A characteristic of the literature of racial and sexual oppression is that it identifies certain generally common features of economic social and psychological disadvantage suffered by members of the oppressed group. The nature and extent of these disadvantages is by no means uniform or constant between groups or within groups over time, and can only be adequately described after detailed empirical investigation. Considerable literature exists to indicate the material disadvantages suffered by disabled people. To take only one recent example, Townsend (1979) produces a picture of low pay, longer hours, worse working conditions and housing, coupled with a higher likelihood of unemployment. For the purposes of this paper I shall assume this study's findings as typical, reliable and valid, and explore this dimension no further. In addition to material and economic disadvantage, another extensive body of work, of which perhaps the most famous example is still Goffman's

Stigma (Goffman, 1963), documents social and psychological disadvantage from what is explicitly or implicitly an Interactionist perspective. From the point of view of a theory of disability as oppression such studies are important in that they can be viewed as identifying and describing the social mechanisms by which the conditions described by social accountants such as Townsend are produced and reproduced. Care must be taken in 'translation', since a common feature of such studies is the assumed inevitability or 'rightness' of what is described. However, taken together and adequately re-interpreted such studies can form an important element in the development of a theory of disability as oppression. For example, Katz *et al.* (1979, 506) found that "Identical behaviours have different social meanings when produced by a normal and by a disabled person. The pleasant competent 'wheelchair bound' group leader aroused anger and got less help because she appeared to violate the stereotyped stigma role requirement which seems to require the disabled person to suffer and be inadequate. When the confederate in the wheelchair was caustic and hostile, this seemed to confirm social expectations and subjects were willing to offer more help."

In commenting on such examples we should endeavour to map out key features of the stereotype of the disabled person which a particular social formation produces and acts towards real disabled people in terms of. Our objective should be the explication of the material conditions which generate such stereotypes, not the mere description found in Interactionist approaches and empiricist psychology.

One key aspect of this stereotype in modern Britain is that whilst his/her 'primary identity' (Shearer, 1981, 23) resides in disability, the legitimacy and value of this identity is simultaneously denied. Whether perceived as 'tragic' or 'brave' a total identity of the person and the disability is assumed—but at the same time the disabled state is taken for granted as necessarily illegitimate to the extent that:

> A crude and obtrusive imitation of a 'normal' body is held to be preferable to an elegant and efficient tool that makes no pretence of being anything other than what it is. (Sutherland, 1981: 75)

and

> There's a tremendous emphasis on a child who's had polio or whatever to walk.... It's like standing up is considered infinitely better than sitting down, even if you're standing by

standing in a total frame that weighs a ton, that you can't move in, which hurts and takes hours to get on and off and looks ugly. It's assumed that that is what you want and that that's what is best for you. (ibid., 73)

The importance of the body in modern western society has been noted, for example in feminist literature and in considerations of youth culture, although any systematic sociological study has until recently been absent (Turner, 1984). For disabled people the body is the site of oppression, both in form, and in what is done with it. The prohibitions upon deaf children signing to each other as "something evil, like wanking-things you do with your hands that you're not supposed to" (Sutherland, 1981: 56) are the mirror image of the unrealisable ideals of physical perfection and competence constantly presented in the media and in conventional sporting and recreational material. But perhaps more significant than the requirements and prohibitions on what you do with your body as a disabled person are the things that are done to it. These 'rapes' and 'carryings off into slavery' correspond for disabled people to the more publicised features of sexual and racial oppression, and are often perpetuated in everyday life by the actions and the gaze of 'normal' people.

Interactionist studies, because of their failure to link interpersonal relations with the material base upon which interactions take place, can never proceed beyond the level of a descriptive and implicitly justificatory account. Impairment, taken as a given 'natural' property rather than a social product ultimately 'explains' discrimination and disadvantage for such analyses via appeal to some social mechanism parallel to the posited 'basic ethnocentrism' employed in some studies of race.

A further significant point to emerge from the consideration of such studies is the degree to which they produce and propagate a misidentification of who disabled people are. While the stereotype of disabled people, (as implied and in turn produced by the disability logo appearing on lavatory doors and motor cars) is of young people in wheelchairs as a result of MS, amputation, etc. This is far from the reality of the vast majority of disabled people.

The mean age of the 'young chronic sick' on Wood's (Wood, 1978) calculation was in 1978 50.3 years, only 9.8% disabled people being less than 45, a fact which has prompted a minor terminological amendment in the most recent literature, with 'young' renamed 'younger' (Royal College of Physicians, 1986b: 4).

Causes of impairment were also found to be at odds with the stereotype.

Causes of severe disability

Arthritis	31%	Amputation	1.5%
Stroke or Parkinson	15%	Paraplegia	1.3%
Cardio-respiratory	13%	Polio	0.7%
MS	2.8%		

(derived from Bury 1979, similar calculations can be made on the basis of data in Royal College of Physicians, 1986a).

There are a number of implications significant for a theory of disability as oppression which arise from this misidentification. Given the prevalent causes of impairment, the significance of the activities or inactivity of the medical agencies should not be underestimated, as it frequently is in certain sociological studies, and by those members of the general public who claim to view disabled people as 'just like everyone else'. Were the majority of disabled people subject to relatively stable conditions for which no medical interventions were appropriate such positions would be more tenable, but the predominant biological causes of impairment are conditions for which modern medicine at least lays claim to some ameliorative competence.

The stereotype addresses itself to people who, were they not disabled, would be expected to work—thus the Poor Law concerns with legitimacy described by Stone (1984) surface again, in public perception and concern if not in statistical reality (on Bury's calculation 57.9% of impaired adults were over 65 years of age). This group is also that identified in the Royal College of Physicians' report (1986a) as the one for whom provision is least adequate, and who are also identified in more anecdotal sources as subject to the most demeaning of 'tests' in seeking mobility allowances (*The Guardian*, letters, Aug. 1986).

This misidentification, while merely puzzling to Bury, can be seen as performing a number of important functions for the present social system. First, by directing attention away from impairment associated with ageing, it naturalises this aspect of the situation, and reduces the amount of perceived disability in society, so that disability appears as 'exceptional'. In reality about five and a half million, or one in ten people, in Britain today are disabled, approximately the same as the proportion of the workforce who are currently suffering from unemployment.

Secondly, it focuses on that aspect of disability, namely its ability to effect potential workers, which is the primary concern of capitalism, for which the 'problem' of disability is why these people aren't productive, how to return them to productivity, and, if this is not seen as economically viable, how to handle their non-productivity in a manner which causes as little disruption as possible to the overriding imperative of capital accumulation and the maximisation of profits. Yet if the primary object of such theories is the 'young' disabled people, their effects reverberate far beyond their immediate subjects. One effect of the downgrading of the disabled state is to lead all people, including the 'young' disabled themselves, to deny their own suffering and to normalise their situation, thus maintaining the existing structures of social organisation and of work. Beyond this, society as a whole is affected, via the propagation of the work ethic and notions of normalcy implicitly contained in such theories. At this level there is a parallel with the argument (Brittan and Maynard, 1984) that racial and sexual oppression are integrally connected to masculine power in the notion of masculinity as mastery over nature. The points raised by Hunt (1966:146), who argues that disabled people challenge the prevailing norms of society in five main ways, "as unfortunate, useless, different, oppressed and sick", indicate how the mode of being of disabled people can be seen as constituting a paradigmatic negation of masculinity as thus conceived.

As in the cases of women and black people, oppressive theories of disability systematically distort and stereotype the identities of their putative subjects, restricting their full humanity by constituting them only in their 'problem' aspects. The more fashionable but equally unacceptable liberal reaction to this view is to deny all differences—similar to the assimilationist perspective in race relations, and thus similarly devaluing and denying the authenticity of an impaired person's experience, dissolving real problems in the soup of 'attitude change'. Both these viewpoints contain the explicit or tacit assumption that 'impairment' is a universally acceptable and primary explanatory factor. This can be seen particularly in the 'mourning' theories criticised by Oliver (1983), and reaches its most refined and nonsensical expression in such pronouncements as "he had the required toughness of mind—despite, or perhaps because of, legs crippled by polio" (Heren, 1984).

As with racism and sexism, a theory of disability as oppression must at some point face the question of who benefits from oppression. Whilst certain individuals and groups can be seen to accrue short-term advantage (a consideration of the manufacture, supply and fitting of artificial limbs in Britain today provides graphic examples of this) the main and consistent beneficiary must be identified as the present social order, or, more accurately, capitalism in a particular historical and national form. These latter distinctions are important ones, if we are to understand variations in policy and attitudes between nations and over time (Mitchell, 1985).

I have largely argued from analogy and through criticism of extant theoretical perspectives on disability. But this analogy has, I hope been a sustained one, and the criticisms have not been random. Taken together they imply a number of things about what an alternative theory, a theory of disability as oppression, will be concerned with and what it will look like, in contrast to oppressive theories. In conclusion I will try to make these points more explicit.

Some of the general effects of the oppression of disabled people are as follows.

(1) It discourages individuals from trying to take up the 'privileges', to use Stone's (Stone, 1984) somewhat curious term, of disability and thus exempt themselves from the work process.

(2) Because of negative stereotypes and material disadvantages connected to disability it encourages people, where possible, to normalise suffering and disease so as not to include themselves in a despised and disadvantaged sub-group.

(3) It helps to constitute part of a passive 'sub-class' of welfare recipients (Leonard, 1984) which serves as a powerful warning against falling off the achievement ladder.

(4) By presenting disadvantage as the consequence of a naturalised 'impairment' it legitimises the failure of welfare facilities and the distribution system in general to provide for social need, that is, it interprets the effects of social maldistribution as the consequence of individual deficiency.

In contrast to this, a theory of disability as oppression will attempt to flesh out the claim that historically specific categories of the 'disabled people' were constituted as a product of the development of capitalism, and its concern with the compulsion to work. This remained until the late nineteenth century largely the task of legal agencies, but the rise of scientific medicine resulted in the transfer of policing from legal to medical authorities. While this clearly led to certain transformations in the situation of disabled people, medical ideology too devalues the impaired modes of being, at the same time as it naturalises the causes of impairment.

A theory of disability as oppression, then,

(1) recognises and, in the present context, emphasises the social origins of impairment;

(2) recognises and opposes the social, financial, environmental and psychological disadvantages inflicted on impaired people;

(3) sees both (1) and (2) as historical products, not as the results of nature, human or otherwise;

(4) asserts the value of disabled modes of living, at the same time as it condemns the social production of impairment;

(5) is inevitably a political perspective, in that it involves the defence and transformation, both material and ideological, of state health and welfare provision as an essential condition of transforming the lives of the vast majority of disabled people.

While the political implications of such an analysis are apparent, the conceptual consequences are also profound, since such a notion of disability as oppression allows us to organise together into a coherent conceptual whole heretofor isolated and disparate area of social research, and potentially to correct the results of such theoretical myopia.

In summary, to usefully apply the notion of oppression to the complex of impairment, disability and handicap involves the development of a theory which connects together the common features of economic, social and psychological disadvantage with an understanding of the material basis of these disadvantages and the ideologies which propagate and reproduce them. Only such an account, specific and systematic, can move discussion beyond the level that it has reached so far, by bringing to bear the tools of today's social science, rather than those of the day before yesterday.

ACKNOWLEDGEMENTS

I would like to thank Sue Abberley, Caroline Freeman, Dee Northover and Christine Webb for their various contributions to the genesis of this paper.

REFERENCES

ARTHRITIS AND RHEUMATISM COUNCIL (N.D.) *Arthritis Research: the way ahead* (London, ARC).

BARKER, R.G. (1948) The social psychology of physical disability, *Journal of Social Issues,* 4(4), pp. 28-42.

BARRETT, M. (1981) *Women's Oppression Today* (London, Verso).

BATTYE, L. (1966) The Chatterley syndrome, in: HUNT, op. cit.

BOTTOMORE, T. (Ed.) (1983) *A Dictionary of Marxist Thought* (Oxford, Blackwell).

BRITISH LEAGUE AGAINST RHEUMATISM (1977) *Rheumatism: the price we pay* (London, BLAR).

BRITTAN, A. & MAYNARD, M. (1984) *Sexism, Racism and Oppression* (Oxford, Blackwell).

BURY, M.R. (1979) Disablement in society, *International Journal of Rehabilitative Research,* 2, pp. 33-40.

CAMPLING, J. (Ed.) (1981) *Images of Ourselves* (London, Routledge & Kegan Paul).

CHESLER, M.A. (1965) Ethnocentrism and attitudes towards the physically disabled, *Journal of Personality and Social Psychology,* 2, pp. 877-82.

COMMITTEE ON CHILD HEALTH SERVICES (1976) *Fit for the Future,* Vol. 1 (London, HMSO).

CONFEDERATION OF INDIAN ORGANISATIONS (U.K.) (1986) *Double Bind—to be disabled and Asian* (London, CIO).

DARTINGTON, T., MILLER, E. & GWYNNE, G. (1981) *A Life Together* (London, Tavistock).

DAVEY, A. (1983) *Learning to be Prejudiced* (London, Edward Arnold).

DAVIE, R. *et al.* (1972) *From Birth to Seven* (London, Longman).

DAVIS, F. (1961) Deviance & disavowal, *Social Problems,* 9.

EISENSTEIN, Z. (1979) Developing a theory of capitalist patriarchy and socialist feminism, in: *Capitalist Patriarchy and Socialist Feminism* (New York, Monthly Review Press).

FRY, E. (1986) *An Equal Chance for Disabled People?—A study of discrimination in employment* (London, The Spastics Society).

GOFFMAN, E. (1963) *Stigma* (New Jersey, Prentice-Hall).

HANDEL, A.F. (1960) Community attitudes and adjustment to disability, *Outlook for the Blind,* No. 54, p. 363.

HEREN, L. (1984) *The Observer,* London, 30 December.

HUNT, P. (1966) A critical condition, in: P. HUNT (Ed.) (1966) *Stigma,* pp. 145-159 (London, Chapman).

KATZ, M. *et al.* (1979) *Journal of Personality,* 46, pp. 606-609.

KAUFERT, J. & KAUFERT, P. (1984) Methodological and conceptual issues in measuring the impact of longterm disability, *Social Science and Medicine,* 19, pp. 609-619.

KINNERSLEY, P. (1973) *The Hazards of Work* (London, Pluto Press).

LEONARD, P. (1984) *Personality and Ideology,* Ch. 8 (Basingstoke, Macmillan).

MITCHELL, P. (1985) *A Comparison of Social Provision For People with Disabilities in the Netherlands and the U.K.* (London, RADAR).

MULLER, M. (1982) *The Health of Nations* (London, Faber).

NAVARRO, V. (1982) The labour process and health international, *Journal of Health Services,* 12, pp. 5-29.

NEW SOCIETY (1985) Findings, 7 June.

NICHOLS T. (1986) Industrial injuries in British manufacturing in the 1980s, *Sociological Review,* 34, pp. 290-306.

OLIVER, M. (1983) *Social Work with Disabled People* (Basingstoke, Macmillan).

OLIVER, M. (1986) Social policy and disability: some theoretical issues, *Disability, Handicap and Society,* 1, pp. 5-18.

PEARSON COMMISSION REPORT (1978) Vols 1 and 2 (London, HMSO).

RICHARDSON, S.W. & GREEN, A. (1971) When is black beautiful? Coloured and white children's reaction to skin colour, *British Journal of Educational Psychology,* 41, pp. 62-9.

ROYAL COLLEGE OF PHYSICIANS OF LONDON (1986a) *Physical Disability in 1996 and Beyond* (London, RCP).

ROYAL COLLEGE OF PHYSICIANS OF LONDON (1986b) *The Young Disabled Adult* (London, RCP).

SADGROVE, J. (1985) I deserve this cigarette, *New Statesman,* 109(2830),14 June, pp. 9-11.

SHEARER, A. (1981) *Disability: whose handicap?* (Oxford, Blackwell).

SHIRLEY, O. (Ed.) (1983) *A Cry for Health—poverty and disability in the Third World* (Frome, Third World Group & AHRTAG).

STONE, D. (1984) *The Disabled State* (Basingstoke, Macmillan).

SUTHERLAND, A. (1981) *Disabled We Stand* (London, Souvenir Press).

THUNHURST, C. (1982) *It Makes You Sick—the politics of the NHS* (London, Pluto Press).

TOWNSEND, P. (1979) *Poverty in the United Kingdom* (London, Penguin).

TURNER, B.S. (1984) *The Body & Society* (Oxford, Blackwell).

WOOD, P.H.N. (1978) Size of the problem and causes of chronic sickness in the young, *Journal of the Royal Society of Medicine,* 71, PV. 437-441.

CHAPTER 11

Stars are not born:
an interpretive approach
to the politics of
disability

Helen Liggett

(First published 1988)

INTRODUCTION

Familiar ways of thinking about disability treat disability as one or more of
any number of conditions which limit the participation of individuals in the
normal activities of society. This kind of definition is based on the unexamined
presupposition that disabilities are various forms of impairment which exist in
individuals. Philanthropic versions of this way of thinking include the notion
that enlightened societies have an obligation to facilitate the lives of disabled
citizens. Public policy responses to this way of viewing disability vary;
including among other activities, income maintenance and rehabilitation
programs, legislation requiring physical accessibility, and the inclusion of
classes on designing accessible environments in the curriculum of architecture
schools.

Definitional issues play a major role in both theoretical and policy-oriented
studies of disability. For example, historical accounts are often concerned with
how the meaning of disability has changed over time (Blaxter, 1976; Stone,

1983). Policy studies typically focus on measuring disability and developing coherent criteria for relating types of disability to eligibility requirements and benefit schedules (Berkowitz, 1979b; Howards *et al.*, 1980). Even the literature of the helping professions is organized to a certain extent by discussion of how disability should be determined and administered.

The purpose of this paper is to show how such discussions are politically relevant. A Foucaultian analysis is presented which links the politics of disability to discursive practices in which disability is constituted. I argue below that the politics of disability entails the production and administration of the notion of disability. Becoming conscious of the institutionalized practices in terms of which disability is constituted broadens the arenas within which political strategies can be promoted and legitimated.

I. FOUCAULT'S CONTRIBUTION TO THE POLITICS OF INTERPRETATION

> . . . if interpretation is the violent or surreptitious appropriation of a system of rules, which in itself has no essential meaning, in order to impose a direction, to bend it to a new will, to force its participation in a different game, and to subject it to secondary rules, then the development of humanity is a series of interpretations.

In the statement reproduced above Foucault links interpretation and truth to politics. Foucault's interpretative approach is part of a larger movement within contemporary thought in which meaning is connected to systems of interpretation which organize human experience. An exposition of the variations within the interpretative perspective is a project beyond the scope of this paper. Generally, however, proponents of the interpretative point of view see meaning and truth as social productions connected to particular language games or discursive practices within the human community. The interpretative position on the role of language in the production of meaning differs from the view of other epistemological perspectives which have currency in contemporary social thought.

In positivism truth claims are based on observations which connect concepts to objects. The positivist view explicitly neglects interpretation because, among other things, it regards objects as isolated 'facts' existing independently of systems of interpretation. Research based on methodologies derived from this view is organized around verifying relations among concepts which are first defined theoretically and then operationalized so they can be observed. That is, concepts are translated into indicators, which are used to measure objects and the relations among them. For positivism, disability presents itself as a problem of definition. The issue becomes one of indicating the relevant physical impairment. A disabled individual is one who has some 'medically' *observable* impairment; and medical science is not considered to be an interpretative system, but a value free mode of measuring physical impairment (Nagi, 1979; Mashaw, 1979).

Phenomenologically derived methodologies differ from positivist approaches because they emphasize the process by which objects are constituted. Two better known forms are symbolic interactionism and ethnomethodology, both practiced in sociology. Instead of investigating the relationships between pre-existing objects, symbolic interactionists focus on the process by which subjects define objects. For example, symbolic interaction approaches to disability study the experience of disability from the viewpoint of disabled people. Typical questions include: How do individuals come to see themselves as disabled? How do disabled people handle their relations with social welfare agencies (Blaxter, 1976; Scott, 1969)? Because symbolic interactionists and ethnomethodologists ask about "definitions of the situation" from the viewpoint of individual actors, they share with positivists the disinclination to problematize interpretative contexts.

Those who use interpretative approaches do problematize interpretative contexts. These epistemological positions differ from both positivist views which connect truth to objects outside of language and also from phenomenological derived views which connect truth to the consciousness of individual knowers because truth is connected to language use, i.e. to meanings produced in the course of human affairs. Subjects and objects are seen as 'object-effects' of institu-tionalized social practices. Instead of being prior to language the existence of subjects and objects are inseparable from language use. The truth of objects is assumed to be more or less in flux (depending on the situation) because truth is embedded in the commerce of everyday life. Researchers working within an interpretative approach trace the appearance and disappearance of disability as an available identity within particular societal conditions (Stone, 1983).

For Michael Foucault these kinds of questions relating to how we know and what kinds of knowledge become institutionalized in established practices are of interest to political theorists because knowledge, and the constitution of available identities, are connected to the operation of power in society.

Interpretations do not exist separately from the practices of social life. Instead they are embedded in systems of meaning which *are* our social life. Because definitions are part of constitutive practices, definitions do more than just 'label' people. They constitute identities and in so doing, participate in the maintenance of relations of dominance.

In Foucault's thinking the traditional distinction between the 'individual' and 'society' is misguided because it assumes that 'individuals' have natural or pure identities whlch are separable from the possibilities constituted by society. Foucault and others who adopt such a view see no individuality separate from systems of meaning.

Foucault has developed two metaphors to describe the production and control of subjects in modern life. They are "the carceral network", which he develops in *Discipline and Punish* (1977a) and "the normalizing society" which he emphasizes in *The History of Sexuality* (1978). He uses both to characterize the processes by which identities (he uses the word 'subjects') are constituted by modern society.

In *Discipline and Punish* (1977a), Foucault connects notions of crime, of what criminals are, and of appropriate forms of treatment with the development and ascendancy of modern discursive practices which manage criminality. The locus of authority for dealing with criminality is now lodged in specialized practices in which bases of legitimacy are tied to science. Other modes of thinking, those tied to morality, for example, are still present, but in altered forms. Criminality is a project (in a sense) of the shifting forces which competed to constitute the criminal justice system. Religious and secular courts; Protestant, Catholic, and free thinking reformers; various scientific disciplines and helping professions have all had a hand in producing criminality. Foucault's genealogy of criminality records its emergence during the course of particular disputes over jurisdiction, struggles to institutionalize reform, and the development of new mechanisms of administration. There has been a shift from inflicting punishment externally (e.g. public execution and torture) to administering criminality by first separating the criminal from the normal population and then trying to rehabilitate him.

Modern rehabilitation practices begin by separating 'the criminal' from members of normal society and then watching over or 'disciplining' all aspects of the prisoner's life. The monitoring of criminality involves and goes beyond crude forms of control such as the ability to physically watch every prisoner. It includes the contemporary equivalent of watching over and transforming each prisoner's soul. The work of rehabilitation is to teach delinquents to discipline themselves. This work is successful when the monitoring function has been internalized so that the burden of producing a normal identity is carried by the prisoners themselves. Rehabilitated delinquents are no longer delinquent; assuming the expectations of normal life, they become . . . normal.

In talking about 'the normalizing society', Foucault means to emphasize that disciplinary practices qualify identities both inside and outside of the individuals. He uses the phrases "instruments of perpetual assessment" and "the carceral network" to describe our society. This is his way of talking about universal participation in discipline. "Perpetual assessment", i.e. the various expectations according to which subjects produce themselves and others, is legitimatized and provoked by the authority of scientific truth which is attributed to the various 'social science' disciplines, professions and practices involved. Criminology is only one example. Demography, educational psychology, and social work are others. The inescapable terms of everyday life, in this model of society, are organized in terms of various distinctions between normal and deviant identities.

In *The History of Sexuality* (1978) Foucault develops these ideas further and shows how discipline and the formulation of identities work as relations of control even in areas of life we think of as natural, such as sexuality, or motherhood. He also shows how inescapable the normalizing society is. The so-called normal identities are just as much products of discipline as are deviant identities. Subjects that rule are as thoroughly disciplined as any graduates of prison rehabilitation programs. The normalizing society is a structure of dominance that involves all its members.

In *Discipline and Punish* (1977a) Foucault reproduces a dialogue between a judge and a juvenile delinquent that illustrates the normalizing society in action.

Judge: One must sleep at home.

Be'asse: Have I got a home?

J: You live in perpetual vagabondage.

B: I work to earn my living.

J: What is your station in life?

B: My station: to begin with, I'm 36 at least; I don't work for anybody. I've worked for myself for a long time now. I have my day station and my night station. In the day, for instance, I hand out leaflets free of charge to all the passers-by; I run after the

> stage coaches when they arrive and carry luggage for the passengers. I turn cart-
> wheels on the avenue de Neuilly; at night there are the shows; I open coach doors;
> I sell pass-out tickets; I've plenty to do.
>
> *J:*   It would be better for you to be put into a good house as an apprentice and learn a
>   trade.
>
> *B:*   Oh, a good house, an apprenticeship, it's too much trouble. And anyway the
>   bourgeois . . . always grumbling, no freedom.
>
> (1977a, pp. 290-291)

One response to this exchange would be to point out that it represents a romanticized, short-term, childish, etc. view of life, or to say that Be'asse's cheekiness is annoying. Foucault emphasizes the force of the latter, namely the challenge to codes of normal behavior that Be'asse presents. Be'asse challenges the whole system which opposes normal to deviant by cheerfully describing his life in positive terms. In modern life this is a privilege usually restricted to literature. Otherwise,

> One must live in a home, have a station in life,. . . a recognizable identity.... In short one
> should have a master, be caught up and situated within a hierarchy; one exists only when
> fixed in definite relations of domination.
>
> (1977a, pp. 290-291)

Foucault suggests that Be'asse was delinquent because of 'indiscipline', not because of criminal activity. (Be'asse was sentenced to two years in a reformatory. His response: "Two years, that's never more than 24 months. Let's be off, then".)

Where some social theorists use an organic or systems model to talk about social order, Foucault's model is based on relations of force. He does not present society as a normatively integrated or mutual-benefit system in the same way a structural-functionalist theorist might. The normalizing society is a structure of dominance.

The carceral functions of the normalizing society are not mechanisms of oppression, as vulgar Marxism might have it. Foucault ties surveillance to productivity, but in a broad sense. In the *History of Sexuality* (1978) Foucault connects the deployment of sexuality within discursive practices such as psychoanalysis to the emergence of the bourgeois as a new ruling class. " . . . they first tried it on themselves" (1978, p. 122). "The primary concern was not repression of the classes to be exploited, but rather the body, vigor, longevity, progeniture, and descent of the classes that 'ruled'" (p. 123).

If the opposition between normal and delinquent or deviant operates as a system of control, what does all this have to do with what we usually assume is a natural distinction between the able-bodied and the disabled? In other words, how does the opposition between disabled and able-bodied function in our society of perpetual assessment? Can Foucault's interpretative perspective provide a useful discussion of what disability is and how it is produced as part of the contemporary political order?

II. AN INTERPRETATIVE ANALYSIS OF DISABILITY

The problem of living with a stroke is not a new one, but there has been a very significant change in emphasis in recent years in relation to the management of such patients. People with this condition should not be allowed to wait for recovery. They should be encouraged to live the fullest life possible, consistent with their disability.

(J. C. Somerville, Medical Director,
London and Farnham Park Rehabilitation Centre)

"People with this condition" are different kinds of people, different, for example, from men like Somerville who try to rehabilitate them and different from the rest of normal society, which is identified implicitly with a 'full life'. If a patient remarked that she had a very full life dealing with the aftermath of her stroke she would have more in common with Be'asse than with the respectful and compassionate voices that struggle to manage disability.

Similarly, we can imagine an interaction between a disabled or unemployed person and the civil servant assigned to her. It would be unusual, as the system is currently organized, to hear the case worker called "My good man" by his client and then be asked about the health of the wife and kids. As a society we have decided to insure our members against certain extenuating circumstances, yet we are conventionally institutionally ill-mannered when it's time to pay up. The explanation of this behavior may have something to do with how disability (and unemployment) are produced and managed. If the practices which constitute disability are part of the carceral network that Foucault talks about, then they operate as relations of domination, in the very act of what we otherwise might only think of as dispersing agreed upon payments.

The discussion below interprets current public policy literature on disability in order to address these issues. This literature is interrogated as a data source for understanding the production and maintenance of disability, as we know it.

There is widespread agreement in the social science literature on disability that disability isn't managed as well as it should be.

(1) In some studies the American political system is seen as the source of the current crisis. According to this view, interest group politics is the wrong tool for the job of formulating a rational disability policy. For example, Social Security Disability Insurance is presented as the result of discontinuous and incremental processes extending over fifty years. Current policy is said to reflect the varying and sometimes competing interests of the many groups which have been involved in formulating it. These include, among others, the Chamber of Commerce, the insurance industry, the American Medical Association, organized labor, the Department of Commerce, Congress, and private organizations for blind people. From the point of view of this criticism, "the reality of interest politics" over "inner bureaucratic logic" is regrettable (Berkowitz, 1979a, p. 10). Current policy represents "the sum of all that accumulated rather than a rational or comprehensive policy".

The solution to the irrationality of the disability system which is suggested most often in the literature is to make the system which administers it more rational. A typical suggestion is to improve the determination of disability by institutionalizing more scientific definitions. Nagi (1979), for example, considers impairment an 'objective' condition which medical science can measure while disability has been determined more 'subjectively'. If disability is defined as "reduced ability to perform competitive employment or other significant individual roles" (p. 11), determining whether or not disability exists depends on the context. Nagi recommends developing operational definitions of disability which would have the exactness of measures of impairment but which would also take working conditions into account. "Specific norms and mechanisms in decision making structures" are needed for more exact specification of disability.

Howards, Brehm & Nagi (1980) study of Social Security Disability Insurance is an example of a comprehensive rational remedies approach to the management of disability. They ask whether the problem with disability isn't that it is plagued by a lack of correspondence between "underlying social problems", "social policy", and "social programs". Their conclusion is that this is indeed the case; the relative importance of "the ability to work" and the "medical impairment" components of disability insurance have become reversed. Whereas the original legislative intent was that citizens who are unable to work because of physical impairment should receive financial support. SSDI is administered in such a way that clients are assessed in terms of their need first, and then in terms of their disability. Furthermore, applicants self-select themselves on the basis of whether they do actually hold jobs. The number of applicants increases during bad times and in sections of the country which are economically depressed. In addition, strong economic incentives exist for continuing to receive disability insurance once enrolled and substantial penalties are connected with re-enrolment especially for those with regular medical expenses. In other words, participation in and the overall costs of disability programs are closely related to prevalent economic trends (Hahn, 1983, p. 8).

Howards, Brehm & Nagi (1980) suggest rationalizing the system by bringing the three segments of disability in line with each other. Functional definitions of "the ability to work" would make "social policy" correspond with "the social problem". Adjustments to the earning test component would bring "the social problem" on line with "social policy". In addition, they recommend changing eligibility and re-enrolment criteria so that beneficiaries would no longer be encouraged to become permanently dependent on Disability Insurance. SSDI would function "as originally intended", i.e. as insurance which meets the problem of the inability to work caused by disability (instead of functioning as welfare) (Howards et al., 1980).

The Howards and Nagi studies and others like them (Mashaw, 1979; Berkowitz, 1979a,b) make disability into a scientific problem. For example, the force of Nagi's argument is to bring the contextual elements of disability under the mantle of science. He is saying, in effect, that because disability is a complex phenomenon tied to shifting employment conditions, it is all the more important that we tie it down. In epistemological terms, he is interested in devising ways of knowing disability for the object it really is. The effect of structuring investigations in terms of "lack of correspondence" (Howards et al., 1980) and "operational definitions" (Nagi, 1979) is to produce disability within scientific discourse. Solutions of the problem of disability which call for bringing the problem under control with more precise information follow from a scientific perspective. This type of solution, in turn, leads to recommendations for reform based on increased monitoring of disabled people.

Calling for more detailed qualifications from applicants authorizes further discursive involvement in determining and administering disabled identities. From a Foucaultian point of view, the relational remedies approach reinforces surveillance in the disciplinary society.

Concern with the cost of disability programs is typical in studies which present disability as a management and control problem. There are references throughout the literature to the danger of malingerers, of creating dependency, of the coming fiscal crisis. The rising cost of disability programs is often presented as the rationale for recommending further control. The cost of the proliferation of mechanisms of control is rarely discussed.

(2) There are studies of disability which do not see the problem of disability as a problem of cost resulting from the irrationalities of interest group politics. These studies are concerned with how disabled people are treated and they tend to see politics as a solution, rather than as the problem. But as discussed below, studies of disability which attempt to reproduce the experience of disability and appear to use a different perspective to understand the problem of disability also contribute solutions which reinforce the disciplinary society.

Studies which are concerned with the experience of disability are usually written from symbolic interaction or ethnomethodological perspectives. Disability is not interpreted as a static operationalizable condition: instead it is seen as a process involving a change of consciousness (Blaxter, 1976; Edgerton, 1974; Scott, 1969). Where researchers working within a behavioral view talk about the problem of controlling and managing disability, symbolic interactionist studies talk about the problems connected with learning to manage one's own identity as disabled. Blaxter treats disability as a 'career', rather than as a 'category'. Scott takes the more radical position that 'blind men' are produced as the result of relations with blindness agencies.

The authors of these studies sometimes speak as if the formulation of identities only occurred inside individuals' heads. Some seem to implicitly accept the idea that disability is a real condition (Blaxter, 1976; Edgerton, 1974). Nevertheless, the evidence they present also supports the interpretative view which privileges discursive practices. For example, there is widespread evidence that the smoother the adoption of a disabled identity, the smoother the processes of dealing with the agents of rehabilitation (Blaxter, 1976; Boswell and Wingrove, 1974; Scott, 1969).

Blaxter (1976), found that her subjects tended "to rewrite their own medical history in the light of subsequent events" (p. 11). Subsequent events included relations with normals both inside and outside of social agencies who treated subjects as disabled. The treatment could either be benign (helping people to qualify for benefits) or pernicious (denying people employment). Scott shows how social roles and behavior patterns which are appropriate to interactions with sighted people are assumed in the context of agencies authorized to administer blindness. Even Howards *et al.* (1980) show how disability programs are active producers of disability. Widows who do not meet the specified criteria of the Social Security Administration are "for practical purposes 'non-widows'" (p. x). What they don't say and what symbolic interactionist studies record is that women who do meet the qualifications are encouraged by their engagement with the system to constitute themselves as widows in its terms.

Remedies to the problem of disability as it is formulated by symbolic interactionists are based on empowering the disabled. Disabled people, in this view, would be encouraged to participate in their own administration. Hahn (1983) is representative of those who recommend "new social-political definitions of disability". This means that the disabled should get into decision-making processes on the basis of their claims to be a special group. Proponents of this minority group strategy argue that it gives the disabled a basis upon which to make claims for certain adjustments in the environment (e.g. access to public buildings) instead of always accepting adjustments of the individual to the environment. The Rehabilitation Act of 1973 is a victory of those who see disability as a minority group status entailing certain rights.

The minority group approach basically argues that disabled people should be brought into the American political system as another interest group. The structure of decision making isn't attacked. Instead the idea is to improve the odds that the disabled will be recognized as having legitimate demands.

The minority groups approach is not satisfactory from a management view because it introduces complexities which cannot be controlled and which are often expensive. Hearings and appeals are opposed on the grounds that they favor the tenacious rather than the worthy (Rock, 1976). A 'litigious atmosphere' is considered undesirable, because it introduces irrationality. It also challenges the current power relations.

From the viewpoint of those concerned with how disabled people are treated, challenging the current power relations appears to be desirable. The minority group approach to disability gives disabled people a legitimate voice within the American political system. As disabled people become an established interest group they can change some of the agents of dominance which manage and administer them.

(3) From an interpretative view the minority group approach is double-edged because it means enlarging the discursive practices which participate in the constitution of disability. In other words, the price of becoming politically active on their own behalf is accepting the consequences of defining disability within new perspectives, which have their own priorities and needs. The new perspectives then become involved in disciplining disability. For example, disability as a problem of legal rights exists within the ways of thinking and prejudices that constitute legal discourse.

The interest groups politics critique, the rational remedies approach, the symbolic interaction critique, and the minority groups strategy all operate on the basis of their own kind of distinctions between disabled and not disabled people. In that way they participate in and reinforce a disciplinary society. The oppositions that Foucault sees in the normalizing society among normal and various forms of deviance remain intact.

A detailed genealogy of disability would investigate how various shifting social practices constitute and administer disability in the normalizing society. The system as we know it is a legacy of shifting relations among these practices. A detailed genealogy would show exact instances of struggle and transformation. That work would help answer the question of why this age produces disability as we know it.

That project is beyond the scope of this paper, but there is some evidence in the existing literature about how the current opposition between normal and disabled identities operates. The opposition between normal and disabled people in this society differentiates between those who carry on the work of society and those who deserve to receive the charity of society (Blaxter, 1976). Stone (1983) argues that this distinction has important implications for capitalism. The primary distributive system in capitalist societies is work-based. At the same time there are exceptions: i.e. certain classes of people deserve support for other reasons. For example, after wars industrialized nations are faced with the problem of disabled veterans. Disabled veterans are considered to be deserving of some share in the wealth of society, but they are unable to work (Blaxter, 1976; Berkowitz, 1979). Stone (1983) suggests that the creation of 'disability' helps to solve this problem by maintaining boundaries between work and need. The needy deserving should be provided for. But the just plain needy should work for their money, i.e. participate in the primary work-based distribution system. The institutionalization of medical criteria for disability provided clear-cut ways of determining who the deserving needy were (Stone, 1983).

At the present time medical practices contribute to the current crisis in disability. The disinterestedness of the medical profession in boundary maintenance and the recent cycles of recession in industrial nations have produced a situation where disability programs handle and disguise unemployment. Because doctors don't have the same fiscal concerns as disability administrators, new ways of determining and managing disability need to be devised (Stone, 1983).

Even though Stone's analysis is marred by her unjustified assumption that disability is a management problem, she does show what interpretative analysis that treats disability as a production of prevalent discursive practices is like. A more extensive discursive analysis of disability would deal with the question of how the constitution of disability fits with Foucault's notion that disciplinary power produces subjects by operating "directly on bodies".

Scott suggests that blindness agencies remove blind people from the sight of normals. This makes the disabled body an invisible body. A politically oriented study might begin by asking how invisible bodies can participate in society. The disabled body has also traditionally been a non-reproducing body. In a seeming contradiction to this tradition, social science has recently 'discovered' the sexuality of disabled people and a whole literature has emerged on 'the problem' of the sexuality of disabled people. Further study might focus on asking about the relation of this literature to the emergence of the truth of sex as a control mechanism. Further investigation could ask how the distinction between disabled and normal continues to participate in maintaining the normalizing society. How does the normal/disabled difference help produce subjects who exercise responsibility and control as a matter of course, as well as those who are acted upon as a matter of course?

III. VICTIMS WITHOUT CRIMES

Positivist, phenomenological and interpretative perspectives constitute disability differently. These different notions of disability have different possibilities for politics built into them.

The positivist definitions of disability operate as part of a set of established practices which entail some disabling commitments. Even the phenomenological views, which often align themselves with the disabled reinforce distinctions between normal and disabled people. The interpretative approach has the advantage of distancing the researcher from the conventional categories.

The interpretative approach has been used by Foucault to show how deviant identities work as relations of dominance. His model, first developed in the context of investigations into criminality, is relevant to disability because it focuses on practices which operate by producing and managing identities. In the criminality example, some administer justice and some have justice administered to them. Similarly, the disabled as well as the non-disabled participate in the system that binds them to their respective identities.

The politics of disability need to take into account the findings of the interpretative perspective. One way to do this is to investigate further how the perpetuation of disabled identities helps insure that the disabled participate in the normalizing society as victims without crimes. Foucault recently centered his own work around the question, "At what cost can subjects speak the truth about themseves?" The evidence presented above is that in order to participate in their own management disabled people have had to participate as disabled. Even among the politically active, the price of being heard is understanding that it is the disabled who are speaking.

What other kinds of politics are there? If participation in the disciplinary society is inescapable, what else is possible?

Again, this raises issues which are beyond the scope of this paper, particularly in so far as political strategies are tied to specific social formations and need to be assessed in terms of local practices (Liggett, 1988). Political action should be a reflective undertaking in which both the costs and benefits of accepting disabled identities and the available strategies in a given political system are weighted in each situation. Sometimes political action operates within established practices and sometimes it challenges those practices. For example, in some issues, such as physical access, the identity as disabled has been used to good advantage to remove disabling distinctions between those who can move around and those who cannot.

A central contribution of discursive analysis is to recognize a broader scope for political action at the secondary level. Because language practices work to produce disabled identities, the politics of disability entail choosing instances to challenge those practices to work in different ways. Since individual identities are group projects, politics involves questioning the constitutive activities of those groups.

In so far as disabled people exist in society as an excluded category, the struggle will necessarily be arduous and often subversive. When Foucault says that bodies are a battlefield, I do not think he's speaking in hyperbole. He's saying something about how intimately we are involved in conventional social practices. If certain identities are to be permanently disabled this means direct challenge by those who are willing to bear the costs of transgressing their own customary identities. For example, introducing women into university faculties has resulted in various unpleasantries (in the best of circumstances) because academic identities based on sexism are unavoidably threatened. Similarly, a therapist who sits in a wheelchair must deal daily with reactions to his or her upseating conventional notions of fitness.

These activities should be valorized as political action on the individual level. Individual counter-politics to accepting denigrated identities means paying attention to the kinds of practices we allow to go on. Relentless refusals to go along with what appears to come naturally are front-line battles in the politics of disability.

REFERENCES

BERKOWITZ, EDWARD D. (1979a) Introduction, in: E. BERKOWITZ *Disability Policies and Government Programs* (New York, Praeger).

BERKOWITZ, EDWARD D. (1979b) The American disability system in historical perspective, in: E. BERKOWITZ *Disability Policies and Government Programs* (New York, Praeger)

BLAXTER, MILDRED (1976) *The Meaning of Disability: a sociological study of impairment* (London, Heinemann).

BOSWELL, DAVID M. & WINGROVE, JANET (Eds) (1974) *The Handicapped Person in the Community* (London, Tavistock).

EDGERTON, ROBERT B. (1974) Passing and denial: the problem of seeming to be normal, in: D. M. BOSWELL & J. WINGROVE (Eds) *The Handicapped Person in the Community* (London, Tavistock).

FOUCAULT, MICHEL (1977a) *Discipline and Punish: the birth of the prison* (New York, Pantheon).

FOUCAULT, MICHEL (1977b) Nietzsche, Genealogy, History, in: D. F. BOUCHARD (Ed.) *Language, Counter-memory, Practice: selected essays and interviews* (Ithaca, N.Y., Cornell University Press).

FOUCAULT, MICHEL (1978) *The History of Sexuality, Vol. I* (New York, Pantheon).

HAHN, HARLAN (1983) *Public Expenditures for Rehabilitation Policies: toward a politics of disability* (Los Angeles, University of Southern California Press).

HOWARDS, IRVING, BRAHM, HENRY P. & NAGI, SAAD Z. (1980) *Disability: from social problem to Federal program* (New York, Praeger).

LIGGETT, HELEN (1988) Class action in the academy: Penk v. OSBHE, *Thought and Action* (4. pp. 87-100)

MASHOW, JERRY L. (1979) The definition of disability from the perspective of administration, in: E. BEREKOWITZ (Ed.) *Disability Policies & Government Programs* (New York, Praeger).

NAGI, SAAD Z. (1979) The concept and measurement of disabilty in: E. BERKOWITZ *Disability Policies and Government Programs* (New York, Praeger).

RAULET, GERARD (1983) Structuralism and post-structuralism: an interview with Michel Foucault, *Telos*, 55, pp. 195-211.

SCOTT, ROBERT (1969) *The Making of Blind Men: a study of adult socialization* (New York, Russel Sage Foundation).

SHAPIRO, MICHAEL J. (1981) *Language and Political Understanding* (New Haven, Yale University Press).

SOMERVILLE, J.C. (1977) The rehabilitation of the hemiplegic patient, in: D. BOSWELL & J. WINGROVE (Eds) *The Handicapped Person in the Community* (London, Tavistock).

STONE, DEBORAH A. (1983) *The Disabled State* (Cambridge, Mass., MIT Press).

CHAPTER 12

The Politics of Disability:
a new approach

Mike Oliver

Gerry Zarb

(First published 1989)

It is only in recent years that the issue of disability has been transformed from a purely medical problem to a political one, in Britain, at least. Central to this transformation has been the rise of the disability movement and the coming to power of a radical government whose social policies have fractured the post-war welfare consensus. Unfortunately, however, this politicisation of disability has not resulted in the development of a new understanding of the position of disabled people in society. Instead, we have seen the politics of disability reduced to a consideration of pressure group and party political activity. This paper will argue that this is an inadequate basis for understanding either the historical significance or the current relevance of the disability movement. It is only by understanding that the disability movement is centrally placed within the rise of a whole range of new social movements which are characteristic of post-capitalist society, that its significance can be grasped.

THE POLITICAL PARTICIPATION OF DISABLED PEOPLE

That disabled people constitute a potentially powerful political force there can be no doubt. According to Fry (1987), a recent MORI poll found that 9% of the public (18+) considered themselves to be disabled and 27% said that another member of their family was disabled. This study (Fry, 1987) looked at the political participation of disabled people in the 1987 General Election and found that many disabled people did not even appear on the electoral register; others, particularly blind and deaf people, were denied access to all the information necessary to make an informed choice; and other disabled people, postal and proxy voting notwithstanding, found the problem of transport and physical access to polling stations too daunting to allow them to exercise their right to vote.

There are two further ways in which it is difficult for disabled people to participate within the Party system. First, many local constituency headquarters are inaccessible and hence it is very difficult for them to become grass-roots activists and to feed in disability issues at this level. Secondly, although there are examples of disabled politicians at the local and national level, it is also very difficult for many disabled political activists to offer themselves as candidates at local or national elections, for the problems of both campaigning and door-to-door canvassing may prove to be impossible.

Even if these barriers to political participation were removed, it would not necessarily mean that the disabled population would cohere into an active political force to which all political parties would need to take notice. There are a number of reasons for this.

> To begin with there is a great deal of variety within the disabled population as a whole— differences in social class, age, sex, family circumstances and clinical conditions—as well as the fact that disability may have developed after political commitments had been established. In addition, many disabled people do not necessarily regard themselves as disabled, or even if they do, would not contemplate joining an organisation of disabled people. Finally, as a consequence of disability, some people may disengage from political activity, either because their physical impairment poses limitations of a physical or psychological kind, or because they are aware that in many contexts they lack any basis for exercising power, eg. through the withdrawal of their labour. (Oliver, 1984 p. 23)

Extending this analysis, it has been suggested also that the medical approach to disability has fostered artificial divisions within the disabled population (Borsay, 1986).

But these divisions do not arise simply from the medical approach, for the State also provides services in such a way as to foster divisions within the disabled population. Hence, it gives tax allowances to blind people but not to other categories of disability, mobility allowances to those who cannot walk but not for those who can, and higher pensions and benefits for those injured at work or in the services than for those with congenital disabilities or those who have had accidents. This is not an unintentional consequence of State provision but a deliberate tactic which the State has developed in its dealings with other groups and can be summed up as 'divide and rule'.

This idea of disabled people as a group divided amongst itself has obvious implications for any notions of class based political activity.

> The myriad of disability-specific programs and policies, the segregation of disabled people, the inability to gain access to organised society, to experience an integrated and adequate education, to obtain meaningful employment, and to socially interact and participate has resulted in a politically powerless and diffuse class of people who are unable to coalesce with other groups of disabled people on common issues, to vote, to be seen or heard. This class has accepted the stigma and caste of second-hand citizenship and the incorrect judgement of social inferiority. (Funk, 1987, p. 24)

This description of the political situation fits in neatly with the 'underclass thesis' developed to explain the political situation of black people.

The usefulness of this idea of an underclass is still being debated and centres around the issue of whether an underclass is a subgroup of the working class or a group relegated to the margins of society on the basis of personal or group characteristics. In either case disabled people as an underclass are likely to remain powerless and marginalised, at least as far as organised political activity is concerned.

Thus it is unlikely that disabled people can expect the party political process to serve their interests well. We take the issue of anti-discrimination legislation, as an example. While it is true that this issue has been forced onto party political agendas, and indeed, several bills have even been introduced in parliament, all of these have been defeated, usually covertly, but on one occasion overtly, through the operation of the party political system; that is through a sustained campaign by Conservative whips to ensure that their party members voted it down (Oliver, 1985). Hence, disabled people can hardly expect to articulate and achieve their political ends through the party system, and this raises the question of whether they can expect pressure group activity to serve them better.

POLITICS OF PRESSURE GROUP ACTIVITY

From the mid-1960s onwards, it became clear that, despite rising affluence, a number of groups were not sharing in the new material and social benefits that were being created, and that traditional political activity was not even getting these issues onto the political agenda. Hence

> The creation of new kinds of pressure groups like Shelter, the Disablement Income Group and the Campaign Against Racial Discrimination, as well as the Child Poverty Action Group, in the mid-1960's, was more than a sign of the times. It was a reaction to what was perceived to be the fraudulent character of British democracy. There were of course special conditions which explained the new expressions of protest. Public expectations had been running high. The policies of successive Governments had been built on relatively full employment and steadily increasing national wealth. This meant that the views and interests of workers, pensioners and others were believed to weigh more heavily than they had done before the war in the conduct of national affairs . . . Some groups—like the elderly, one-parent families and sick and disabled people—were observed to have been left behind in the race for prosperity. (Townsend, 1986, pp. i-ii)

If, then, disabled people could not get issues onto the political agenda through the normal processes of political participation, then this raises the issue of whether the avenue of pressure group activity was likely to be more successful? The most sophisticated analysis of this so far is provided by Borsay (1986) who draws heavily on the framework provided by Cawson (1982). Cawson suggests that pluralist analyses of pressure group politics are now inadequate because of the nature of the 'corporate state', and that it is necessary to distinguish between competitive groups, whose members share a common interest, and corporate groups, whose members share a common position within the division of labour. Needless to say, it is the latter who have most influence on the political decision-making process. As most disability organisations are of the former kind, their partnership with government (Oliver, 1984) is unlikely to have much influence.

> This partnership does not inevitably banish the needs and opinions of physically disabled people from sight, but the allegiance of corporate professional interests to economic development stacks the cards against their faithful representation in the shaping and administration of policy. (Borsay, 1986, p. 15)

It is not, however, simply the structural location of these disability organisations that leads to such pessimism. As most of these organisations are registered as charities, direct and overt political activity is precluded. But more importantly, these disability organisations have, over the years, built up a relationship with the State, or the 'establishment' as Borsay calls it, which gives them credibility, but little power.

> The string of more formal voluntary organisations or charities, which for many years have doubled up as pressure groups in the field of physical handicap, meet the same structural barriers to change, but the status which flows from their long traditions and their connections with the 'establishment' give them a credibility and aura in government circles which more recent (and perhaps more radical) groups of disabled people cannot easily imitate. (Borsay, 1986, p. 16)

This credibility has been based upon history and tradition rather than the claim to representativeness of these organisations, whose 'key decision-makers' are usually salaried professional staff who articulate their own assumptions about the needs of disabled people rather than the needs of disabled people as they themselves express them. Two recent examples of this are the attempts of the Government with the public support of RADAR to abolish the Quota, established under the Disabled Persons' (Employment) Act 1944, and the opposition of the Spastics Society to anti-discrimination legislation. Pressure from individual disabled people and from organisations controlled and run by disabled people forced public about-turns in both cases.

There is one further aspect of the politics of disability as pressure group activity that needs to be considered; that of minority group politics. In the wake of the Civil Rights and Women's Movements in the United States in the 1960s, it was suggested that disabled people should seek to articulate and claim their rights to full citizenship on the basis of their own particular needs as a minority group (Hahn, 1986). However, there are problems with this approach for:

> The minority group approach basically argues that disabled people should be brought into the American political system as another interest group. The structure of decision making isn't attacked. Instead the idea is to improve the odds that the disabled will be recognised as having legitimate demands. (Liggett, 1988, p. 271)

Using what she calls "an interpretive approach", based on the work of Foucault, Liggett takes her criticisms further than this and argues that the politics of disability is structured by certain discursive practices. Thus the minority group approach

> . . . is double-edged because it means enlarging the discursive practices which participate in the constitution of disability. In other words, the price of becoming politically active on their own behalf is accepting the consequences of defining disability within new perspectives, which have their own priorities and needs. The new perspectives then become involved in disciplining disability. (Liggett, 1988, p. 271)

Thus, accepting disabled people as a minority group also involves the accepting of the disabled-nondisabled distinction; accepting the 'normalising' society.

This has implications for disabled people seeking to gain control over their own lives for

> . . . in order to participate in their own management disabled people have to participate as disabled. Even among the politically active, the price of being heard is understanding that it is the disabled who are speaking. (Liggett, 1988, p. 273)

While not disagreeing with this analysis of the politics of disability as minority group activity, Liggett's problems arise when she suggests alternative political strategies. These strategies involve 'reflection' and sometimes the acceptance and sometimes the rejection of disabled identities depending upon the specifics of particular situations.

However, such strategies would inevitably look like special pleading and further, move away from the strategies disabled people have chosen for themselves; that is the personal and public affirmation of disabled identities and the demands that disabled people be accepted by and integrated into society as they are; that is, as disabled people.

Thus, the structural position of these organisations, their relationship to the State, their non-representativeness in terms of the needs and wishes of disabled people and their acceptance of the normalising of society, lead to the inevitable conclusion that

> . . ., for disabled people,. . ., the chances of immediate and radical reform of social policies are slim. (Borsay, 1986, p. 19)

It is hard to disagree with this conclusion when analysing disability pressure group activity from a pluralist, corporatist or minority group position, but an analysis based upon the idea of 'new social movements' within late capitalism can lead to very different conclusions indeed. However, that is the subject of later sections of this paper and no discussion of pressure group activity would be complete without some discussion of the single, most sustained example of pressure group activity within the field of disability; the campaign for a national disability income.

A NATIONAL DISABILITY INCOME

The campaign for a national disability income began in 1965 with the formation of the Disablement Income Group (DIG) by two disabled housewives. This group provided a major focus for pressure group activity and published plans for a national disability income comprising two elements; a disablement costs allowance and an income maintenance scheme. A decade later, the Disability Alliance was formed, initially comprising over 50 voluntary organisations, which has now grown to over 90, and they put foward their own proposals which were broadly similar to those of DIG. Recently both have updated their plans (DIG, 1987; Disability Alliance, 1987), which are again broadly similar, except that the Alliance proposals plan to incorporate a separate, independent benefit for those who care for a disabled person, whereas DIG argue that if disabled people were given a proper, adequate income, it would be unnecessary to pay carers separately.

There are difficulties in assessing the success or failure of these pressure group activities over the last 20 years, though it has to be said that a national disability income has not yet become a reality. On the other hand, all of the major political parties have made public commitments to the establishment of such a scheme (Disability Alliance, 1987, pp. 4-5), but have couched these pronouncements with get out clauses such as 'when economic circumstances permit' and 'as a matter of priority'.

> Despite these expressed commitments, no substantial progress has been made towards the introduction of a comprehensive disability income scheme. The past decade has instead seen a series of piecemeal changes which, although sometimes useful, have failed to correct the longstanding anomalies in social security provision for people with disabilities. Furthermore, in a number of vital areas, benefits have been cut and new anomalies created. (Disability Alliance, 1987, p. 5)

So, during the past 20 years there have been some incremental improvements, usually connected to the performance of the economy, but there have also been reversals.

There are a number of reasons why this sustained campaign has been unsuccessful. To begin with, both DIG and the Alliance have suffered from the problem already referred to, in that as registered charities, they have been unable to campaign in an overt political way. They have therefore found it necessary to divide their organisations into two component parts in order to retain their charitable status and to continue with political activities. In addition, both organisations have found it necessary to set up information and advisory services in order to steer disabled people through the maze of benefits and to help individuals to receive all the benefits they are entitled to. Finally, they have carried out research to demonstrate that the financial position of disabled people is considerably worse than that of their able-bodied counterparts. Hence, neither organisation has been able to concentrate solely on pressure group activities.

Both groups can also be criticised for taking a somewhat naïve view of the political process in that their campaigning is based upon three assumptions: that evidence must be produced to show the chronic financial circumstances of disabled people; that proposals for a national disability income must be properly costed to show that the burden on the economy will be marginal; and that sustained pressure must be mounted to hammer these points home to the political decision-makers.' This approach has been called 'the social administration approach' and has been criticised for its assumptions about consensual values, rational decision-making, its unproblematic view of the State and its failure to acknowledge, let alone consider the role of, ideology. Perhaps the only thing that can be said in its favour is that

> If the empiricist study of consensual solutions to defined social problems did not exist, it would be necessary to invent it: democratic welfare capitalism presupposes the social administration approach. (Taylor-Gooby & Dale, 1981, p. 15)

What the income approach to disability fails to understand, therefore, is that political decisions are not made on the strength of particular cases, but in ways whereby the capitalist system itself benefits, regardless of the appearance of consensual values concerning the need for a national disability income. The establishment of such a scheme implies the paying of one group of people a sufficient income for not working to enable them to have a qualily of life comparable to another group of people who do work. This, of course, has enormous implications for any system which requires its members to produce sufficient goods and services to sustain the material life of the population, and indeed for its ideological underpinnings which emphasise the value of those who do work and denigrates those who do not. In short, the fundamental question of whether a national disability income is achievable within capitalism has never been addressed.

It is this failure to address fundamental issues which has brought criticism of both DIG and the Disability Alliance from the more 'populist' organisation, the Union of the Physically Impaired Against Segregation (UPIAS). The two major criticisms of this approach are that it concentrates on a symptom (i.e. the poverty of disabled people) rather than the cause (i.e. the oppression of disabled people by society), and that both organisations have moved away from representing disabled people and instead presenting an 'expert' view of the problem. The logical conclusion to this approach, according to this analysis, is to make things worse, not better.

> Thus in practice the Alliance's assessment plans, developed logically from the narrow incomes approach, can be seen to increase the isolation and oppression of physically impaired people. We would be required to sit alone under observation on one side of the table, while facing us on the other side, social administrators would sit together in panels. We would be passive, nervous, deferential, careful not to upset the panel: in short, showing all the psychological attributes commonly associated with disability. It would be the social administrators who would gain strength, support and confidence from colleagues on the panel. A token number of the more privileged physically impaired people might be included, as they are in the Alliance. But the whole approach would reinforce the historical and traditional situation whereby physically impaired people are made dependent upon the thinking and decisions of others. (UPIAS, 1976, p. 18)

This debate about 'expert or 'mass' representation in respect of pressure group activity has continued into the 1980s, with Townsend (1986) claiming that these groups can only be 'representative' in certain senses.

> But what they can do is commit themselves unreservedly to the interests of millions of poor people, call representative injustices to public notice and exchange blow with blow in an expert struggle with the Government over the effects, implications and constitutional niceties of policy. (Townsend, 1986, p. v)

But like UPIAS before it, BCODP denies the claims of such groups to be representative in any sense, suggests that expert representation can only be counter-productive and argues that the only way forward is to fully involve disabled people in their own political movement.

If this analysis is correct, then it is, perhaps, fortunate that a national disability income is likely to be unachievable within capitalist society. The crucial issue from a political point of view, however, is whether the traditional, single-issue, pressure group campaign for a national disability income is, any longer, a relevant tactic for the post-capitalist world to which we are moving. The following sections will suggest that the politics of disablement can only be properly understood as part of the new social movements which are a part of post-capitalist society and that this casts severe doubt on the relevance of single-issue pressure group politics.

THE EMERGENCE OF NEW SOCIAL MOVEMENTS

Changes in the economy to one driven by consumption rather than production, the rise in technology, changing occupational patterns, social disorganisation affecting family and social life, increasing crime and hooliganism, crises in the welfare state, the ecological crisis and various kinds of political unrest have all been features of capitalism in the late twentieth century. This has led some commentators to characterise the end of the twentieth century as the era of late capitalism or to herald the coming of post-industrial or post-capitalist society.

This has had an influence on the political system and since the 1970s there has been an emergence of many new movements comprising neighbourhood groups, environmentalists, the unemployed, welfare recipients, minority groups and "the generally disenfranchised" (Castells, 1978; Touraine, 1981; Boggs, 1986). These movements have been seen as constituting the social basis for new forms of transformative political action or change. These social movements are 'new' in the sense that they are not grounded in traditional forms of political participation through the party system or single-issue, pressure group activity targeted at political decision-makers.

Instead, they are culturally innovative in that they are part of the underlying struggles for genuine participatory democracy, social equality and justice, which have arisen out of "the crisis in industrial culture" (Touraine, 1981). These new social movements are consciously engaged in a critical evaluation of capitalist society and in the creation of alternative models of social organisation at local, national and international levels, as well as trying to reconstruct the world ideologically and to create alternative forms of service provision. It is in this sense that Touraine (1981) defines such movements as "socially conflictful" and "culturally oriented forms of behaviour".

THE DISABILITY MOVEMENT AS A NEW SOCIAL MOVEMENT

There are four characteristics of new social movements that can be considered as relevant to the disability movement as a new social movement. The first of these is that they tend to be located at the periphery of the traditional political system and, in fact, sometimes they are deliberately marginalised (Hardin, 1982). This is certainly true of the disability movement which does not have the same relationship to the State as do the organisations for the disabled, either in terms of consultation procedures, lobbying, or indeed resourcing. For example, RADAR, the umbrella 'organisation for', is usually given a grant of £225,000 per year by the DHSS, whereas its 'organisation of' counterpart, BCODP, is lucky to get £10,000 per year.

However, this does not mean that the political significance and meaning of the disability movement can be taken to be marginal, nor, indeed, its transformative potential. New social movements in general do have great significance and meaning in the changing political circumstances that are currently occurring.

> The changing nature of political interests is most clearly focused around what have come to be termed as 'new social movements' .... The new social movements are characterised not only by a greater willingness to employ a wide variety of forms of political action, but also by an underlying orientation towards political values that have widespread ramifications. In particular their underlying scheme of values stress the importance of political participation and personal self-actualisation in ways that have implications for the forms that political behaviour takes. (Weale, 1988, pp. 1-2)

This definition accurately fits in with the emergence of self-help/populist groups within the disability movement, both in terms of the importance such groups place on personal self-actualisation, and their willingness to follow pro-active strategies towards what, ultimately, become political goals.

> Self-help groups were slow to develop . . .but they have flourished and have become a powerful source of mutual support, education and action among people affected by particular health concerns or disabilities . . . while learning and working together, disabled people can combine their power to influence social and political decisions that affect their lives. (Crewe & Zola, 1983, pp. xiii-xiv)

However, the development of self-help strategies can initially be purely practical, rather than explicity political. One case study highlights the way in which the selfhelp approach is often a response to the perceived failings in professional service provision. Thus while the initial impetus was to encourage disabled people "to solve their problems themselves and not have them solved for them", there was also a further aim which was 'to identify the needs of the membership as a whole and articulate them, both to statutory agencies and political parties at both a local and a national level" (Oliver & Hasler, 1987, p. 116).
Hence,

> The self-help movement is, however, but one part of the struggle. It is a pre-requisite for change, but neither the sole nor the sufficient avenue. We must deal as much with social arrangements as with self-conceptions; one, in fact, reinforces the other. (Zola, 1979, p. 455)

This link between the personal and the political is often an integral feature of these new social movements

> To varying degrees and in varying ways the new movements also seek to connect the personal (or cultural) and political realms, or at least they raise psychological issues that were often submerged or ignored . . . (Boggs, 1986, p. 51)

A specific form of self-help, more or less unique to the disability movement and, perhaps, the clearest practical illustration of the ways in which the disability movement corresponds with general definitions of new movements, can be found in the increasing numbers of Centres for Independent and Integrated Living (CILs) being established both in the UK and in other countries, including the United States, Australia, Canada and Japan. CILs represent both an attempt to achieve self-actualisation, and a form of direct action aimed at creating new solutions to problems defined by disabled people themselves (Oliver, 1987).

The second characteristic of new social movements is that they offer a critical evaluation of society as a part of "a conflict between a declining but still vigorous system of domination and newly emergent forms of opposition" (Boggs, 1986, p. 4). Ideologically, the Independent Living Movement, which led to the establishment of the first CILs in California and other parts of the United States in the late 1960s, also represents an explicit critique of prevailing social structures and the position of disabled people within them. The rationale behind the Independent Living Movement was that the obstacles to self-actualisation were perceived to be the result of living in hostile physical and social environments and the fact that what services were provided were restricting rather than enabling. The movement set about attempting to change this situation, first by redefining the problem in this way and then by setting up alternative kinds of service provision under the control of disabled people themselves.

The third characteristic of new social movements resulting from fundamental changes in the constitution of the political agenda has been

> an increasing predominance of. . . 'post-materialist' or 'post-acquisitive' values over those that have to do with income, satisfaction of material needs and social security. (Offe, 1980, p. 12)

While it is certainly true that the disability movement is concerned with issues relating to the quality of life of disabled people, it is also true that many disabled people still face material deprivation as well as social disadvantage and the movement is centrally concerned with this. It would be inaccurate to attempt to characterise the disability movement as stemming from a middle-class, disabled élite concerned only with their own quality of life, as Williams (1983) attempts to do in his critique of the Independent Living Movement.

A final characteristic of new social movements is that they sometimes tend to focus on issues that cross national boundaries and hence they become internationalist. This is certainly true of the disability movement and at Disabled People's International (DPI) Second World Congress, the objectives and strategies underlying the international movement were clearly defined around the central issues of empowerment and of disabled people acting collectively to achieve collective goals. It was noted by the Congress that

> ... political action aimed at governmental bodies—or at private groups or individuals, was more likely to produce results than through a legislative or constitutional route. Countries which had passed legislation favourable to disabled people, did not necessarily find that improved conditions followed—or that disabled people had more control over their lives as a result. The prerequisite for successful action lay in the proper organisation of disabled persons groups, and the development of a high level of public awareness of disability issues.... This did not necessarily mean that disabled people's organisations were in an antagonistic relationship to established organisations which were not controlled by disabled people. But it did mean that our own organisations should assert that they were the true and valid voice of disabled people and our needs. (DPI, 1986, p. 21)

The significance of these other social movements is that they are taken as evidence of the emergence of a 'post-materialist paradigm'. The common denominator amongst these movements, including the disability movement, is that they typically emerge as a response to the perceived failure of existing political institutions and strategies to achieve the objectives of a particular social group as they themselves define them. This has been particularly true in the United States where the civil rights tradition has profoundly influenced the disability movement.

> The civil rights movement has had an effect not only on the securing of certain rights but also on the manner in which these rights have been secured. When traditional legal channels have been exhausted, disabled people have learned to employ other techniques of social protest. (De Jong, 1983, p. 12).

Lacking such a tradition in Britain, and not even having basic rights enshrined in law through anti-discrimination legislation, the disability movement in this country has been more circumspect in terms of tactics, although the lessons of the American movement have been noted and there have been a few organised boycotts, sit-ins and street demonstrations.

The discussion so far has indicated that the disability movement can, indeed, be considered as part of a new social movement generally. The crucial question this therefore raises is what does it mean for political action in general and the possibility of improving the quality of life for disabled people in particular?

NEW DIRECTIONS FOR THE FUTURE

Thus far, attempts to consider the meaning and significance of these new social movements generally (Laclau & Mouffe, 1985; Boggs, 1986) have usually taken place within a framework derived from the work of Gramsci (1971). Within this framework there are three discrete areas that need to be considered—the economy, the State and civil society—all given a sense of unity by the concept of hegemony. For Gramsci, the economy referred to the dominant mode of production; the State consisted of all State-funded institutions including the political, the bureaucratic and the means of violence; the term civil society

> connotes the other organizations in a social formation which are neither part of the processes of material production in the economy, nor part of state funded organizations, but which are relatively long-lasting institutions supported and run by people outside of the other two major spheres. (Bocock, 1987, pp. 33-34)

The importance of the concept of hegemony in Gramsci was that it claimed that dominance, or leadership of all the people, could never be simply reduced to dominance in the economic sphere, but could be established within the State or civil society. Thus, politics, not economics, can have a central role in the establishment of hegemony, and within Gramsci's framework this politics can take place both within the State and civil society, although

> The borderline between state and civil society is a constantly shifting one and one which has to be negotiated, maintained and continually readjusted over time. (Bocock, 1987, p. 34)

To put the matter simply, political activity within the State comprises traditional party politics and corporatist pressure group activities; political activity within civil society comprises the activities of the new social movements. The crucial issue for these new social movements thus becomes one of how far they can effect political and social change, either by shifting power across the borderline and away from State political institutions, or by exerting greater and greater external influence on these existing institutions. It is within this framework that consideration can be given to the significance of the disability movement as a new social movement.

A major factor to be considered in the development of post-capitalist society is the influence of new technological developments on the economic, social and material needs of disabled people. Finkelstein (1980), while not specifically calling Phase 3 of his model post-capitalism, is clear where both the problem and the solution, lies.

Disabled people, also, no less than able-bodied people, need to express their essential human nature by moulding the social and material environment and so influence the course of history. What stands in the way, (at a time when the material and technological basis for solving the human and material needs of disabled people have mostly been solved), is the dominance of phase 2 attitudes and relationships. Such attitudes take society and, indeed, the dependency relationship as given. (Finkelstein, 1980, p. 39)

But not all commentators see the issue as one of out-dated attitudes, moulding technology in particular directions but point to the fact that technology itself will not necessarily produce or equally distribute its benefits (Habermas, 1971; Illich, 1973). These technological developments have not been universally welcomed either in terms of health care in general (Reiser, 1978; Taylor, 1979) or disability in particular (Oliver, 1978). Zola, writing from his own experience, has suggested that

Technology can do too much for those of us with disabilities. The machines that technology creates may achieve such completeness that they rob us of our integrity by making us feel useless. (Zola, 1982, p. 395)

And he applies this analysis not just to the development of machines, gadgets and prostheses, but also to what he calls "the over-technicalization of care".

To be handled by a machine or animal, where once I was handled by a person can only be invalidating of me as a person. (Zola, 1982, p. 396)

Further, in terms of its effects on the work system and the material and social environments, it may be oppressive rather than liberating. In a review of changes in the work system in what he calls "post-industrial society", Cornes (1988) discusses both the optimistic and pessimistic views of the effects of new technology on the work opportunities of disabled people. He suggests that such developments can be viewed optimistically,

New jobs and new opportunities to organise and locate work on an entirely different basis using new technologies are increasingly being perceived as offering even more grounds for optimism. This is because such new jobs, in which physical requirements are replaced by electronic skill, strength and precision are particularly suitable for people with disabilities, and because new developments in communications have increased opportunities for home-based employment. (Cornes, 1988, p. 15)

But he then sounds a cautionary note, suggesting that many disabled people may not have the educational opportunities or training potential to take advantage of such opportunities. Further, the new skills that will be required to master new technology may require a degree of confidence and independent thinking that many disabled people currently lack. Finally, he suggests that many disabled people are already falling behind in the mastery of these skills "because of problems of access, mobility, finance and discriminatory attitudes" (Cornes, 1988).

He agrees with Finkelstein's (1980) analysis that the probiem is that while we are in Phase 3 in terms of economic and technological developments, we, nonetheless, remain locked into Phase 2 attitudes, or in his terms, that "existing policies, programmes, attitudes and expectations may be too dependent on the institutional arrangements, values and ideals of an industrial society" (Cornes, 1988). And he goes on to locate the solution as being in the hands of the disability movement itself.

> Their successful participation in all spheres of life within post-industrial society— economic, cultural and political—will depend greatly on the extent to which they themselves and their supporters can lay claim to and exercise that right not only during the transition from school to work but throughout their lifetimes. (Cornes, 1988, p. 17)

If then, the disability movement is central to ensuring that technology is used to liberate rather than further oppress disabled people, then a clear understanding of its double-edged nature needs to be developed within the movement. A start in this direction has been made by recognising that the mentality which allows technology to be used for evil purposes is the very same mentality which facilitates the oppression (and indeed, even the creation) of disabled people.

> Relentlessly, the connection between disability and the bomb becomes clear. The mentality that made Cheshire a compliant participant in the mass creation of disability at Hiroshima is the same mentality which made him the instigator of the mass incarceration of disabled people in a chain of segregated institutions. In the first case he went over the tops of the heads of disabled people in a B29 bomber, in the second he went over our heads in the name of charity. Increasingly, over the years, both actions have come to attract our abhorrence . . . we have to find the strength to *INSIST* that our representative organisations are fully involved in decisions about the dismantling of disabled apartheid. And we have to add our INSTANT voice to the clamour for WORLD DISARMAMENT—with the aim of removing for all time, this particular and horrifying cause of unnecessary disability. (Davis, 1986, p. 3)

But in order to challenge what might be called attitudes (Finkelstein, Cornes), mentality (Davis) or more properly, in the context of this analysis, ideology, then clearly the disability movement must work out an appropriate political strategy. As has already been indicated, this cannot be done through traditional political participation in parties or pressure groups, but has to be addressed in terms of the relationship between the disability movement and the State, the second element within Gramsci's (1971) framework.

The relationships of these new social movements in general to the State have been considered in some detail and raise crucial issues of political strategy.

> If social movements carry forward a revolt of civil society against the state—and thus remain largely outside the bourgeois public sphere—they typically have failed to engage the state system as part of a larger democratizing project. In the absence of a coherent approach to the state, political strategy is rendered abstract and impotent. (Boggs, 1986, pp. 56-7)

On the other hand, to engage in an uncritical relationship to the State, is to risk at best, incorporation and absorption, and at worst, isolation and marginalisation and perhaps, ultimately, oblivion.

Leaving aside the question of whether the State represents specific interests or is relatively autonomous, the disability movement has to decide how it wishes such a relationship to develop. Should it settle for incorporation into State activities with the prospect of piecemeal gains in social policy and legislation with the risks that representations to political institutions will be ignored or manipulated? Or, should it remain separate from the State and concentrate on consciousness-raising activities leading to long-term changes in policy and practice and the empowerment of disabled people, with the attendant risks that the movement may be marginalised or isolated?

In practice it cannot be a matter of choosing one or the other of these positions, for the disability movement must develop a relationship with the State so that it can secure proper resources and play a role in changing social policy and professional practice. On the other hand, it must remain independent of the State to ensure that the changes that take place do not ultimately reflect the establishment view and reproduce paternalistic and dependency-creating services, but are based upon changing and dynamic conceptions of disability as articulated by disabled people themselves. Such is the nature of a crucial issue facing the disability movement over the next few years and the complexities of the task should not be underestimated.

In order, however, to develop an appropriate relationship with the State, all new social movements, including the disability movement, must establish a firm basis within civil society.

> The important point is that these movements, as emergent, broad-based agencies of social change, are situated primarily within civil society rather than the conventional realm of pluralist democracy. Further, the tendency toward convergence of some movements (for example, feminism and the peace movement) gives them a radical

potential far greater than the sum of particular groups. Even though their capacity to overthrow any power structure is still minimal, they have begun to introduce a new language of critical discourse that departs profoundly from the theory and practice of conventional politics. (Boggs, 1986, p. 22)

Thus, because these movements are developing within the separate sphere of civil society, they do not risk incorporation into the State, nor indeed do they need to follow a political agenda or strategy set by the State. Hence, they can engage in consciousness raising activities, demonstrations, sit-ins and other forms of political activity within civil society. Further, they can develop links with each other so that their potential as a whole is greater than that of their constituent parts. Finally, the relationship to organised labour needs to be renegotiated, which means that labour will have "to confront its own legacy of racism, sexism and national chauvinism" because

The complex relationship between labour and social movements, class and politics—not to mention the recomposition of the workforce itself—invalidates any scheme that assigns to labour a hegemonic or privileged role in social transformation. (Boggs, 1986, p. 233)

As far as the disability movement is concerned, its growth and development have been within the realm of civil society. It has used consciousness and self-affirmation as a political tactic and has begun to be involved in political activities such as demonstrations and sit-ins outside the realm of State political activities. By reconceptualising disability as social restriction or oppression, it has opened up the possibilities of collaborating or co-operating with other socially restricted or oppressed groups.

But it has also crossed the borderline between the State and civil society by developing its own service provision, sometimes in conflict and sometimes in co-operation with State professionals, and has, on occasions, engaged in interest representation within the State political apparatus. The issue of crossing the borderline to the economy and establishing links with organised labour, however, has yet to be properly addressed. It could be said that as well as overcoming its racism, sexism and chauvinism, organised labour has to overcome its disablism too. While the labour movement has been broadly supportive in wishing to retain the Quota, established by the Disabled Persons (Employment) Act 1944, it has been disablist in its resistance to changing work practices to facilitate the employment of disabled people and to re-writing job specifications to enable disabled people to get the kind of personal support they need to live better lives in both the community and residential care.

COUNTER-HEGEMONIC POLITICS

The concept of hegemony is a unifying one in that it contextualises the relationships between the economy, the State and civil society. While hegemony may be exercised in all three realms,

> In any given historical situation, hegemony is only going to be found as the partial exercise of leadership of the dominant class, or alliance of class fractions, in some of these spheres but not in all of them equally successfully at all times. (Bocock, 1987, p. 94)

And this of course raises the possibility of counter-hegemonic tendencies emanating from civil society rather than from traditional political institutions or changes within the economy, for

> Contemporary social movements are thus hardly marginal expressions of protest but are situated within the unfolding contradictions of a rapidly changing industrial order, as part of the historic attempts to secure genuine democracy, social equality, and peaceful international relations against the imperatives of exploitation and domination. (Boggs, 1986, p. 3)

And it is not unrealistic to suggest that only when peace, democracy and equality have been secured, can the social restrictions and oppressions associated with disability be eradicated. This article has suggested that the disability movement has a central role to play in the eradication of these restrictions and oppressions as part of the emergent new social movements.

It has to be admitted that nowhere in the world have these new movements been successful in overturning the status quo. Their significance has been in placing new issues onto the political agenda, in presenting old issues in new forms and, indeed, in opening up new areas and arenas of political discourse. It is their counter-hegemonic potential, not their actual achievements, that are significant in late capitalism.

> To say that the new movements have a counter-hegemonic potential is also to suggest that they have emerged in opposition (at least partially) to those ideologies that legitimate the power structure; technological rationality, nationalism, competitive individualism, and, of course, racism and sexism. (Boggs, 1986, p. 243)

It is a pity that the ideology of disablism has not been incorporated into this quote, for clearly this has been central to the issues that the disability movement has begun to address. In its short history, the disability movement has had considerable impact on policy formulation and is beginning to influence service provision in Britain. This process will undoubtedly gain in strength in the next few years and its significance within changing political processes will gradually emerge. This will have a wider significance in that it will challenge the dominant ideologies of individualism and normality upon which post-capitalist society is based. Hence, the disability movement will come to have a central role in counter-hegemonic politics and the social transformation upon which this will eventually be based.

ACKNOWLEDGEMENT

This paper is based upon a broader consideration of disability in society presented in *The Politics of Disablement* (London, Macmillan, 1990).

REFERENCES

BOCOCK, R. (1987) *Hegemony* (London, Tavistock).

BOGGS C. (1986) *Social Movements and Political Power* (Philadelphia, PA, Temple University Press).

BORSAY, A. (1986) *Disabled People in the Community* (London, Bedford Square Press).

CASTELLS, M. (1978) *City, Class and Power* (Basingstoke, Macmillan).

CAWSON, A. (1982) *Corporatism and Welfare: social policy and state intervention in Britain* (London, Heinemann).

CORNES, P. (1988) The role of work in the socialisation of young people wlth disabilities in a post-industrial society paper presented at *OECD Conference Adult Status for Youth with Disabilities*, Sigtuna, Sweden.

CREWE, N. & ZOLA, I. (1983) *Independent Living for Physically Disabled People* (London, Jossey-Bass).

DAVIS, K. (1986) DISABILITY and the BOMB—the connection, Clay Cross, Derbyshire, *Coalition of Disabled People Newsletter.*

DE JONG, G. (1983) Defining and implementing the independent living concept, in: N. CREWE & I. ZOLA (Eds) *Independent Living for Physically Disabled People* (London, Jossey-Bass)

DIG (1987) DIG's National Disability Income (London, DIG)

DISABILITY ALLIANCE (1987) *Poverty and Disability: breaking the link* (London, Disability Alliance).

DPI (1986) DPI—*Calling, European Regional Newsletter*, 1, March.

FINKELSTEIN, V. (1980) *Attitudes and Disabled People: issues for discussion* (New York, World Rehabilitation Fund).

FRY, E. (1987) *Disabled People and the 1987 General Election* (London, Spastics Society).

FUNK, R. (1987) Disability rights: from caste to class in the context of civil rights, in: A. GARTNER & T. JOE (Eds) *Images of the Disabled, Disabling Images* (New York, Praeger).

GRAMSCI, A. (1971) *Selections from the Prison Notebooks* (London, Lawrence & Wishart).

HABERMAS, J. (1971) *Toward a Rational Society* (London, Heinemann).

HAHN, H. (1986) Public support for rehabilitation programs: the analysis of US disability policy, *Disability, Handicap & Society*, 1(2).

HARDIN, B. (1982) *Collective Action* (Baltimore, MD, Johns Hopkins University Press).

ILLICH, I. (1973) *Tools for Conviviality* (London, Calder & Boyars).

LACLAU, E. & MOUFFE, C. (1985) *Hegemony and Socialist Strategy. Towards a Radical Democratic Politics* (London, Verso).

LIGGETT, H. (1988) Stars are not born: an interactive approach to the politics of disability, *Disability, Handicap & Society*, 3(3).

OFFE, C. (1980) The separation of form and content in liberal democratic politics, *Studies in Political Economy*, 3.

OLIVER, M. (1978) Medicine and technology: steps in the wrong direction, *International Journal of Medical Engineering and Technology*, 2(3).

OLIVER, M. (1984) The politics of disability, *Critical Social Policy*, 11.

OLIVER, M. (1985) Discrimination disability and social policy, in: M. BRENTON & C. JONES (Eds) *The Yearbook of Social Policy 1984-5* (London, Routledge & Kegan Paul).

OLIVER, M. (1987) From strength to strength, *Community Care*.

OLIVER, M. & HASLER, F. (1987) Disability and self-help: a case study of the spinal injuries association, *Disability, Handicap & Society*, 2(2), pp. 113-125.

REISER, S. (1978) *Medicine and the Rise of Technology* (New York, Cambridge University Press).

TAYLOR, R. (1979) *Medicine Out of Control* (Melbourne, Sun).

TAYLOR-GOOBY, P. & DALE, J. (1981) *Social Theory and Social Welfare* (London, Edward Arnold).

TOURAINE, A. (1981) *The Voice and the Eye: an analysis of social movements* (Cambridge, Cambridge University Press).

TOWNSEND, P. (1986) Democracy for the poor, Foreword in: M. MCCARTHY (Ed.) *Campaigning for the Poor: CPAG and the Politics of Welfare* (Beckenham, Croom Helm).

UPIAS (1976) *Fundamental principles of disability* (London, Union of the Physically Impaired Against Segregation).

WEALE, A. (1988) *New social movements and political change*, Draft Initiative Proposal prepared for ESRC (Society and Politics Research Development Group).

WILLIAMS, G. (1983) The movement for independent living: an evaluation and critique, *Social Science & Medicine*, 17(15).

ZOLA, I. (1979) Helping one another: a speculative history of the self-help movement, *Archives of Physical Medicine & Rehabilitation*, 60.

ZOLA, I. (1982) Social and cultural disincentives to independent living, *Archives of Physical Medicine and Rehabilitation*, 63.

CHAPTER 13

Cultural Representation of Disabled People:
dustbins for disavowal?

Tom Shakespeare

(First published 1994)

INTRODUCTION

The majority of sociological renderings of disablement gloss over aspects of normality, conformity and difference, and focus instead on the performative aspects of impairment. Radical views of disability have sought to situate their analysis firmly within sociology: thus Oliver draws on Comte, Marx and Weber in a very conventional analysis of the disability experience. With an explicit rejection of methodological individualism goes a rejection of 'psychologically inclined' explanations: in their place Oliver puts a 'materialist' approach, focusing on societal structures. In some part this is a reaction to psychological research on attitudes to disability, which has never questioned individualistic understandings of impairment (the 'individual medical tragedy theory'). However, the effect is to neglect the potential contribution of social psychology and anthropology to the understanding of disability: to bracket, that is, questions of culture, representation and meaning.

Oliver devotes just two pages to issues of cultural imagery in his major monograph on disability. Writers such as Finkelstein, and the prevailing orthodoxy of the 'social oppression' theories underpinning the political movement of disabled liberation are generally in accord with Oliver's position. Only recently have writers, predominantly feminists, reconceptualized disability. I would suggest that some of the lack of weight given to cultural imagery and difference stems from the neglect of impairment: Liz Crow has recently suggested that the Social Model needs to be developed, in order to conceptualize this experience (Crow, 1992). If Social Model analysis seeks to ignore, rather than explore the individual experience of impairment (be it blindness, short stature or whatever), then it is unsurprising that it should also gloss over the cultural representation of impairment, because to do otherwise would be potentially to undermine the argument.

However, this is clearly not an inevitable outcome of stressing the role of impairment. Robert Connell, in the context of sex/gender distinction, illustrates how there is no necessity of a causal linking between biological and social processes: the latter centrally concerns issues of meaning, which are socially invested:

> In fact the social practices are not reflecting natural differences with these diacritical marks of gender. They are weaving a structure of symbol and interpretation around them, and often vastly exaggerating or distorting them. (Connell, 1987, p. 80)

In this article I will first explore the role of impairment imagery, and subsequently discuss cultural representation of disabled people in terms of ideology, otherness, anomaly and liminality.

IMAGERY AND IMPAIRMENT

Here I will examine some meanings given to impairment in western culture. Subsequently, I will try and develop theoretical insights into this process, before going on to ask why impairment becomes so significant for human culture.

Some recent texts on disability have covered aspects of cultural representation. In general, these approaches are more likely to be feminist-inspired, and follow on from feminist concerns with social representation of femininity, cultural stereotypes, norms of physical beauty and so forth. From this perspective, the particular situation of disabled people, women especially, is a more extreme version of the general experience of all women.

Thus the feminist discussion of media representation, *Out of Focus* (Davies *et al.*, 1987) included a chapter discussing views of disability. Contemporary attitudes, for example the tendency to exaggeration and romanticization of disability, are compared with the prevailing focus on beauty and normality. The latter values are deeply divisive for all women, but particularly oppress those whose bodies do not fit the stereotype. Media treatments depoliticize struggles of disabled people by always taking an individualized perspective, focusing on disability as personal misfortune.

In *Disability, Whose Handicap,* Ann Shearer (1981) takes a more historical approach to representation, highlighting the moral attitudes underlying discrimination. In Classical drama, the villain had red hair; in Victorian children's books, crippled young people teach messages of courage, forgiveness and generosity; witches were always ugly, and villains generally have had impairment—Captain Hook, Long John Silver and all.

I would point to the ubiquity of disability within wider literary sources, ranging historically and culturally: thus Shakespeare uses impairment, symbolically and metaphorically, in plays such as *Richard III* and *King Lear*, while the Bible employs such techniques extensively (Holden, 1991). Certain forms of impairment are almost exclusively used in these ways, while others are ignored. Epilepsy, restricted growth and sensory impairments, together with the figures of the cripple and the leper, are the common stock of cultural representations of disability, being conditions with specific resonance and literary utility.

The focus on literary and cultural representation is developed in an American collection, *Images of the Disabled, Disabling Images.* Kriegel suggests that

> The world of the crippled and disabled is strange and dark, and it is held up to judgement by those who live in fear of it. The cripple is the creature who has been deprived of his ability to create a self. ... He is the other, if for no other reason than that only by being the other will he be allowed to presume upon the society of the "normals." He must accept definition from outside the boundaries of his own existence. (Kreigel, 1987, p. 33)

He goes on to outline stereotypes such as the Demonic Cripple, the Charity Cripple and the Realistic Cripple, referring to a wide range of literary sources, including *Lady Chatterly's Lover* and *Moby Dick.*

These typically negative renderings are especially oppressive for women, as Deborah Kent suggests:

> Disability seems to undermine the very roots of her womanhood. Not surprisingly, therefore, the disabled women in these works frequently feel inferior to others and regard themselves with loathing. (Kent, 1987, p. 63)

She shows how it is not the disabled person themselves that the author is concerned with, as subjects, but the disabled person as vehicle, as object:

> In many instances, the disabled woman is little more than a metaphor through which the writer hopes to address some broader theme. (*ibid.*, p. 60)

This point is made also by Kriegel, when he suggests that Clifford Chatterley is a cipher: the impotent industrialist into whom Lawrence pours everything that he abhors about modern industrial society. Not one of the many books centring on disabled women that Kent analyses is actually written by a disabled woman (although more recently several collections have been published).

A third essay in this collection illustrates how disability imagery is prevalent in contemporary film and television, yet is rarely recognized as such: Paul Longmore points out how even popular cartoon characters like Porky Pig and Elmer Fudd carry messages about impairment and identity. He argues that it is fear of disability which underlies these presentations:

> What we fear, we often stigmatize and shun and sometimes seek to destroy. Popular entertainments depicting disabled characters allude to these fears and prejudices or address them obliquely or fragmentarily, seeking to reassure us about ourselves. (Longmore, 1987, p. 66)

I suggest that these analyses, albeit individualist and fragmentary, are beginning a process parallel to that epitomized by Kate Millet in *Sexual Politics*, or Mary Ellman in *Thinking About Women*, two works of feminist literary theory that, for the first time, devoted attention to the ideologies of women evident in much mainstream literature.

Two British works have developed the analysis of disability within cultural theory. From a mainstream social research perspective, Cumberbatch & Negrine's (1992) content analysis of British TV, *Images of Disability on Television*, reinforces many of the conclusions made in the American collection. Disabled people are either absent from the 'TV population' or else occur in a limited number of roles. Colin Barnes (1992) study for the British Council of

Organizations of Disabled People certainly holds to this philosophy. In an examination of disabling imagery, Barnes isolates the same series of one-dimensional portrayals of disabled people, within newspapers, television, film and other areas of popular culture. Barnes' conclusions summarize this situation, and are welcome evidence that the official disability movement is recognizing the need for work in this area:

> Disabling stereotypes which medicalise, patronise, criminalise and dehumanise disabled people abound in books, films, on television, and in the press. They form the bedrock on which the attitudes towards, assumptions about and expectations of disabled people are based. They are fundamental to the discrimination and exploitation which disabled people encounter daily and contribute significantly to their systematic exclusion from mainstream community life. (Barnes, 1992, p. 39)

A recent work from within the movement, which develops the theme of cultural representation further than most such publications, is Jenny Morris' *Pride Against Prejudice* (1991): here, she isolates the assumptions regarding disabled people, both the absences within culture, but also the distortions.

> Surely, the representation and exploration of human experience is incomplete as long as disability is either missing from or misrepresented in all the forms that cultural representation takes. It is fear and denial of the frailty, vulnerability, mortality and *arbitrariness* of human experience that deters us from confronting such realities. Fear and denial prompt the isolation of those who are disabled, ill or old as "other," as "not like us." (Morris, 1991, p. 85)

Her book is a vital development, coming out of her perspective as a feminist, as well as a disability activist and researcher: the suggestions she makes here parallel the arguments I will be developing later in this article.

I want to conclude this section by referring to the work of Susan Sontag, a non-disabled American critic, in her books *Illness as Metaphor* (1991) and *AIDS and Its Metaphors* (1991). She shows the way in which disease functions as a metaphor, focusing on tuberculosis, cancer and AIDS: while she argues strongly that illness is not a metaphor for anything, she shows that this is the way in which it has been used. Her focus is on the resonance of illness itself, not with the experience of people with illness: nevertheless, she suggests that the people with illness are the ultimate victims. But Sontag skirts the real process: it is disability which is the most active and prominent metaphor of all, and disabled people become ciphers for those feelings, processes or characteristics with which non-disabled society cannot deal. As a result, those negative aspects become cemented to disabled people.

OBJECTIFICATION

Here I want briefly to underline a key theme of this article, namely the objectification of people with impairment. Earlier, I have suggested that disabled people are 'objectified' by cultural representations: it is also clear that processes described above assume that disabled people are passive, akin to animals, objects rather than subjects. In seventeenth, eighteenth and nineteenth century British society, the freak-show is a clear example of the way that human beings were seen as non-human, as potential exhibits in what was perhaps a cross between a zoo and a museum: in this connection, see *The True History of the Elephant Man*. Roland Barthes wrote:

> The Other becomes a pure object, a spectacle, a clown. Relegated to the confines of humanity, he no longer threatens the security of the home. (quoted in Sontag, 1982, p. 142)

I would suggest that the term 'fetishism' is useful in capturing the reality of this process. Marx, of course, used fetishism to refer to the way that social relationships are regarded as things (or reified) and such a conception has been employed by writers such as Michael Oliver, to capture the way in which disability is a relationship between people with impairment and a disabling society. Freud used the term to describe the projection of sexual drives into objects, and I suggest this is parallel to disability, in the sense that disabled people within cultural representation are ciphers. Disabled people are objects, on to which artists project particular emotions, or which are used to represent specific values or evils.

Another example of this objectification, or fetishism, is evident in the way that contemporary societies provide for disabled people by means of charities, filling the gap left by the unwillingness of statutory bodies to meet their obligations to disabled citizens. Charities operate by presenting extremely demeaning images of disabled people, intended to engender pity and sympathy in 'normal' people, who are then motivated to donate money. Pity is an expression of superiority: it can also be the obverse of hatred and aggression, as the post-structuralist psychologist Lacan has suggested in *The Mirror Stage:*

> For such a task, we place no trust in altruistic feeling, we who lay bare the aggressivity that underlies the activity of the philanthropist, the idealist, the pedagogue, and even the reformer. (Lacan, 1977, p. 7)

> Only saints are sufficiently detached from the deepest of the common passions to avoid the aggressive reactions to charity. (*ibid.*, p. 13)

Disabled people enable able-bodied people to feel good about themselves: by demeaning disabled people, non-disabled people can feel both powerful, and generous. Disabled people, on the other hand are viewed as passive and incapable people, objects of pity and of aid. Similar arguments have been suggested to account for imagery of developing world people's in charity campaigns: I would suggest that the same processes of colonization and imperialism are involved in both instances.

That fetishism is not an inappropriate description is evidenced by the sexual nature of much imagery surrounding disability, whether within cultural or pornographic stereotypes: through exoticism and voyeurism, disabled people, like black people, and women in general, are presented as sexualized objects, for instance in representation of amputees. The objectification of disabled people in charity advertising parallels the objectification of women in pornography. In each case the gaze focuses on the body, which is passive and available. In each case, particular aspects of the body are exaggerated: sexual parts, in pornography, or 'flawed' parts in charity advertising. In each case, the viewer is manipulated into an emotional response: desire, in the case of pornography, fear and pity in the case of charity advertising, as David Hevey has argued.

More generally, everyday interaction involving disabled people involves an invasion, by 'normal' people, of disabled people:

> It is not only physical limitations that restrict us to our homes and those whom we know. It is the knowledge that each entry into the public world will be dominated by stares, by condescension, by pity and by hostility. (Morris, 1991, p. 25)

Jenny Morris' quotation captures some of this experience, in which stares, comments and unwanted attention are seen as legitimate tactics in respect to disabled people, in a way which would be wholly inappropriate for any other group except women, and perhaps black people in certain communities.

Freudians argue that the gaze is a phallic activity, a form of sadistic mastery. John Berger, in *Ways of Seeing*, discusses the ways in which women are perceived differently from men, the fact that "men act and women appear" (Berger, 1972, p. 47). In his analysis of the female nude, which he distinguishes from the naked woman, he shows how male voyeurism has always been implicit in such paintings, which present the woman as available and objectified in a way comparable to that of pornography. Disabled people, both within paintings, but also through film and media portrayals, and everyday patterns of the gaze, are similarly displayed and objectified, so that we can again use Berger's phrases: "the social presence of a woman is different in kind from that of a man," (*ibid* p. 45) and "Her own sense of being in herself is supplanted by a sense of being appreciated as herself by another," (*ibid.*, p. 46), exchanging the terms woman/man with disabled person/ able-bodied person.

It has often been suggested that the gaze is a power relationship. Rosalind Coward argues:

> The ability to scrutinise is premised on power. Indeed the look confers power; women's inability to return such a critical and aggressive look is a sign of subordination, of being the recipients of another's assessment.
>
> Women, in the flesh, often feel embarrassed, irritated or downright angered by men's persistent gaze. But not wanting to risk male attention turning to male aggression, women avert their eyes and hurry on their way. (Coward, 1984, p. 75)

Harassment is a problem for disabled people as well as for women.

THEORETICAL MODELS

Here, I will briefly explore some theoretical models for understanding the processes of cultural representation and objectification which have been outlined above. My intention is not necessarily to present a clear answer or comprehensive explanation, but to raise the important questions, and suggest some suitable channels for investigation: theory has been neglected in the analysis of disabling imagery, and this analysis is a preliminary to filling that gap.

1. Ideology

Social Model theorists such as Oliver, Finkelstein, Abberley, etc, have not devoted particular attention to the question of meaning and representation. Where it is necessary to cover the issues, they have done so fairly schematically using an approach which I would suggest is close to the Marxist conception of ideology. That is, ideas about disabled people are consequences of the material relations involving disabled people. Ideology is a system of theoretical domination, which justifies oppressive social relations. A determinist view, this privileges the material level of explanation, and does not give much explanatory space or autonomy to the realm of culture and meaning.

As a consequence of this position, Social Model writers have rejected social psychologists, anthropologists, and even feminists, all on the basis that such theorizations are 'idealist', and fail to pay attention to material processes and social relations. I would support any argument which suggests that it is vital to consider material relations: a theoretical explanation which neglects the disabling role of society, which ignores socio-economic structures, is a mere fantasy. However, I would equally suggest that mono-linear explanations, reducing everything to economic factors, are misguided.

Disability is a complex process, which involves a number of causal components. Within this, the role of culture and meaning is crucial, autonomous and inescapable. In many societies, disabled people are viewed in significant ways—not always negatively—regardless of the particular socio-economic relationships. But to say this, is not to posit some universal feature of human psychology, nor to suggest that progressive change is impossible. As an example of the type of awareness I am trying to develop, I would indicate the debates within feminism, between marxist-feminists and radical feminists, which have covered very similar ground.

While the concept is useful, and any analysis has to give attention to the role of ideas in justifying material processes, ideology is nevertheless inadequate as a tool for understanding disabling imagery and representation.

2. Otherness

The inspirational text of second wave feminism, *The Second Sex* (de Beauvoir, 1976) introduced the concept of otherness as a useful way of conceptualizing the position of women within culture. Simone de Beauvoir was paralleling the work of Sartre in the use of otherness: existentialism itself had borrowed the approach, ultimately, from Hegel.

The term, more common in French social theory than in British sociology, has been clearly and succinctly defined by Ludmilla Jordanova: I will quote at length because this will set out the basis for subsequent developments.

> The term helps us to think about the ways in which groups and individuals distance themselves from each other, often by unconscious means. Such separating devices are only needed, however, when the two parties are also deeply bound together, implicated in each other's characteristics. Otherness, then, conveys the kinships, the fascination and the repulsion between distinct yet related categories of person. (Jordanova, 1989, p. 14)

In my view, the suggestion of parity and equivalence in this formulation is inaccurate: subsequently Jordanova is more explicit about the power relations involved in otherness,

> ... the distancing of what is peripheral, marginal and incidental from a central norm, of illicit danger from safe legitimacy. Women are other to men, as blacks are to whites, as animals are to human beings, as death is to life—although different degrees and modes of otherness are here involved.

> ... The idea of otherness is complicated, but certain themes are common: the treatment of the other as more like an object, something to be managed and possessed, and as dangerous, wild, threatening. At the same time, the other becomes an entity whose very separateness inspires curiosity, invites enquiring knowledge. The other is to be veiled and unveiled. (*ibid.*, p. 109ff)

Such formulations indicate how the disability experience discussed above can usefully be theorized as an example of 'otherness'.

The concept has exceptionally wide usage in Continental philosophy. While it is perhaps most familiar as the key theme of *The Second Sex* (discussed below), the term also crops up in a range of writers from varying theoretical standpoints: thus Barthes and Foucault commonly refer to an implicit understanding of 'otherness', which they leave unexplored. Lacan makes alterity a key element in his structuralist psychoanalysis in the form of the *petit a*, or *alter*. Feminists too, such as Kristeva, commonly adopt the expression.

Ironically, in view of its adoption by structuralists and their successors, 'otherness' originates within a humanist philosophy—widely used by Sartre as well as by de Beauvoir, it was adopted from Hegel's master/slave dialectic in the *Phenomenology of Spirit*.

> Sartre elaborates Hegel's idea that there is an unavoidable power-struggle at the heart of self-consciousness into the claim that it is only in so far as each is opposed to the Other that they grasp themselves as selves, as having "being for itself". Confronting the Other, each asserts his right of being an individual self. (Lloyd, 1983, p. 5)

Subsequently Sartre discusses the gaze, to which I referred earlier, where he suggests that the experience of being looked at is a denial of transcendence: the transformation into a "degraded consciousness".

De Beauvoir had started her 1943 novel, *L'Invitée*, with the Hegelian statement that "Each consciousness seeks the death of the other", and *The Second Sex* is permeated with Sartrean existentialism (a main criticism of later feminists). De Beauvoir's crucial move was to suggest that the process of alterity, the experience of objectification through the gaze, could be specifically applied to the situation of women, who were the "generalised other" within human culture. One sex was always the "looked at": but for de Beauvoir, women were complicitous in this oppressive relationship, having accepted the benefits of their objectification—in this sense they were guilty of "bad faith".

The statement that women are other, generalized rather than as individuals, is the conclusion of a line of reasoning which starts with the observation that the masculine has been presented as the absolute human type:

> In actuality the relation of the two sexes is not quite like that of two electrical poles, for man represents both the positive and the neutral. (de Beauvoir, 1976, p. 15)

Through citation of a range of Classical and early Christian writers, de Beauvoir shows how women have always been defined in relation to male humanity, as imperfect men (St Thomas), as suffering a lack (Aristotle). The Christian enmity to the body, as representative of original sin becomes translated into an opposition to women, as the precise expression of that flesh. Women represent Nature, with all the ambivalent feelings that the Natural arouses.

Repeatedly, de Beauvoir stresses that it is not biology, but the meaning attributed to biology, and also the way women view their biology, which is implicated in their subordination.

> Just as the penis derives its privileged evaluation from the social context, so it is the social context that makes menstruation a curse. (ibid., p. 50)

De Beauvoir therefore argues that the position of women is not natural or biological but cultural and contingent: in this she is placing herself in a tradition of historical materialism, with the consequent view of humanity as creating its own reality: "Humanity is not an animal species, it is a historical reality". (ibid., p. 84) and hence the classic statement: One is not born a woman, one becomes one.

Men construct themselves in opposition to women, who play the vital role of Other in this process of identity formation.

> Once the subject seeks to assert himself, the Other, who limits and denies him, is none the less a necessity to him: he attains himself only through that reality which he is not, which is something other than himself. (ibid., p. 171)

Therefore, women's oppression is not merely advantageous and economically and socially beneficial to men: in patriarchal societies it is a vital part of what it is to be a man, a major component of male identity and culture. As Okeley has written:

> The individual necessarily uses 'the other' for self-definition. He or she needs the other's gaze and presence as a confirmation of existence. (Okeley, 1986, p. 57)

The role of cultural imagery and stereotype is central to De Beauvoir's analysis:

> Everything helps to confirm this hierarchy in the eyes of the little girl. The historical and literary culture to which she belongs, the songs and legends with which she is lulled to sleep, are one long exaltation of man.
>
> (De Beauvoir, 1976, p. 27)

Much of her book analyses literary and cultural sources.

The Second Sex links the experience of women to that of "American Negroes": similarly oppressed, associated with nature, powerless. I would argue that there is a general process by which the subordinated person becomes 'the other', common to a range of groups in society: women, black people, and also disabled people. Here, for the first time, de Beauvoir is identifying the tendency to use association with nature to undermine the status of the subordinate group. It is from this fundamental insight that the subsequent feminist literature and debate on Nature versus Culture ultimately originates: de Beauvoir first; isolated this crucial dichotomy, and explained what was at stake in the process.

These statements, on the role of the body, and the role of nature, and the way that women are identified as both body and nature, and hence as Other, are crucial to my understanding of disability. If you were to substitute 'disabled people' for women in the argument as outlined above, I suggest that the fundamental sense of the analysis would remain. I am not denying what de Beauvoir has to say about women. I am, however, suggesting that disabled people could also be regarded as Other, by virtue of their connection to nature; their visibility as evidence of the constraining body; and their status as constant reminders of mortality. If original sin, through the transgression of Eve, is concretized in the flesh of woman, then the flesh of disabled people has historically, and within Judaeo-Christian theology especially, represented divine punishment for ancestral transgression. Furthermore, non-disabled people define themselves as 'normal' in opposition to disabled people who are not.

The message of *The Second Sex* is that genuine subjectivity, the goal of all existentialist philosophy, is unattainable for women, who (like disabled people) are confined to the status of object, of other:

> It is a strange experience for an individual, who feels himself to be an autonomous and transcendent subject, an absolute, to discover inferiority in himself as a fixed and preordained essence: it is a strange experience for whoever regards himself as the One to be revealed to himself as otherness, alterity. (op. cit., p. 35)

One of the criticisms of this position is the fixity, the inescapability of the identity as Other. Certainly, at the time de Beauvoir was writing, there was no feminist movement to give even the hope of positive social change for women. However, because of the firmly anti-biologistic stance of the book, the negative scenario is not as debilitating to the message as subsequent critics have suggested.

Perhaps a more effective criticism has been that de Beauvoir, in stressing meaning, culture, and using literary sources primarily, has developed an idealist position, which would have been better rooted in material realities and evidences. In the context of disability, I have already argued that there has been a firm stress on the materiality of the disabled person's oppression: in devoting attention to questions of culture and meaning, I am seeking both to give a context for the economic and political processes, but also to centre issues of identity which are crucial to the lived experience of disability by individuals.

It is clear that few would accept the Existentialist stress on freedom, choice and subjectivity as the ultimate possibility for all: the structural obstacles to such liberation, which de Beauvoir does outline consistently, can not merely be wished away. But I suggest that the analysis can be accepted, without its individualistic and voluntarist overtones: after all, the concept of alterity, as I have argued above, is familiar to many other, more structuralist, French philosophers also. My remaining doubt is over the universalistic message of the 'otherness' analysis: that this is the fundamental dichotomy. Thus when de Beauvoir states that "... the temptation to dominate is the most truly universal, the most irresistible one there is ..." (op. cit., p. 183) I feel concerned at the essentialist implications, close to some sociobiology arguments. Nevertheless, it is a suggestion with which I have a lot of sympathy, given the historical realities of patriarchal, racial and disability domination.

3. Anomaly and Liminality

This conceptualization, which I would argue has strong parallels with the concept of otherness, and overlaps with much of the foregoing discussion, originates in the work of Mary Douglas. She is diametrically opposed to Simone de Beauvoir, as a British, Catholic, structuralist anthropologist. But her work *Purity and Danger* (1966) which discusses the prevalence of pollution ritual in culture, and follows on from the insights of Levi-Strauss in *The Raw and the Cooked*, contains relevant insights.

De Beauvoir takes a binary dichotomy, between subject and other, in which the identity of the former is constructed in opposition to the latter: thus men define themselves in opposition to women, whites to blacks, straights to gays. Another way to look at this process, is to suggest that identity is being strengthened by the isolation and rejection of anomaly—that which is different, which stands out. Thus Douglas writes, "When something is firmly classed as anomalous, the outline of the set in which it is not a member is clarified." (Douglas, 1966, p. 50). What is being suggested here is not a dichotomous, conflictual situation, but a comparison between the dominant, normal, ordered structure, and that which disturbs or conflicts with it. For there to be normality, it is necessary for there to be an abnormality. When Allison James discusses identity development in children, I think that similar processes are involved:

> Much of the children's social life is spent in talking, telling jokes and singing songs and it is through this medium that they instruct each other in an agreed and commonly held set of norms for the physical body. Jokes. tales and rhymes abound concerning those who are physically or mentally afflicted. (James, 1986, p. 160)

Such playful interaction is important for laying down standards, centred on the body and invariably gendered. The work of the Opies has demonstrated the range of such material within children's culture, and also the extent to which important processes of socialization and identity formation are embedded in such games.

When boundaries are breached, and identities seem threatened, behaviour is devoted to re-establishing the fixities, reinforcing categories and power relations. Kate Purcell has described the constant presence of sexual tension in a factory where both men and women worked on the shopfloor: women in such work are deviating from expected gender roles, and their subordination has thus to be enforced:

> In fact, the observations at NICO suggests that a major reinforcement of women's perpetual gender consciousness is the fact that, in the factory at least, they were rarely allowed to forget that they were women. They were addressed, responded to and handled, both literally and metaphorically, as women rather than as people or as workers. (Purcell, 1988, p. 170)

I would hypothesize that prejudice, in the context of everyday interaction, media and charity imagery, popular assumptions, etc, plays a similar role in reinforcing a subordinate position for disabled people who enter mainstream society. A particular example is provided by the massive advertising hoardings and full-page newspaper advertisements of impairment charities (for example the MS Society).

Hawthorn dismisses Douglas in terms of her "suppressed psychological premises of a need for cognitive order" (Hawthorn, 1976, p. 3): I would not be so quick to such sociological élitism, because it seems clear that the need for security is an important aspect of human consciousness. It is this requirement for order and fixity which Douglas argues underlies the extraordinarily complicated Mosaic Law, in the Biblical book of Leviticus: where of course blind people, dwarfs and menstruating women are unclean just as much as the wrong food can be contaminating. Using concepts of anomaly and order, Douglas is able to explain how the complicated and seemingly irrational prohibitions work to reinforce a monist, logical view of the world.

The arguments I have made concerning the need for dualistic conceptions, the denial of the continuum of difference, the urge to make qualitative rather than quantitative distinctions, are parallel to Douglas' argument:

> It is only by exaggerating the difference between within and without, above and between, male and female, with and against, that a semblance of order is created. (Douglas, 1966, p. 15)

This underlies the difference between having an impairment (a common experience) and being disabled (a specific social identity of a minority): or between various sexual practices, and between specific gay and straight identities.

I suggest that any history of disability could be categorized along the lines by which Douglas suggests primitive peoples react to anomaly: by reducing ambiguity; by physically controlling it; by avoiding it; by labelling it dangerous; by adopting it in ritual. Historical experiences—such as the freakshow, the court jester, the asylum, the Nazi extermination and so forth —can be conceptualized straightforwardly using such categories, and it is in this way that disability can be usefully regarded as anomalous, as ambiguous.

Disabled people are seen to be ambiguous because they hover between humanity and animality, life and death, subjectivity and objectivity. The disabled anthropologist, Robert Murphy, explains this situation, not with reference to Douglas, but to Victor Turner's related concept of liminality:

> The long-term physically impaired are neither sick nor well, neither dead nor alive, neither out of society nor wholly in it. They are human beings but their bodies are warped or malfunctioning, leaving their full humanity in doubt. They are not ill, for illness is transitional to either death or recovery.... The sick person lives in a state of

> social suspension until he or she gets better. The disabled [sic] spend a lifetime in a
> similar suspended state. They are neither fish nor fowl; they exist in partial isolation
> from society as undefined, ambiguous people. (Murphy, 1987, p. 112)

Thus people with restricted growth could be children or adults; mentally ill people historically were lunatics, people of the moon. In the eighteenth century there were long debates as to whether deaf people were fully human, or if they had souls. In the fourteenth century the *Malleus Maleficarum*, a catalogue of witchcraft, links the birth of deformed and disabled children to the devil, hence the concept of the changeling. Douglas herself uses the example of the Nuer peoples, who view impaired infants as 'hippotamus', not humans, and consequently place the babies in the river "where they belong".

Alison James and Jennifer Hockey's recent anthropological work on childhood has shown how physically impaired adults are subject to infantilization: adults whose bodies, due to incontinence or immobility, function like young children's bodies, typically find themselves viewed as 'children', with a consequent loss of social power.

Turner suggests that,

> Liminal entities are neither here nor there; they are betwixt and between the positions
> assigned and arrayed by law, custom, convention and ceremonial. (Turner, 1969, p. 95)

Turner suggests that liminal peoples have particular resonances within cultural representation, have a licence to criticize or to strip off the pretensions of society and power-holders, citing the example of the court jester. It is for this reason that

> Members of despised or outlawed ethnic or cultural groups play major roles in myths
> and popular tales as representatives on expressions of universal human values. (ibid.,
> p. 110)

Both these anthropological approaches can be used to explain the particular processes involved in cultural imagery and social practices surrounding disabled people, both historically and in contemporary societies. People with impairment are the ultimate non-conformists, and as such are perpetually threatening to the self-image of the average, so-called 'normal' population. Strategies are needed to explain the prevalence of such conditions—and these are often based on cosmological explanations, on myth, and on folklore. Such processes legitimate the exceptions and ensure that the overall world-view is not damaged by the existence of these anomalous or liminal phenomena. Both Douglas and Turner, as cultural anthropologists, conclude in a reference to the basic structures of such societies, the cognitive desire for order which Hawthorn has referred to. In failing to ground their analyses in specific socio-economic contexts, in failing to develop a link between culture and material relations, they are making the opposite error to those deterministic, marxian-inspired Social Model theorists whom I criticized at the outset of this article.

DISABILITY AND PREJUDICE

The Social Model needs to be reconceptualized: people with impairment are disabled, not just by material discrimination, but also by prejudice. This prejudice is not just interpersonal, it is also implicit in cultural representation, in language and in socialization.

In order to explain prejudice against disabled people, I argue that disabled people are other because people with impairment can represent the victory of body over mind; of nature over culture; of death over life. Nothing, I would add, is fixed about this, because we are discussing the values attributed to social phenomena, not the essential meanings of this or that. But in practice, the peculiar and particular fascination—the fear and loathing—that disability has for human beings is because impairment represents the physicality and animality of human existence. Nature is the enemy, women are the enemy, black people are the enemy, disabled people are the enemy: this is why there is so much in common between these different experiences, as Cynthia Cockburn and other feminists have already perceived.

Kim Chernin's analysis of *The Tyranny of Slenderness* suggests:

> One of the great advantages to men, in a culture they dominate, is the ability to assign to those they oppress whatever it is they wish to disown or ignore in their own condition. (Chernin, 1983, p. 124)

She herself quotes Susan Griffin, author of *Women and Nature,* who summarizes her argument thus, in her book on *Pornography and Silence*:

> For we hunt down, suppress or attempt to inflict harm upon whatever might call us back to nature, whether this call arises from our own body or from a people to whom we have attributed those qualities of instinctual life we wish to separate from ourselves. (quoted Chernin, 1983, p. 129)

Griffin relates this argument to the role of women and black people, explaining their oppression in terms of their association with the body, with instinct, and with sensuality. I would expand the analysis to include disabled people, and also gay men and lesbians.

The process described here can be analysed from a psychoanalytical perspective as a form of projection, defined as an

> operation whereby qualities, feelings, wishes or even objects, which the subject refuses to recognise or rejects in himself, are expelled from the self and located in another person or thing.

Thus able-bodied people are perpetually anxious to deny their own mortality and physicality, and disabled people are the group onto whom these difficult feelings are projected.

Jenny Morris has developed a similar argument:

> Our physical characteristics evoke such strong feelings that people often have to express them in some way. At the same time, they feel able to impose their feelings on us because we are not considered to be autonomous human beings (Morris. 1991, p. 29)

She reiterates this position towards the end of *Pride Against Prejudice*:

> Our disability frightens people. They don't want to think that this is something which could happen to them. So we become separated from common humanity, treated as fundamentally different and alien. Having put up clear barriers between us and them, non-disabled people further hide their fear and discomfort by turning us into objects of pity, comforting themselves by their own kindness and generosity. (Morris, 1991, p. 192)

But it is not our disability, but our impairment which frightens people. And it is not us, it is non-disabled people's embodiment which is the issue: disabled people remind non-disabled people of their own vulnerability.

The key features of this argument are firstly, the equation of certain groups with nature and the body, and secondly, the establishment of a normal identity through separation from the Other. Thirdly, and arising out of these developments, is the projection of negative attributes onto the Other, either as part of a denial of those elements in the self, or as part of a general denigration of disturbing, contradictory, anomalous or threatening phenomena. I believe this is what Hevey is talking about in the following extract:

> What is happening is that non-disabled people are getting rid of their fear about their mortality, their fear about the loss of labour power and other elements in narcissism. The point I am making is that disabled people are the dustbin for that disavowal. (Hevey, 1991, p. 34)

People project their fear of death, their unease at their physicality and mortality, onto disabled people, who represent all these difficult aspects of human existence. Paul Longmore, whose cultural criticism was referred to above, has suggested:

> As with popular portrayals of other minorities, the unacknowledged hostile fantasies of the stigmatizers are transferred to the stigmatized. The non-disabled audience is allowed to disown its fears and biases by "blaming the victims," making them responsible for their own ostracism and destruction. (Longmore, 1987, p. 67)

Disabled people are scapegoats. It is not just that disabled people are different, expensive, inconvenient, or odd: it is that they represent a threat—either, as Douglas suggests, to order, or, to the self-conception of western human beings—who, since the Enlightenment, have viewed themselves as perfectible, as all-knowing, as god-like: able, over and above all other beings, to conquer the limitations of their nature through the victories of their culture.

I have drawn upon feminist work to analyse the extent to which disabled people can be regarded as other, and as analogous to women in certain key areas. It therefore seems appropriate to end by suggesting that this ethic of invincibility or perfectibility that I have outlined, the separation of mind and body and so forth, should not strictly be viewed as a human trait, but should perhaps be specifically identified with masculinity which is the real focus of concerns with potency, with supremacy, and with domination. This notion can only be a hypothesis at this stage, but it is one which is powerfully suggested by the evidence at our disposal.

NOTE

Acknowledgements to David Hevey for the phrase "dustbins for disavowal."

REFERENCES

BARNES, C. (1992) *Disabling Imagery and the Media* (Halifax, Ryburn/BCODP).
BERGER, J. (1972) *Ways of Seeing* (Harmondsworth, Penguin/BBC).
CHERNIN, K. (1983) *Womansize: the tyranny of slenderness* (London, Women's Press).
CONNELL, R. (1987) *Gender and Power* (Cambridge, Polity Press).
COWARD, R. (1984) *Female Desire* (London. Paladin).
CROW, L. (1992) Renewing the Social Model of disability, *Coalition*, July, pp. 5—9.
CUMBERBATCH, G. & NEGRINE, R. (1992) *Images of Disability on Television* (London, Routledge).

DAVIES, K., DICKEY, J. & STRATFORD, T. (1987) *Out of Focus* (London, Women's Press).

DE BEAUVOIR, S. (1943) *L'Invitée* (Paris, Gallimard).

DE BEAUVOIR, S. (1976) *The Second Sex* (Harmondsworth, Penguin).

DOUGLAS, M. (1966) *Purity and Danger* (Harmondsworth, Penguin).

ELLMAN, M. (1979) *Thinking about Women* (London, Virago).

HAWTHORN, G. (1976) *Enlightenment and Despair* (Cambridge, Cambridge University Press).

HEVEY, D. (1991) From self love to the picket line, in: S.LEES (Ed.) *Disability Arts and Culture Papers* (London, Shape Publications).

HOLDEN, L. (1991) *Forms of Deformity* (Sheffield, JSOT Press).

JAMES, A. (1986) Learning to belong: the boundaries of adolescence, in: A. P. COHEN (Ed.) *Symbolising Boundaries: identity and diversity in British cultures* (Manchester, Manchester University Press).

JORDANOVA, L. (1989) *Sexual Visions* (New York, Harvester Wheatsheaf).

KRIEGEL, L. (1987) The cripple in literature, in: A. GARTNER & T. JOE (Eds) *Images of the Disabled, Disabling Images* (New York, Praeger).

KENT, D. (1987) Disabled women: portraits in fiction and drama, in: A. GARTNER & T. JOE (Eds) *Images of the Disabled, Disabling Images* (New York, Praeger).

LUCAN, J. (1977) *Ecrits: a selection* (Tavistock, London).

LEVI-STRAUSS, C. (1970) *The Raw and the Cooked* (London, Cape).

LONGMORE, P.K. (1987) Screening stereotypes, images of disabled people in television and motion pictures, in: A. GARTNER & T. JOE (Eds) *Images of the Disabled, Disabling Images* (New York, Praeger).

LLOYD, G. (1983) Masters, slaves and others, *Radical Philosophy*, 34, pp. 2-9.

MILLET, K. (1972) *Sexual Politics* (London, Sphere).

MORRIS, J. (1991) *Pride Against Prejudice* (London, Women's Press).

MURPHY, R.F. (1987) *The Body Silent* (London, Phoenix House).

OKELEY, J. (1986) *Simone de Beauvoir: a re-reading* (London, Virago).

PURCELL, K. (1988) Gender and the experience of employment, in: D. GALLIE (Ed.) *Employment in Britain* (Oxford, Blackwell).

SHEARER, A. (1981) *Disability, Whose Handicap?* (Oxford, Blackwell).

SONTAG, S. (1991) *Illness as Metaphor/AIDS and its Metaphors* (London, Penguin).

SONTAG, S. (1982) *A Barthes Reader* (London, Jonathan Cape).

TURNER, V. (1969) *The Ritual Process* (London, RKP).

PART THREE

CHAPTER 14

Disability and the Myth of the Independent Researcher

Colin Barnes

(First published 1996)

At a recent seminar on the relationship between medical sociology and disability theory I was struck by the response from some non-disabled and disabled academics to a call from a disabled delegate from an organisation of disabled people for guidelines on how to deal with requests from researchers for information and collaboration on disability-related research. Although the enquirer was clearly concerned about the ease with which researchers can easily misrepresent disability, those who responded used the request as an opportunity to put forward their own positions as independent researchers. They were concerned that in disability research, as in research generally, researchers must be free of all external considerations and controls in order to produce valid and unbiased results.

Now, given the history of disability research and the way that some disabled people have argued that it has played a role in the oppression of disabled people (see, for example, Hunt, 1981; Oliver, 1990, 1992; Morris, 1992; Abberley, 1992; Rioux and Bach, 1994), it seems quite understandable to me that disabled people and their organisations should be wary of researchers.

What is more difficult to understand, however, is the way in which some academics continue to argue for the idea of the 'independent researcher' without qualification. In my view this is a strategy which is, at best, naïve and, at worst, misleading.

Setting aside the apparently never ending and seemingly irreconcilable debates about value freedom, 'objectivity' and appropriate methodologies within social science (see Pawson, 1989; Sayer, 1992), in Britain the myth of the independent researcher has its roots in the university system. Historically, British universities have fulfilled at least two main functions. Besides providing a particular form of advanced education for a certain section of the population, they have provided the necessary facilities for a select group of individuals to conduct research on a whole range of issues unfettered by the mundane demands of everyday life. Although this frequently abused privilege was almost exclusively reserved for the middle and upper classes, most universities, in accordance with their charitable status [sic] provided some form of support through sponsorship and bursaries for those considered worthy, but without.

Today, this tradition finds expression in postgraduate training programmes and fellowships sponsored by either Government funded research councils, such as the Economic and Social Research Council (ESRC), for example, or independent grant-making charities and trusts. Moreover, as long as certain academic standards are adhered to and maintained, these schemes give students and academics a unique opportunity to develop their own interests and ideas.

However, the opportunities for students and researchers to pursue and develop controversial and radical new ideas are limited, and, in my view, diminishing. Due mainly to the sustained critique of the social sciences by successive right-wing governments during the 1980s and early 90s, and the introduction of market forces into the university system, postgraduate training programmes are increasingly geared toward the acquisition of 'generic' rather than specific research skills. Also, established scholars with a good publication record are far more likely to get study leave or a research fellowship than their less illustrious colleagues with few or no publications. Furthermore, the recent erosion of job security within the university system, due mainly to the introduction of short-term contracts for new academic staff, can be seen as an implicit if not explicit incentive for anyone pursuing a career in academia to kow tow to convention.

Moreover, this situation has been exacerbated further by the Higher Education Funding Council's (HEFC) Research Assessment Exercise. Introduced in 1992 to bring the 'benefits' of market forces into the university svstem, and conducted every four years, the scheme grades university departments from one to five. High scoring departments receive significantly more funding from the HEFC than low scoring ones. Hence, those achieving a grade five, termed 'centres of excellence', have far more resources at their disposal than those deemed grade one or two. For academics, this can mean the difference between good working conditions and relative job security or possible redundancy. The two criteria used in the HEFC grading process are: the number and 'quality' of publications produced by individual academics working in a particular department and the amount of research they do. As a consequence, academic staff are 'encouraged' to produce at least four publications every 4 years, and to do as much research as possible.

The 'quality' of publications is judged by the level of 'scholarship' they exhibit. As a general rule, this means that complex and sophisticated analyses spread over hundreds of pages carry far more weight than relatively short single issue monographs and research reports. Articles published in 'academic' journals which are edited and refereed by academics, are rated far higher than those which appear in 'popular' magazines and newspapers like the Greater Manchester Coalition of Disabled People's *Coalition* or Scope's *Disability Now*. Thus, the more sophisticated and, in most cases, the more inaccessible an academic's work is the more highly rated it is by the academic community.

In other words, the university system, implicitly if not explicitly, compels academics and researchers to write primarily for other academics and researchers rather than for the general public. Or, to put it another way, and with regard to disability research, university based researchers are far more likely to write for other university based researchers than they are for their research subjects—disabled people.

Furthermore, postgraduate training programmes and research fellowships account for only a relatively small part of a research active university department's research activities. Most do research for external organisations on a subcontract basis. Additionally, the more money they can earn from research contracts, the higher their rating on the HEFC Research Assessment Exercise. With disability research this usually means policy related projects funded by health authorities, social services departments, charities and government departments.

For most of these organisations, disability remains a profoundly medical problem which warrants traditional individually based 'rehabilitative' type solutions that are both politically and professionally expedient. In many cases, these organisations are quite specific about their requirements and impose extensive constraints on what researchers can and cannot actually do. This is particularly evident with reference to government funded projects such as those initiated by the Department of Health (DH), National Health Service (NHS), and the Department of Employment (DE), for example.

Indeed, the main principle governing any Government funding of R&D (Research and Development) is the Rothschild principle, laid down in Cmd 4814 and reiterated in the White Paper 'Realising our potential: A Strategy for Science, Engineering and Technology', 'the customer says what he [sic] wants, the contractor does it, if he [sic] can and the customer pays' (DH, 1994a, p. 1).

According to the DH's code of practice, research and development commissioned by the Department should be commensurate with its policy and management aims. Furthermore, to ensure quality, research requirements must be informed by 'expert' advice, projects should follow a 'well defined protocol, be subjected to expert peer review, seek to maximise value for money, and meet agreed targets' (DH, 1994a, p. 1). A typical contract for DH funded research is about nine pages long and in several key areas is very explicit. Besides covering general arrangements for funding, administration and the staffing of projects they include instructions relating to research methodologies. For example, 'Any questionnaire, or forms used in surveys or both which are to form part of the research shall be submitted in draft to RDD (Research and Development Division)...together with explanatory notes, covering letters to respondents and any other relevant documents' (DH, 1994b, p. 4).

Additionally, if, for some reason, the DH, is unhappy with how the research is being conducted then they have a legal right to terminate it as and when they feel appropriate. At the same time, if the research findings 'are vitiated by methodological problems. . .or otherwise'(?) (DH, 1994b, p. 7) then they are under no obligation to publish them.

It should also be remembered that the pressure on university-based researchers to subscribe to this type of control is intensified by the commercialisation of social research. There are a number of research institutions, both large and small, which operate on a purely commercial basis tendering for lucrative research contracts.

Clearly, then, university based researchers are not free of external considerations and controls. To suggest otherwise is to misrepresent social research in the 1990s. Furthermore, in my view, to maintain the myth of the 'independent researcher' within the context of disability research—or any kind of social research, for that matter—can only exacerbate the gulf between researchers and research subjects—the very opposite of what is needed.

If disability research is about researching oppression, and I would argue that it is, then researchers should not be professing 'mythical independence' to disabled people, but joining with them in their struggles to confront and overcome this oppression. Researchers should be espousing commitment not value freedom, engagement not objectivity, and solidarity not independence. There is no independent haven or middle ground when researching oppression: acdemics and researchers can only be with the oppressors or with the oppressed.

REFERENCES

ABBERLEY, P. (1992) Counting Us Out: A Discussion of the OPCS Disability Surveys, *Disability Handicap and Society*, 7, pp. 139-157.

DH (1994a) *Department of Health Code of Practice for the Commissioning and Management of Research and Development* (London, Research and Development Division, Department of Health).

DH (1994b) *Specimen: conditions of approved cost contract* (London, Research and Developmemt Division, Department of Health).

HUNT, P. (1981) Setting Accounts with the Parasite People, *Disability Challenge London, Union of the Physically Impaired Against Segregation*, No. 2, pp. 37–50.

MORRIS, J. (1992) Personal as political: a feminist perspective on researching physical disability, *Disability, Handicap & Society*, 7, pp. 157-166.

OLIVER, M. (1990) *The Politics of Disablement* (London, Macmillan).

OLIVER, M. (1992) Changing the Social Relations of Research Production, *Disability Handicap and Society*, 7, pp. 101-115.

PAWSON, R. (1989) *Measure for Measure: a manifesto for empirical sociology* (London, Routledge)

RIOUX, M. & BACH, M. (1994) *Disability is Not Measles* (Ontario, L'Institut Roeher Institute)

SAYER, A. (1992) *Method in Social Science: a realist approach*, 2nd edn. (London, Routledge).

CHAPTER 15

Disability and the Myth of the Independent Researcher:
a reply

Mike Bury
(First published 1996)

At the seminar Colin Barnes mentions in his article, a considerable amount of time was spent arguing about the relationship between politics and social research. One of the issues, which remained unresolved, was whether those struggling for political rights or for resources needed to bother with research in the first place. Surely people who are 'oppressed', the argument seemed to go, already know it and battle against it. Some people at the seminar were so hostile to academic research in any form, viewing it as no better than 'rape' or 'voyeurism', to use one contributor's rather unfortunate language, that the answer for some was fairly clear; such research had nothing to offer. Others felt that academic research was necessary. In his article, Colin speaks in less intolerant terms of disabled people being wary of researchers, but he is still in favour of social research under specific circumstances, which is under-standable given his position as a university academic.

Perhaps the first point to note is that most people are probably already wary of researchers, and for all kinds of reasons, both good and bad. Some people fear intrusion and surveillance, others (notably politicians and the wealthy) fear exposure of their activities, or the social costs of their actions or policies. Colin is playing to the gallery in this respect.

The central issue raised in the article is, however, what degree of independence and accountability should researchers have, in responding to this ambivalence about research in society. On this point, Colin seems to offer a confusing answer.

On the one hand, Colin seems to be objecting to academic research operating within an ivory tower of 'researchers speaking to themselves' yet, on the other hand, he spends considerable space in his article castigating the threat to research posed by government sponsored edicts and procedures.

Though Colin states that contributors at the seminar voiced the concern that researchers 'must be free of all external considerations and controls', I, personally cannot remember anyone putting the point in such an overdrawn manner. I know of no social researcher who would argue along these lines. Research is always conducted in a social context, and researchers must always operate within a professional code of ethical conduct, and cannot expect to be 'free of all controls'. Moreover, social researchers must provide opportunities for people to refuse to take part in research, as 'refusal rates' in research reports routinely testify they do.

Social researchers are also mindful of the nature of the 'contract' that may be set up in the research relationship and the need to be aware of the impact of the research process on the participants. Numerous books on research methods discuss these issues and it seems strange that Colin should write as if these matters are not thought about, or dealt with, by researchers. In recent years, as he must know the trend is towards a greater level of participation and accountability in research, partly as a result of outside pressure, but also as a function of greater 'consumerism' in official policy. Funding bodies, including the Department of Health R&D initiatives, now expect researchers to involve the relevant client group in the research process. While this may not go as far as some would wish it is misleading to convey the impression that researchers can or wish to be entirely free of 'external considerations', or of responsibilities towards those with whom they are researching.

Having said this, I have considerable sympathy with many of the points made in the article about the attitude towards research proffered by government and funding agencies. The desire among some funding bodies that all social research should demonstrate how it helps (in a post-Thatcherite manner) to promote 'wealth creation', for example, seems invidious if not ridiculous. Certainly Margaret Thatcher thought that research should serve specific interests. However, criticising such views, surely, speaks to the need for more independent research, not less.

The idea of independence in this context does not mean, as Colin seems to want to portray it, a complete absence of commitment or accountability. Indeed, it can mean quite the reverse. Social researchers may often be committed (especially in the health and welfare fields) to revealing social inequalities, the effects of the lack of power, or the inappropriateness, as well as appropriateness of official responses. However, there must always be room for argument and counter-argument, and crucially for researchers, to reveal matters that may be uncomfortable, for specific interest groups and even for those funding the research.

Research on disability is, in this sense, no different than any other area of social life. Social research in the past has revealed a great deal of the inequalities that comprise the disadvantage and discrimination experienced by disabled people, and the complexities of the social and cultural attitudes that underpin such disadvantage. However, some work has been explorative and descriptive. Indeed, writers such as Colin Barnes and Mike Oliver use this social research themselves. They have, for example, recently spoken of 'the struggle for equal rights and opportunities for Britain's 6.5 million disabled people' (*Disability & Society*, 10, 1, 1995, p. 111), thereby using the estimates of the extent of disability from the 1988 national OPCS study, which elsewhere they, and others, have been at such pains to criticise.

What needs to be recognised is that social research has often involved challenging a number of entrenched interests, especially within medicine and government circles. The idea that social research relies on a notion of disability as a 'profoundly medical problem' is to completely misrepresent the history of research on disability and to attempt to elevate the 'social oppression' model as the only one that can govern research.

It is for this reason that voices were raised at the seminar in defence of independence. The idea that a particular section of the disability movement should control the research agenda on a 'you are either for us or against us' basis, as the final comment in Colin's article implies, sounds like a thinly veiled threat.

Surely Colin, and others who are interested in research, want it carried out well and in the most convincing manner. Poorly conducted research helps neither the researchers or those wishing to use it. Good research needs people (whether 'disabled' or 'able bodied') who are trained properly to do so. It also requires that the researcher can be confident that findings that do not please specific interest groups or funders will not be dismissed or suppressed.

For example, research on representative samples of disabled people might reveal that relatively few subscribe to the 'oppression' theory of disability, or find it relevant to their everyday experiences. Or research might reveal that activists identify with it more than others. Or, indeed, it might find that it is widely adhered to by disabled people. Would Colin object to see negative as well as positive findings emerge from such research? It would certainly be of interest to know how many of the 6.5 million disabled people in Britain (most of whom suffer from chronic illness) either understand or subscribe to the 'oppression theory', and if so, which version of it. To argue that research could not test out such assumptions, and that it must pursue a certain line of 'confronting and overcoming oppression', suggests that one approach should be privileged over others. Even if one accepted such an approach to research there would be a need to operationalise 'oppression theory' in a researchable manner, if only to secure the necessary funds. In this sense all social researchers are in the same boat.

In my own career, I have rarely come across anyone who views social research as merely a technical or neutral process. As I have suggested, it must of necessity occur within a social context and be influenced by it. Universities, notwithstanding Colin's characterisation of them, provide one of the few spaces within capitalist societies where issues can still be addressed with a degree of independence. This means that a range of issues need to be tackled in disability research including mapping disadvantage, the need for health and welfare services, and variations in experience. I would also argue for the right for research that does not always have an immediate practical outcome. Without at least some fundamental research, basic questions may not be asked and conceptual frameworks not developed. Colin is right to regard threats to research in universities as worrying. I would suggest that this means that disabled people and social researchers should work collaboratively together, where possible, to influence the research agenda in a positive and pluralistic direction, to tackle the range of issues involved in disability. From this viewpoint I would argue that the language of 'oppressors' and 'oppressed' does not do justice to the problems, and possibilities, involved.

CHAPTER 16

Rules of Engagement:
changing disability research

Tom Shakespeare

(First published 1996)

First, let me agree with many of the points raised by Colin Barnes, and share his concern at the danger of 'academic independence' being employed as a spurious cloak for research which reinforces, rather than challenges, the subordination of disabled people. However, I want to take issue with various points, and challenge the simplistic and reductionist analysis of the research process which I feel he is in danger of perpetuating. I think there is a risk of positivism within Barnes' stance, which reproduces the positivism of the so-called 'independent' researchers he criticises. I write this as a disability activist; as an academic trained in a traditional establishment context; as a researcher who believes that parallels with other movements can give us clues as to the development of Disability Studies; as a sociologist who finds the whole field under-theorised. I think there are particular questions about the types of research, the relationships to disabled people and organisations, the techniques of research and the roles of researchers. In this piece I will concentrate on a couple of these issues.

FOR COMMITMENT

A key influence on my development as a sociologist has been the work of feminist theorists and researchers, and it is feminist models of the research relationship and the role of academic knowledge which have informed my approach. For example, Ann Oakley's work is important to me for several reasons. First, she departs from the traditional paradigm of 'objective' and 'positivist' social research, and develops an altogether more equal and balanced style of interviewing (Oakley, 1993). Secondly, she combines her academic publications with more accessible versions of the same research, intended to be used by the type of women who form her sample. These principles inform the best sociology currently being undertaken within the Disability Studies context, and underlined the special research issue of this journal (Various, 1992). Personally, I value my articles in *Coalition*, and *The Pink Paper* as much as those in *Disability & Society* or *The Times Higher Educational Supplement*.

However, within feminist work, it is clear that a variety of positions coexist and that numerous debates and disagreements have taken place: this is the mark of a mature and sophisticated discipline, and shows that it is unnecessary (and dangerous) for there only to be one voice. Sometimes, within Disability Studies, there is a risk of an orthodoxy being established, or dissenting voices being marginalised, or challenging opinions being ignored. Additionally, the relationship between feminist academic work and the women's movement has been less formalised and unilinear than has sometimes been proposed in the case of disability. Arguments there have certainly been, but the expectation of accountability has been altogether more diffuse and generalised, and the notion of commitment has been rather more important. Within lesbian and gay studies, as Vance indicates, there has also been dissent from the orthodoxy of the lesbian and gay political movement (Vance, 1989).

I believe there is a difference between accountability to one's research subjects, and accountability to the disability movement or specific organisations within it. When I do qualitative research, I aim to represent fairly the experiences of my interviewees. I explain exactly what the research is about; I give them the opportunity to revise what they have said and I offer them the opportunity to ask me questions, either about the research or about myself. Equally, I do not use techniques which obscure the voice of participants, for example formal structured interviews or questionnaires. In these ways, I aim to equalise the research relationship, and give participants some control over the process, over their words and over their participation. I try to be accountable to research participants, and I am committed to representing interviewees and giving them a voice within my publications. At the end of the day, I am not naïve enough to imagine I have completely equalised the relationship, because I believe this is ultimately impossible. I write the articles; I have the academic voice and authority; I have the education and the language which contributes to the acceptability of what I write.

These points, especially my espousal of 'experience' and 'authenticity', could be interpreted as suggesting that I am engaged on a search for truth. Often, researchers justify their own behaviour by reference to an external reality of this kind. However, feminist and especially post-structuralist theories have challenged the notion of a singular, unitary set of truths which are openly accessible to the researcher. I support this theoretical approach, which leads me to suggest that respondents views will themselves be subject to deconstruction and analysis. I acknowledge the tension between my espousal of accountability to respondents, and my epistemological anti-foundationalism, a dynamic which I am currently working through and exploring. My consolation is that I am not alone in this process:

> S, I think my problem, and 'our' problem, is how to have simultaneously an account of radical historical contingency for all knowledge claims and knowing subjects... *and* a non-nonsense commitment to faithful accounts of a 'real' world... (Haraway, 1988, p. 579).

AGAINST ACCOUNTABILITY

In terms of the movement, I have a commitment, which is different from accountability. I support the cause of disability rights, I support the principle of self-organisation and I support the disability movement. This is an ethical or a political position, which informs everything I do, professionally and personally. I think it is clear from my published work that I am not a disinterested observer, but a participant in the processes I describe. I recognise that this could lead to criticism in sociological terms, because I might be perceived to be too close to processes which I seek to analyse. However, independent research is indeed ultimately a fiction, and my own engagement gives me insights which can be useful in the research, and enable me to get closer to the people and experiences which I try to analyse.

I do not feel I owe loyalty to BCODP, to my local self-organised groups or to other organisations within the movement. As an academic, I have the luxury of reflection, and the possibility of looking in from outside. I believe it is sometimes my duty to be critical, to raise questions and consider issues which may have been overlooked in the heat of political debates. Sometimes, an organisation may become unrepresentative, or may act in ways which do not seem to be in the best interests of the disability community as a whole or sections of it. In that context, it is the right, indeed, possibly the duty of academics, to take an independent line. However, while I aim to be independent, I do not confuse this with being neutral or being objective.

Incidentally, the tension that has existed between disabled academics and disabled activists, and which perhaps contributes to a certain defensiveness on my part, can be compared to an issue which seems to me to be more problematic. As an academic, one is subject, not just to the institutional and financial constraints which Colin outlines, but also to peer review and evaluation. The intellectual work one performs is scrutinised for its accuracy, effectiveness and consistency, in a process which is meant to ensure quality and integrity. Disabled academics are thus subject to at least two monitoring processes: academic colleagues and movement comrades. Compare this to the legions of self-employed, self-appointed consultants who now operate in the disability field. Some are also leading members of the disability movement, many are not. The latter may be more obviously feathering their own nests, but even the former have conflicts of interest and may, indeed, be profiting personally from the collective endeavours of disabled people. As a disabled academic, I do not depend on disability for my career and I do not exploit the disability movement for advancement. I research disability, but equally I teach and research on a number of other social issues.

ACCESSIBILITY AND ADEQUACY

This all relates to a broader point, which was an underlying issue at the Leeds University seminar to which Colin refers. Academic work on disability may not always be accessible. I believe writers should use plain language, but this does not equal a duty to be immediately comprehensible. Theories and concepts, and social reality itself, will often be complex, nuanced and difficult. If Disability Studies is to capture this richness, it will have to be able to use ideas and develop analyses which may not be transparent and simple. Mike Oliver has spoken of the dangers of a 'Noddy Guide' to disability, and elsewhere I have quoted Einstein, who said 'Make everything as simple as possible. But not simpler'. This was in the context of reviewing a book by a disability arts practitioner, not a professional sociologist which highlights the point that the autodidact may be more obscure than the academic.

Within sociology, the distinction between 'common sense' and sociology is absolutely central, and refers to the greater rigour, the formalised language and the urge to deconstruct and uncover which is central to academic social science. Sociology has to be adequate, and accurate, and precise. Disabled people certainly need access to sociology and we need more disabled sociologists, but Disability Studies is an academic investigation of the social world, and as such is more than simply common sense (Giddens, 1989). Sociological discourse is a critical discourse but also a reflexive discourse, because it is critical upon itself. In this, it differs from political language.

I have major reservations with the concept of emancipatory research, even while admiring the motivation and commitment of those engaged in it. I am cynical about the possibility of research achieving major change, whether it be radical and emancipatory, or traditional social policy research. Ideas clearly have a role, but actions decide the day, and while it is possible to make the research process more balanced, grandiose claims for its revolutionary potential seem to me to be over-optimistic. Furthermore, while few would now argue in terms of objectivity, a notional independence and balance is still seen as critical to the academic endeavour. Given the political context, there is little point in developing progressive research which is rejected out of hand by government and media alike as being contaminated by ideological prejudice. That is not to say that research is ever uncontaminated by politics, but merely to highlight the reality that academics cannot be perceived to have axes to grind. Neither is it to support the current arrangements for funding (or not funding) research in this country, which Colin is right to characterise as unfair and misguided.

My current research concerns sexuality and disability, and is not emancipatory research. I hope it is research which reflects the reality of disabled people, and which acts as validation and affirmation for disabled people who read the book. It may have some indirect policy outcomes, but I do not think it should be judged on instrumental grounds, and I defend the right of researchers to undertake research and develop theory for its own sake. This is not the same as offering researchers *carte blanche* to parasitise disabled people's experience and develop careers on the back of disabled people's lives.

PARTNERSHIP OR PRAXIS

Many of the points I have made here may not sit easily with the prevailing orthodoxy of Disability Studies. It may be that my persona as an academic, and my academic socialisation, is outweighing my activist persona. However, in my view, it is necessary for there to be a division of labour between academics and activists: notions of accountability and representation are relevant in the political context, while notions of engagement and commitment are more relevant in the sociological context.

Ultimately, political action achieves change. Intellectual activity contributes to a climate in which change becomes possible and offers theoretical support to practical debates. Clearly, this dichotomy is not as clear cut as this statement implies, especially when many academics are also activists, and other academics are actually in opposition to the disability movement. Politics is often about pragmatism, instrumentalism, and rhetoric: sociology must be about different things, and sociologists must have the space and the integrity to tell it how it is. Gramsci's concept of praxis, the dialectical relationship of theory and practice, is an important principle in this context (Gramsci, 1985, p. 365). However, I find equally useful the approach of Michel Foucault:

> I dream of the intellectual who destroys evidence and generalities, the one who, in the intertias and constraints of the present time, locates and marks the weak points, the openings, the lines of force, who is incessantly on the move, doesn't know exactly where he (*sic*) is heading nor what he will think tomorrow, for he is too attentive to the present; who, wherever he moves, contributes to posing the question of knowing whether the revolution is worth the trouble and what kind (I mean, what revolution and what trouble), it being understood that the question can be answered only by those who are willing to risk their lives to bring it about (Foucault, 1990, p. 124)

REFERENCES

FOUCAULT, M (1990) *Politics, Philosophy, Culture* (New York, Routledge).
GIDDENS, A. (1989) *Sociology* (Cambridge, Polity).

GRAMSCI, A. (1971) *Selections from the Prison Notebooks* (London, Lawrence and Wishart).

HARAWAY, D. (1988) Situated knowledges: the science question in feminism and the privilege of partial perspective, *Feminist Studies*, 14, pp. 757-799.

OAKLEY, A. (1993) Interviewing women: a contradiction in terms? in *Essays on Women, Medicine and Health* (Edinburgh, University Press).

VANCE, C. (1989) Social construction theory: problems in the history of sexuality, in: ALTMAN, D. *et al.* (Eds) *Homosexuality, Which Homosexuality?* (London, Gay Men's Press).

VARIOUS (1992) Special issue: researching disability, *Disability, Handicap and Society*, 7, No. 2.

CHAPTER 17

Fighting Two Different Battles: unity is preferable to enmity

Ayesha Vernon

(First published 1996)

INTRODUCTION

This article is in response to Oliver's (1995) critique of the polemics in the work of Hill (1994) and Stuart (1994). These centre around three particular themes: that the experience of 'black' disabled people has been ignored; that the disability movement is racist and that the theoretical developments in disability have misunderstood or misrepresented the real nature of racism.

I will, first, discuss each of the above in turn and, secondly, suggest a way forward on dealing with what has become an extremely contentious and a divisive issue.

First, some terminological clarification is necessary. In keeping with the debate on the diversity of the minority ethnic communities in Britain and a widely expressed dissatisfaction with the commonly used term 'black' to refer to all those who experience racism on the basis of their skin colour, the dual terms black and minority ethnic are here used together to refer to all those who experience discrimination on the grounds of their ethnic/national origins as well as skin colour and culture. This is in order to take account of groups such as Irish people, Jews and gypsies who have a long history of experiencing a form of racism based on their culture and way of life which has hitherto gone unnoticed by the use of the term 'black' as racism is not just based on skin colour, although it makes one more visible as a target than minority ethnic groups who share their skin colour with the majority ethnic group in Britain. The singular term 'black', will, hence, appear in single quotation marks only when referring to the work of other writers, as will the term 'race' to indicate it is a socially constructed category and not a biological one as previously assumed. I will also break with usual convention by referring to disabled black and minority ethnic people rather than the usual tradition of 'black disabled people' in that it is linguistically correct to proceed with the adjective 'disabled' rather than 'black' as well as to minimise the differences between disabled black and minority ethnic people, and disabled white people in the movement. It is also more descriptive of the emphasis placed by the social model of disability which is that we are disabled by society and not our bodies (Sutherland, 1981; Oliver, 1990; Barnes, 1991), which I feel is better described by the term disabled 'black' rather than 'black', disabled people.

ANALYSING CONTEMPORARY RACISM

The proponents of 'new racism' have shifted the frontier of difference from skin colour to culture (Barker, 1981). For new racism, British culture and British way of life is the absolute, valued identity, to be promoted. This shift in emphasis can be seen clearly in such examples as: the call in spring 1995 by the government's adviser on school curriculum for schools to promote a sense of British identity in all children. Witness also the case of Henderson (1995) claiming that only the exclusive presence of 'unequivocal Englishmen' in England's cricket team can have the best formula for success; and the recent government measures to toughen up on illegal immigrants which gives free reign to all racists employed in the public sector to question the status of anyone who is 'not British' in appearance. This means that anyone whose skin colour is not white will be scrutinised both overtly and covertly, regardless of where they were born. This has the effect of marginalising everything that is un-British as 'alien', as well as giving the message that British is superior and anything else is inferior. As Tariq Modood comments: 'The empire legacy–the view that we are on top and all the others are lucky to be civilised and are lucky to be allowed into this country . . . I don't really think that we have left that behind' (Race Matters, BBC Radio 4, 1995).

Thus, it appears that while things seem to be marginally improving for disabled people, generally (increased public and media awareness of discrimination against disabled people and the introduction of, albeit inadequate, Disability Discrimination Bill), for black and minority ethnic people the pendulum is swinging in the opposite direction. Therefore, for disabled black and minority ethnic people there is an increased pressure resulting in discrimination and victimisation from the fact of their 'race' in accessing health services, education or welfare benefits, they will first have to prove their right to entitlement based on their immigration status because they are not visibly British'. Being British and being white are both inseparable and anyone who is not white is therefore assumed to be a potential illegal immigrant, here to 'scrounge' off the state. Such racist imagery is widely portrayed by government policies and the media and has the effect of making disabled black and minority ethnic people particularly vulnerable in accessing social and welfare services.

DUAL OPPRESSION OR SOMETHING ELSE?

The effects of racism and disablism, thus, leads to disabled black and minority ethnic people experiencing a form of 'double' disadvantage in Britain (Confederation of Indian Organisations, 1987; McDonald, 1991). That is, they experience disabling barriers the effects of which are to exclude people with any form of physical, sensory or intellectual impairment from full participation in economic and social life (Barnes, 1991), and as members of a minority ethnic group, racism operates to exclude them from participating as full citizens of Britain (Brown, 1984; Donald and Rattansi, 1992; Jones, 1993). Thus, it can be argued that disabled black and minority ethnic people in Britain experience a kind of 'double' exclusion, though this is a rather simplistic equation (Stuart, 1993; Begum, 1994). Instead, it is argued that what they experience is a form of 'simultaneous' oppression, that is, they experience disablism and racism at the same time. This state of affairs is widely accepted by disability writers (Oliver, 1990; Barnes, 1991). I would suggest, that the experience of disabled black and minority ethnic people is both multiple and simultaneous since on an individual level, from day to day, racism and disablism are not always experienced at the same time. It varies from situation to situation—sometimes, disablism is the experience and obviously so. At other times, it may be racism or a combination of both which is disadvantaging an individual either in a social or economic context. In this sense, what is unique about our experience is that we cannot always locate the actual cause of our exclusion, for instance, from a job or why it is that someone would rather stand than sit next to you on the bus.

RACISM IN THE DISABILITY MOVEMENT

The widely accepted definition of racism is prejudice plus power. Given this definition disabled black and minority ethnic people can be said to be at a disadvantage in the disability movement on two grounds. First, black and minority ethnic people generally are disadvantaged in Britain by the virtue of their skin colour/culture which tender them as 'other' and thus politically and economically powerless. By the same token, white people as the dominant/superior group are in a position of power over black people. This is borne out in the fact that black people, historically and at present, have unequal access to jobs, education and other resources (Brown, 1984; Jones, 1993). Therefore, the disability movement, as consisting in the main of white people, has power and advantage over black people. This is not to deny the economic and political marginalisation of disabled people generally in society and that they too are accorded the status of 'other' and, hence, not fully classified members of the white able-bodied élite. Secondly, the disability movement and the white individuals taking part in it are a microcosm of white society and they are equally subject to stereotypes and the generally negative imagery of black and minority ethnic people portrayed in the media.

In addition, disabled black and minority ethnic people are an 'other' within an 'other' both as a minority within the black 'other' and as a minority within the disabled 'other'. As such, it appears that in the disability movement, white society at large is reflected. That is, all the positions of power and influence are held by white people (the majority) and white culture and white norms dominate it to the exclusion of minority groups.

A WAY FORWARD

Social model writers have long since engaged in drawing parallels between the experience of disablism and other oppressions such as racism (Abberley, 1987; Oliver, 1990; Barnes, 1991). There are similarities between these oppressions but merely to draw parallels does not in itself take account of the experience of disabled black and minority ethnic people. This is what is at the heart of Stuart (1994) and Hill's (1994) claim that 'black' disabled people are ignored in the movement.

However, whilst this was true before, it is increasingly the case that disability writers and researchers are making a conscious effort to include disabled people of minority ethnic background in their work (Morris, 1990; Zarb and Oliver, 1993; Priestley, 1995; Morris, 1996). I believe that writing polemics are a useful way of getting people to think of issues which they may have hitherto omitted to pay attention to. However, it is also important to build bridges and work for joint solutions.

Turning to the polemics of Hill (1994) and Stuart (1994), in particular, I am concerned by Hill's call for 'black' disabled people to keep faith with the 'black' voluntary sector rather than with the disability movement. This type of assertion serves only to marginalise 'black' disabled people further in the movement. What we need instead is to look for a way to work through our differences so that we can work together in the fight against disablism rather than fight each other. Racism is endemic in all parts of society and the disability movement (by which I mean organisations of disabled people) is no exception to the rule. However, disablism is just as important in disabled black and minority ethnic people's lives and Hill's call to unite with the 'black' community rather than the disability movement ignores disablism experienced by 'black' disabled people in their own communities.

Oliver asks at the conclusion of his comment 'anyone want to write a polemic about the rampant disablism in the black voluntary sector?' and thus hinting strongly that black and minority ethnic people are disablist. True, disablism is rife in the black and minority ethnic communities as racism and disablism are both rife in the white community. Two wrongs have never made a right. The white disability movement needs to stop denying racism defensively and acknowledge that racism is prevalent in the white community and that as such it affects the lives of disabled black and minority ethnic people both within and without the disability movement. Denying racism vehemently makes way for unconscious prejudices to creep in. Whereas, ackowledging the potential to be racist means consciously ensuring that one's actions are not racist.

Hill (1994) talks of the importance of disabled "black" people setting up their own organisations to address their own issues because she conceives the disability movement as 'not our brothers'. This is not an adequate solution in itself for it will completely marginalise disabled 'black' people that is, if these organisations are to stay totally separate, as Hill suggests. Organisations and groups based on a common interest are important for sharing experiences and making the 'personal political', and as such disabled black and minority ethnic groups should be formed, but not to stay totally cut off from the wider disability movement. Such groups should be encouraged to form by the disability movement, i.e. local coalitions of disabled people and BCODP (British Council of Organisations of Disabled People), and those that exist should be encouraged to take part in the larger disability movement. Disabled black and minority ethnic people cannot and should not be forced to choose between the lesser of the two evils—disablism or racism. They both play an equal part in our oppression and as such should receive equal attention. Instead of 'black' disabled people segregating themselves into their own organisations away from the disability movement as Hill (1994) is suggesting; there are lessons to be learnt from the 'race' relations field where separate community groups exist such as Pakistani Community Association, Marcus Garvey Association and numerous other groups along specific ethnic identities. However, these associations play an important part in the running of their local racial equality councils which are part of the national anti-racist movement in the UK. Similarly, local groups of disabled black and minority ethnic people such as the Association of Blind Asians in Leeds and in London exist but they do not at present take part in the activities of the national disability movement (Priestley, 1995). These groups should be encouraged to take part and others encouraged to form so that disabled black and minority ethnic people's experiences are addressed more fully rather than just partially. Such groups have a vital role in raising awareness in their own communities on the extent of disablism in society and, hence, aim to improve things for disabled black and minority ethnic people within their own communities as well as campaigning for anti-racist service provision which takes their needs into account. This strategy is consistent with the formation of disabled women's group within BCODP.

The funding of such groups would be seen as an important acknowledgement of the experience of disabled black and minority ethnic people and the part that racism plays in their lives. This is particularly important as McDonald's (1991) experience demonstrates: 'To fight for the rights of black people is one thing, to fight for the rights of disabled people is something else, there isn't enough time and energy to fight two different wars' that of racism and disablism. The disability movement has limited resources and as such it cannot engage in a full-scale battle against racism in the wider community, but what it can and should do is acknowledge its own part in racism, and make a conscious effort to include disabled black and minority ethnic people in all its work. Equally, however, it is vital that disabled black and minority ethnic people claim centrality in the disability movement and join in the fight against disablism and not ghettoise ourselves into corners where we will have no-one to hear our cries of oppression except ourselves, for the 'black' communities are just as disablist as the white and we are not really accepted there either. Thus, as Oliver (1995, p. 371) has stated 'the social model of disability offers a more strategic and collective response to disablism.'

REFERENCES

ABBERLEY, P (1987) The concept of oppression and the development of a social theory of disability, *Disability, Handicap and Society*. 2, pp. 5–19.

BARNES, C. (1991) *A Case For Anti-Discrimination Legislation for Disabled People* (London, BCODP)

BARKER, M. (1981) *The New Racism* (London, Junction Books).

BEGUM, N. (1994) Mirror mirror on the wall, in: BEGUM, N., HILL, M. & STEVENS, A. (Eds) *Reflections: the views of Black Disabled people on their lives and community care* (London, CCETSW)

BROWN, C. (1984) *Black and White Britain* (London, PSI).

CONFEDERATION OF INDIAN ORGANISATIONS (1987) *Double Blind: to be disabled and Asian* (London, CIO).

DONALD, J. & RATTANSI, A. (Eds) (1992) *Race, Culture and Difference* (Oxford, Sage in association with OUP).

HENDERSON, R. (1995) The Sensitive Matters of Racism and National Identity, *Wisden Cricket*, July.

HILL, M. (1994) They are not our brothers, in: BEGUM, N., HILL, M. & STEVENS, A. (Eds) *Reflections: the views of Black Disabled people on their lives and community care* (London, CCETSW).

JONES, T. (1993) *Britain's Ethnic Minorities* (London, PSI).

McDONALD, P. (1991) Double discrimination must be faced now, *Disability Now*, March.

MORRIS, J. (1990) *Pride Against Prejudice* (London, Women's Press).

MORRIS, J. (Ed.) (1996) *Encounters with Strangers: feminism and disability* (London, Women's Press).

OLIVER, M. (1990) *Politics of Disablement* (London, Mcmillan).

OLIVER, M. (1995) in: Book reviews, *Disability & Society* 10, pp. 369–371.

PRIESTLEY, M. (1995) Commonality and difference in the movement, *Disability & Society* 10. pp. 157–169.

SUTHERLAND, T. (1981) *Disabled We Stand* (London, Souvenir Press A&E).

STUART, O. (1993) Double oppression: an appropriate starting point? in: SWAIN, J., FINKELSTEIN, V., FRENCH, S. & OLIVER, M. (Eds) *Disabling Barriers – enabling environments* (London, Open University Press/Sage).

STUART, O. (1994) Journey from the margin: Black Disabled people and the anti-racist debate. in BEGUM, N., HILL, M. & STEVENS, A. (Eds) *Reflections: the views of Black Disabled people on their lives and community care* (London, CCETSW).

ZARB, G. & OLIVER M. (1993) *Ageing With a Disability: what do they expect after all these years?* (London, University of Greenwich).

CHAPTER 18

Defending the Social Model

Tom Shakespeare* & Nicholas Watson†

(First published 1997)

INTERNAL ARGUMENT

Definitive of the disability studies approach is the social model, pioneered by the Union of the Physically Impaired Against Segregation, formalised by Vic Finkelstein (1990) and Mike Oliver (1990), and since codified as the central tenet of the self-organised disability movement, our 'big idea' (Hasler, 1993). In passing, it is important to note that this ideological position should be properly located in British disability politics: the movement in other countries, while adopting a social or minority group approach, have not built their campaign and self-definition around the social model.

Since 1992, however, a range of disabled voices have raised questions and suggested developments which are needed in order to make the model more adequate and more relevant to disabled people's lives (Morris, 1991; French, 1993; Crow, 1996). These critiques have centred on the inclusion of impairment and personal experience within the social model, and have been hotly resisted by other activists and theorists of the movement. For example, Vic Finkelstein (1996) has recently argued strongly and widely that the effect of considering personal experience and impairment is to dilute the effectiveness of the social model. This has to be understood in the context of the historical tendency to explain disabled people's experience with reference to impairment, and the tradition of 'sympathetic biography' (Hunt, 1966).

The current contribution is not intended as a comment on these debates. Our purpose is to suggest that internal differences are actually relatively minor: using examples from academics outside disability studies, we argue that the battle for the social model has by no means been won in the world at large, and that therefore the main priority is to advocate a social analysis of disability, not nit-pick or navel-gaze amongst ourselves. While its details and implications may be contested within the disability movement, there is a broad and vigorous consensus around the social model which should be translated into a renewed attempt to achieve understanding and win acceptance and application of the model within wider society. The views that have to be debunked are not those of other disabled people, but those of the non-disabled academics and commentators who continue to view disability as a personal medical tragedy.

Because of the relative success of the disability movement agenda in achieving coverage in the broadcast media, it is easy to over-estimate acceptance of the civil rights approach in popular thought. The continued focus on medical coverage in both the press and on television is one example of this. Another is the lack of understanding among the (supposedly liberal) press. The opinion columns of the British broadsheets demonstrated this during the campaigns for anti-discrimination legislation in the UK over recent years.

ACADEMIC RESISTANCE

While it is unsurprising to find establishment broadsheets unwilling or unable to understand and accept the social model and civil rights approach, it is regrettable that other academic disciplines are so slow or unwilling to take account of the recent development of disability studies. It is very common to read texts relevant to disability, which fail even to reference the work of Oliver, Barnes, Morris and others. This ignorance might be expected of various of the medical sciences, to whom the social constructionist approach is a fundamental challenge: however, it is more surprising to find disability studies neglected in other human sciences, and even in other areas of sociology.

The following discussion centres on two approaches to disability: psychology and medical sociology. None is adequate or effective in understanding disabled people's experiences: psychology individualises disability whilst medical sociology pathologises disability. Each contributes insights which are, in a limited way, useful. But none provides a substitute for the social model of disability, to which they are a challenge.

PSYCHOLOGICAL

A recent paper by Marie Johnston (1996) illustrates some of the problems we have with approaches to disabled people's experiences within psychology. Our critique centres on factors external to her argument (i), and internal to her argument. This second category of criticisms include flaws within her argument on her own terms (ii), and a broader set of flaws arising from her failure to understand the relevance of a social understanding of the disability experience (iii).

(i) On the external point, we would argue that her approach is extraordinarily arrogant, because it relies solely on the psychological literature on disability, not on the perspectives of disabled people themselves. Her approach is to criticise medical models, such as the WHO/OPCS model, and to propose the relevance of psychological explanations. But first she states

> The main approach to understanding disability arises from the medical model—disabilities occur because of physical impairments which have resulted from the underlying disease or disorder. (Johnston, 1996, p. 205)

We argue that she has taken a reductionist model (WHO) and made it more reductionist, for example by failing to consider what the WHO calls 'handicap' or social disadvantage. Thus she ignores the considerable mainstream social science literature on measuring disability and the debates around the 1988 OPCS Disability Survey.

Moreover, she fails to acknowledge the critique which disabled people and their organisations have made of the WHO/OPCS model (Oliver, 1990; Abberley, 1992). Neither is she familiar with the social model of disability, or the burgeoning disability studies literature: it is neither mentioned, nor referenced. We find this extraordinary, especially in view of the excellent discussion of the psychology of disability developed by Finkelstein & French (1993). While they show the importance of distinguishing between impairment and disability, she chooses to ignore this key point, because it would undermine the basic tenets of her argument, and indeed the approach taken by the discipline of psychology.

(ii) At the outset of her argument, Johnston usefully criticises the linearity of the measurement model proposed by WHO (and implicitly OPCS). Disabled commentators have shown that the scale of severity of disability does not correspond to disabled people's experiences because it ranks non-comparable physical tasks: thus on the OPCS scale, it would be possible to fail the first severity test, but to successfully perform one of the subsequent severity tests, making a nonsense of its testing function.

Johnston adopts a cumulative model of disability, implying a sequential dependence of items, in order to overcome this problem and arrive at an ordinal scale. Thus she argues:

> It is not necessary to decide whether failing to get out of bed is worse than failing to walk one mile: those who cannot get out of bed inevitably have a worse level of disability because they are unable to perform the second item. (Johnston, 1996, p. 205)

However, due to her failure to consider the social context in which people experience their impairment, the scale she employs (Williams *et al.*, 1976) is flawed. For example, the scale suggests that a person who fails a higher item must necessarily have failed lower items, because it is intended to be a cumulative measure. However, while we find item 8, 'Cannot use w.c. or commode without help' may apply to a number of people with quadraplegia, an earlier item, for example item 1, 'cannot use bus or train unaccompanied', might not apply to such persons (given accessible transportation), which means that the scale is neither cumulative nor logical.

This point highlights two problems in Johnston's approach: first, she abstracts on a purely intellectual level, without considering the lived experience and accounts of disabled people. Second, she fails to understand the way in which environment is causally linked to the experience of impairment. In our example, it is because people with quadraplegia could be equipped with suitable power-wheelchairs and could use accessible transport facilities that they would pass item 1, while possibly failing subsequent items.

(iii) Building on the previous two points, we argue that Johnston's failure to acknowledge the social model, and her lack of understanding of disability, are major flaws to the psychological model which she proposes. We will highlight two dimensions of this.

First, she discusses the ways in which disabled people's functional performance can be related to the observations of particular medical personnel, for nurses and physiotherapists respectively. Her argument is that:

> the results [differing measures of function by nurses and physiotherapists] may be due to differences in the behaviours elicited by different professions, due to the different expectations in rehabilitation and nursing settings. (Johnston, 1996, p. 207)

Thus she suggests that the attitudes of personnel affect the effort made by disabled people. In one sense, this is useful, because it shows that there are not objective measures of functional loss, but that this is contingent and reliant on context and environment. As a challenge to clinical approaches, this is helpful.

However, Johnston fails to take account of the different ideologies adopted by the relevant health professionals, or indeed the cultural representations of disability. That is, Johnston individualises the relationship between patient and professional, rather than putting the experiences in social context. The result is implicitly to blame the individual, rather than locate the problem in society. A more useful approach would explore the levels of prejudice and stereotyping adopted by particular health professionals, following researchers such as French (1996), Oliver (1996a), Begum (1996) and Abberley (1995).

Further, while it is important to note that the person measuring functional limitation may influence the measurement made, the obvious next stage in the argument would be to draw on the social constructionism of sociologists such as Kitsuse & Cicourel (1963), or indeed Barry Hindess (1973), and suggest that disability (as she defines it) is an artifact of the measuring system used, not an objective outcome (measured either clinically or psychologically). That is, Johnston is correct to suggest that 'the social circumstances influence the level of disability observed' (Johnston, 1996, p. 207), but she fails to draw the right conclusions from her observations.

The second dimension, which is the key point which we want to make, is that Johnston's psychologism is unable to account for the social creation of disability. As our comments on her scaling argument show, it is essential not to reduce the disability experience to an individual or physical can do/can't do model. Disabled people's functional capacities have to be placed in a broader social and environmental context, which can incorporate issues such as disabling barriers, availability of aids and personal assistance, and financial and material factors. Rather than adopt the normalising and pathologising perspective of Johnston, psychology must accept that people with impairment manage their physical issues in various ways, but that the key problems they encounter are prejudice and discrimination (physical and social barriers).

To conclude this discussion of Johnston's approach to the construction of disability, we wish to make two key points. First, following Finkelstein & French (1993), we acknowledge that psychological arguments do have relevance to disabled people's experience. Disability studies needs to pay attention to the distress caused by people's experience of social disablement

(Keith, 1996), and indeed it has been argued that we need also to explore the impact of impairment itself (Crow, 1996). However, in order to adequately understand these issues, it is vital to start by distinguishing between impairment and disability, and to remove the causal reductionism of which both psychologists such as Johnston, and biomedical clinicians are guilty.

If, like Johnston, we fail either to distinguish impairment and disability, or to take a social model perspective, then the consequence is clear. Rather than moving forward from the limitations of the WHO/clinical model, we are left with a clinical/ psychological model which continues to individualise disability, but also is guilty of 'blaming the victim'. This is because the model attributes disabled people's rehabilitative progress to their motivation or general psychological state, rather than the social context in which they find themselves, or indeed their willingness or otherwise to accept the normalising values of the rehabilitation approach. While it would be incorrect to suggest that motivation or psychological state is irrelevant to rehabilitation, or indeed to other dimensions of the disability experience, it is extremely dangerous to give primacy to such victim-blaming and value laden approaches.

SOCIOLOGY OF MEDICINE

Medical sociology is another discipline that appears to have problems accepting or working within the social model: emphasis is placed squarely on the experience of chronic illness and disability, individualising the experience. The analysis is couched in terms of coping, adaption, identity and how individuals make sense of and come to terms with their impairments and disablement. Two recent papers by Ruth Pinder (1995, 1996) exemplify this approach. In both these papers she uses detailed case studies of two people with arthritis, examining their experiences of managing, or not managing, in the work force.

Each paper analyses the experiences of two informants; one who is able to continue working and one who is forced to give up work. Pinder's sole project appears to be an attack on the social model of disability. Unlike Johnston she does acknowledge the existence of this model, but does so in disparaging terms. Whilst recognising, and sympathising with this approach she feels it provides only a 'limited understanding' (1996, p. 137). Many working within disability studies will have been angered by the tone of these papers. This is unfortunate, because expressed within a less jaundiced account, the interesting aspects of her research would have been better communicated.

An unprejudiced assessment of recent developments in the field of disability would have included two major points. First, the self-organised movement of disabled people, and the social model theory with which this political development is associated, has had a major impact on British society, as elsewhere in the world. Liberal and individualistic analyses and policy interventions have for years failed to make much impact on the problems of disabled people. However, the radicalism disavowed by Pinder has had an incontrovertible effect, resulting in both social improvements and individual empowerment. The proof of the pudding is in the eating, and despite Pinder's hostility, the social model has brought major benefits to disabled people (which does not mean it is not an over-egged pudding). Obviously individual disabled people may not always agree with the radical agenda or analysis, just as individual women have often not supported feminism. But this does not mean that disabled activists, any more than feminists, are wrong.

Second, the social model of disability is in a process of development, exploration and analysis. While Pinder presents a picture of stone-faced ideologues misrepresenting disabled people's lives, in fact we have thousands of disabled people, including academics, discussing the issues and arguing about the best way to theorise disability. As well as the papers by Crow and French which Pinder references, there is published work by Morris (1991) and Shakespeare (1992), and unpublished work and unrecorded debate by many others. As with any other area of political debate, or sociological theory, there is a constant process of criticism, self-criticism and development (Oliver, 1996b). The social model originally underplayed the importance of impairment in disabled people's lives, in order to develop a strong argument about social structures and social processes. No theory emerges into the world fully formed, and getting the balance between the experience of impairment, and the experience of disability is a continuing endeavour. Pinder's analysis elsewhere in her paper will actually contribute to this process, and should be welcomed.

As well as these omissions, there is a misrepresentation of the body of work which Pinder refers to as 'disability theory' and which is commonly described as 'disability studies'. Pinder suggests a neglect of what she calls society's 'sins of commission', and describes discrimination in terms of negative attitudes. In her conclusions she refers to cultural proscription, marginalisation of outsiders and other social processes which she argues are not dealt with within the social model approach. She is entirely right to identify aspects of cultural representation and social attitudes, which are extremely disabling for people with impairment. `

However, far from offering an original analysis, or locating a lacuna within disability studies, she is in fact making an old argument. For example, Paul Hunt discussed such processes in 1966. Jenny Morris described the effects of prejudice in 1991. David Hevey developed a substantial theoretical account in *The Creatures Time Forgot* (1992). Colin Barnes summarised the key issues in 1992. Shakespeare (1994) subsequently published an article which explored cultural representation and theorised prejudice, using the concepts such as anomaly and liminality to which Pinder refers in the current paper. Many other contemporary sociologists within disability studies are exploring the body, impairment, and cultural processes (Barnes, 1995; Shakespeare & Watson, 1995; Oliver, 1996b). Equally, her suggestion that we need to explore closely the relationship between impairment, environment, and social interaction in the employment context has already been acted on by Alan Roulstone (1993) and forms the subject of his forthcoming monograph.

In order to grind her particular axe, Pinder has constructed a picture of the disability studies perspective which few would recognise, and reinforced it by reference to a mere two research informants. Her critique is out-of-date, skewed by her biography, and highly subjective. Pinder's paper, despite numerous merits and points of interest, represents a cul-de-sac.

MOVING ON

We have tried to demonstrate how the social model has had a limited impact, both in the mainstream media, and academic discourses other than disability studies. This failure relates to the ways in which other literature either ignores disability, or misconstrue disabled people's lives. While this may be expected within biomedical and clinical approaches, its prevalence within social sciences should give cause for concern.

What lessons can be learnt from exploring the range of reactions (and non-reactions) to the social model of disability? It could be argued that the continuing ignorance and hostility outside the movement highlights the danger of internal dissension. It has been suggested that questioning, for example the role of impairment, provides a 'hostage to fortune' and that alternative views should be suppressed, in order for the movement to speak with one, social model, voice (Finkelstein, 1996). Often, the disability movement prioritises marching to the beat of a single drum, favouring a united line to competing voices.

Our conclusion is different. We have consistently argued that pluralism is a positive value, within both the disability movement and disability studies. Debates are necessary, and recognising difference within the disability community is overdue. Neither does openness threaten the central political goals of the movement. Post-modernist writers have argued against 'meta-historical narratives' and the modernist pursuit of a universalising and monolithic rationality (Fraser & Nicholson, 1990), and the contemporary experiences of disabled people highlight the value of such critiques. From this perspective, those who develop and refine the social model ensure its renewal and continuing relevance. Particularly, the dominant version of the social model has favoured a materialist, if not marxist, worldview. We argue it is possible (and indeed desirable), to retain the social model within a more nuanced worldview drawing on feminist and post-modernist accounts.

However, it is critical to have clarity about the wider intellectual environment. The differences within the movement on the issue of the social model are as nothing when compared to the hostility and ignorance with which the social model is greeted in the wider world. We suggest, therefore, that while academics and activists can debate amongst ourselves, our main efforts must be to fight for a social model analysis in society as a whole, and to take the insights and evidence we have gathered into other disciplines and areas of public discussion. Rather than putting energy into internal arguments, we need to challenge the continuing complacency of the intellectual establishment, and to win the battle for a social model understanding of society and our lives.

REFERENCES

ABBERLEY, P. (1992) Counting us out: a discussion of the OPCS surveys, *Disability, Handicap & Society*, 7, pp. 139-155.
ABBERLEY, P. (1995) Disabling ideology in health and welfare—the case of occupational welfare, *Disability & Society*, 10, pp. 221-232.

BARNES, C. (1992) *Disabling Imagery and the Media* (Halifax, BCODP/Ryburn).

BARNES, C. (1995) Politics of the "disabled" body, presented at Minding the Body Conference, Leeds University.

BEGUM, N. (1996) General practitioners role in shaping disabled women's lives, in: C. BARNES & G. MERCER (Eds), *Exploring the Divide* (Leeds, Disability Press).

CROW, L. (1996) Including all of our lives: renewing the social model of disability, in: C. BARNES & G. MERCER (Eds), *Exploring the Divide* (Leeds, Disability Press).

FINKELSTEIN, V. & FRENCH, S. (1993) Towards a psychology of disability, in: J. SWAIN *et al.*, *Disabling Barriers-Enabling Environments* (London, Sage).

FINKELSTEIN, V. (1980) *Attitudes and Disabled People* (New York, World Rehabilitation Fund).

FINKELSTEIN, V. (1996), Inside out. Unpublished discussion paper.

FRASER, N. & NICHOLSON, L. (1990) Social criticism without philosophy: an encounter between feminism and post-modernism, in: L. NICHOLSON (Ed.) *Feminism/Postmodernism* (London, Routledge).

FRENCH, S. (1993) Disability, impairment or something in between, in: J. SWAIN *et al.*, *Disabling Barriers-Enabling Environments* (London, Sage).

FRENCH, S. (1996) The attitudes of health professionals towards disabled people, in: G. HALES (Ed.) *Beyond Disability* (London, Sage).

HASLER, F. (1993) Developments in the disabled people's movement, in: J. SWAIN *et al.*, *Disabling Barriers-Enabling Environments* (London, Sage).

HEVEY, D. (1992) *The Creatures Time Forgot* (London, Routledge).

HINDESS, B. (1973) *The Use of Official Statistics in Sociology* (London, Macmillan).

HUNT, P. (1966) *Stigma* (London, Geoffrey Chapman).

JOHNSTON, M. (1996) Models of disability, *The Psychologist*, May, pp. 205-210.

KEITH, L. (1996) Encounters with strangers, in: J. MORRIS (Ed.) *Encounters with Strangers* (London, Women's Press).

KITSUSE, J.I. & CICOUREL, A.V. (1963) A note on the uses of official statistics, *Social Problems*, 11 (2), pp. 131–139.

MORRIS, J. (1991) *Pride Against Prejudice* (London, Women's Press).

OLIVER, M. (1990) *The Politics of Disablement* (Basingstoke, Macmillan).

OLIVER, M. (1996a) Defining impairment and disability, in: C. BARNES & G. MERCER (Eds) *Exploring the Divide* (Leeds, Disability Press).

OLIVER, M. (1996b) *Understanding Disability* (Basingstoke, Macmillan).

PINDER, R. (1995) Bringing back the body without the blame: the experience of ill and disabled people at work, *Sociology of Health and Illness*, 17(5), pp. 605-631.

PINDER, R. (1996) Sick-but-fit or fit-but-sick? Ambiguity and identity in the workplace, in: C. BARNES & G. MERCER (Eds) *Exploring the Divide* (Leeds, Disability Press).

ROULSTONE, A. (1993) Access to new technology in the employment of disabled people, in: J. SWAIN *et al.* (Eds) *Disabling Barriers—Enabling Environments* (London, Sage).

SHAKESPEARE, T. (1992) Renewing the social model of disability, *Coalition*, September, pp. 40–42.

SHAKESPEARE, T. (1994) Cultural representation of disabled people: dustbins for disavowal? *Disability, Handicap and Society*, 9, pp. 283-299.

SHAKESPEARE, T. (1996) Disability, Identity, Difference, in: C. BARNES & G. MERCER (Eds) *Exploring the Divide* (Leeds, Disability Press).

SHAKESPEARE, T. & WATSON, N. (1995) Habeas Corpus? Sociology of the body and the issue of impairment, paper presented at the Changing Organisms: Organisms in Change Conference, Aberdeen University.

WILLIAMS, R.G.A., JOHNSTON, M., WILLIS, L & BENNETT, A.E. (1976) Disability: a model and a measurement technique, *British Journal of Preventative and Social Medicine*, 30, pp. 71-78.

CHAPTER 19

A Reply to Tom Shakespeare and Nicholas Watson

Ruth Pinder

(First published 1997)

Shakespeare and Watson's paper is well conceived and argued. I particularly enjoyed the way that the debate about the social model was set in a wider context, as this contained some features that I had not previously fully appreciated. In many respects there is more to agree than to disagree with in this critique.

SETTING THE SCENE

Firstly, for the sake of brevity I will refer to the two papers upon which Shakespeare and Watson's critique concentrates as the SHI paper, (Pinder, 1995, 'Bringing back the body without the blame...'), and the B. and M. Collection (Pinder, 1996, 'Sick-but-fit or fit-but-sick? Ambiguity and Identity in the Workplace'). Secondly, as readers may have less easy access to the more arcane academic journals, let me retrace my steps in more detail.

In SHI, I explored the employment stories of two informants disabled with rheumatoid arthritis as they attempted to 'make it'—or not—in the workplace. One, whom I called 'Elaine', was forced out of her much loved secretarial job after the onset of arthritis; the other, 'Sally', despite substantial difficulties, was still managing to hold down her post as a systems analyst at the BBC. In the B. and M. collection, a similar technique was adopted (I, too, enjoy arguing from oppositions), which illustrated the work narratives of two more informants disabled respectively with rheumatoid and psoriatic arthritis. 'Philip' had been abruptly dismissed from a career in the police force he had set his heart upon since early childhood; whilst 'Lucy' was a disability consultant in a local disability organisation, a job which she had found after many difficulties with previous employers over the thorny question of sick leave. Although the social model of disability explained some aspects of their experiences, it left others unaccounted for.

Disability study critiques have emphasised the way in which medical sociologists' work on the experience of illness have often underplayed the influence of structures; and simultaneously how, in their desire to move away from the individualised 'tragedy' model of disability, much of their own work has concentrated on structures, and rather less on the subtleties and complexities of lived experience. The Leeds Conference 'Exploring the Divide' in March 1996 was organised precisely to address these issues and to see if a more sensitive rapprochement might be found between the two. Both my papers were conceived in the light of these two polarities and have attempted, albeit modestly, to explore the agency-structure dialectic through the use of two detailed case histories apiece in a way which, to the best of my knowledge, had not previously been attempted. In my view, their strength lies less in any great claims to originality than in their usefulness in illustrating this dialogue. I'm glad that, despite criticisms, Shakespeare and Watson can see some merit in my efforts.

Shakespeare has argued elsewhere (1992) that one of the achievements of the Disability Movement has been to separate impairment from disability. Whilst I appreciate the force of these arguments, and their grounding in disabled people's experience of marginalisation and exclusion from mainstream society, my two papers argue that attempts to treat the two as discrete entities glosses over the complexity of individual lives. As fast as I pulled out one variable in analysing the data, another tugged at my sleeve. Rather than looking at them in isolation, the task, as I saw it, became one of illustrating how the variables interpenetrate and interweave. My argument throughout has been that if we want to fully understand the ambiguities of lived experience, we need to come to grips with the many interlocking webs of significance in which impairment and disability are embedded. On their own, neither tells the whole story. The picture I have tried to paint is a holistic one, avoiding both the 'undersocialising' of an individualistic psychologising approach and the 'oversocialising' of a more deterministic analysis (Williams, 1996). I stand by these arguments.

WHAT IS AT STAKE

Let me turn to the particular criticisms which Shakespeare and Watson have raised, and acknowledge the depth of feeling which the social model, as a source of identity and pride, as well as a strong political vocabulary which focuses and interprets disabled people's struggles, raises in a way that I had perhaps insufficiently appreciated prior to the Leeds Conference.

Criticism almost always has some kernel of truth in it, so a point of agreement is in order. Gillian Parker (1993), in a sensitive account of caring within marriage, speaks of her 'puzzlement' which the social model engendered in her own attempts to care for a partner with a potentially life-threatening illness: a happy word, and one which I gather is not altogether unacceptable amongst disabled academics. My feelings can most honestly be described as ones of frustration, as I tussled to fit the refractory experience of some (but not all) of the informants studied into a model which sought to provide an explanatory framework for disabled people's lives. It was certainly not my intention to 'grind an axe' against the Disability Movement, and if this is inadvertently the way the texts reads, I regret that.

Neither was it my intention when I commenced this research for *Arthritis Care* to make exploring the social model my 'sole project' (and funding difficulties often preclude writing as fully on a research topic as one might wish). However, the more I learnt of people's experiences, the more this emerged as the 'proper' topic of investigation. Although some informants in the research positioned their lives fully within the social model, others found it less comfortable to relate to. My qualitative social scientific training has alerted me to pay attention to anomalies, or 'deviant cases' in any research study: they often tell us more about the world than those who are more 'typical'. Increasingly I felt it was important to give voice to those experiences which seemed to sit on the margins of disability discussions.

My critics claim not to be able to recognise the four informants' stories (I have not thought to defend case study methods here when Shakespeare and Watson so ably draw upon a similar methodology!). The lack of recognition seems to me to be telling: these are the stories of other people with impairments 'out there', two of whom found a 'social oppression' model of disability unable to account adequately for their predicament; and one of whom was, perhaps, only on the threshold of framing her experiences differently. I am puzzled if the fourth informant, 'Lucy', portrayed in B. and M., is not recognisable, working as she does as a disability consultant in a disability organisation. Her narrative focused on the way in which, with the support of the disability community, she has re-framed the sick leave question—for the moment—in a way that 'Philip' so conspicuously could not. It raises the important question of how far, and on what basis, we can legitimately speak for others, an issue I had started to think about in B. and M., stimulated as it was by debates about difference in feminism.

To a final point of misunderstanding I feel, rather than disagreement. Shakespeare and Watson refer to a phrase I used in SHI regarding the 'limited usefulness' of the social model, when my intention was its use as an heuristic device. Oliver (1996, p. 40) suggests that

> . . . models are merely ways to help us to better understand the world, or those bits of it under scrutiny. If we expect models to explain, rather than aid understanding, they are bound to be found wanting . . . we cannot assume that models in general and the social model in particular can do everything, that it can explain disability in totality.

No one way of classifying a phenomenon is appropriate to every purpose. I was certainly not commenting on the efficacy of the social model as a political tool: indeed, the many gains which have been made by the Disability Movement in raising awareness and legislating towards civil rights can only impact positively on my own disability situation. The fact that such misunderstanding arises in the first place seems to lie in a tension in disability studies, already ably debated (Barnes, 1996; Shakespeare, 1996), between the academic enterprise and political activism. Certainly there are some medical sociologists—and perhaps rather more medical anthropologists—who wish to put their analyses directly to work to improve the lot of those whose lives they study, to do action research. It is my own particular foible that I am more comfortable with 'diagnosis' than I am with 'treatment': whilst I can appreciate the arguments of those in the Disability Movement who feel that there have been understandings enough, in the ebb and flow of events, interpretations always beget new interpretations. The infinite variety of people's experiences never ceases to beckon.

Shakespeare and Watson have treated the two papers as though they were identical, and have made little allowance for the fact that we all travel between writings. My later B. and M. chapter reflected this journey, both in tone and in argument: above all I had found a framework for understanding the differences that I have tried to grapple with in a way that makes sense, both experientially and intellectually.

A BETTER CONCEPTUALISATION

Perhaps the tension that is highlighted most sharply by Shakespeare and Watson's critique is that between the search for clear-cut, univocal messages crucial for the success of any political movement, and the necessarily more complex and subtle reality of people's lived experience. As Levine (1985, p. 38) argues 'the institutions and ideals of modern culture are seriously dependent on unambiguous modes of expression'. In the avalanche of information which characterises our contemporary world, people have neither the time nor the inclination to pursue the meanings behind the words, to sleuth for complexity.

Indeed, the search for that coherence and predictability we all struggle for to make sense of our world is bound up precisely in the way we establish boundaries between what is and what is not: we classify and re-classify, we say a person is this or that. But the mind is simultaneously many things. As Perin (1988) and Sibley (1995) have argued (and Mary Douglas before them), the human tendency is not to look too kindly upon blurred boundaries. Yet, as Baumann (1991) argues 'ambiguity cannot be wished out of existence'. And to ignore it excludes the richness of difference. The informants' stories presented in my two papers are above all stories about mixed categories, about transition —with all the discomfort this may imply for those who are unequivocally and safely 'there'. As I see it, their narratives have put confusion on the map.

TOWARDS A COMMON GROUND

The pluralism and 'nuanced worldview' to which Shakespeare and Watson refer in their critique is where fruitful common ground may surely be found between us. I return to the universalising themes discussed particularly in my B. and M. chapter, which owe much to the works of the disability theorist, Irving Zola (see also Williams, 1996). Let me raise anew the question: cannot a more holistic version of the social model, one which fully recognises the way in which agency and structure are intricately knit together, and which acknowledges that we are both producers and products of our social and cultural world, enhance the impact of a Movement committed to valuing and enhancing human life? As feminists have discovered, the experience of difference-within-difference, the multiple voices which are in our midst, need to be more fully recognised. I wrote in B. and M. 'A more holistic definition of disability, of the way in which disability is intimately linked to other structural relationships which differentially disadvantage social actors, is the hallmark of a Disability Movement which has truly come of age'. We need to nourish both the clarity of message necessary for the achievement of political gains, *and* the ambiguity and complexity inherent in a sensitive appreciation of the many differences in our midst.

I came across this evocative piece by the German sociologist and 'philosopher in transition', Georg Simmel in Levine's book (op.cit):

> 'Whoever is not for me is against me' is only a half-truth. Only the indifferent person is against me—one whom the ultimate questions for which I live move neither to a For nor an Against. But whoever is against me in a positive sense, one who ventured onto the plane where I exist and combats me on that plane, that person is in the highest sense *for* me.

Does this not have much to teach us?

ACKNOWLEDGEMENTS

I gratefully acknowledge the support of *Arthritis Care* in helping to fund the research upon which this work is based.

REFERENCES

BARNES, C. (1996) Disability and the myth of the independent researcher. *Disability & Society*, 11, pp. 107-110.
BAUMAN, Z. (1991) *Modernity and Ambivalence* (Oxford, Blackwells).
DOUGLAS, M. (1966) *Purity and Danger: an analysis of the concepts of pollution and taboo* (London, Routledge).

LEVINE, D. (1985) *The Flight from Ambiguity: essays in social and cultural theory* (Chicago, University of Chicago Press).

OLIVER, M. (1996) *Understanding Disability: from theory to practice* (Basingstoke, Macmillan Press).

PARKER, G. (1993) *With this Body: caring and disability in marriage* (Buckingham, Open University Press) .

PERIN, C. (1988) *Belonging in America: reading between the lines* (Madison, Wisconsin, University of Wisconsin Press).

PINDER, R. (1995) Bringing back the body without the blame? The experience of ill and disabled people at work, *Sociology of Health and Illness*, 17, pp. 605-631.

PINDER, R. (1996) Sick-but-fit or fit-but-sick? Ambiguity and identity at the workplace, in: C. BARNES & G. MERCER, *Exploring the Divide: illness and disability* (Leeds, The Disability Press).

SHAKESPEARE, T. (1992) A Response to Liz Crow. *Coalition*, September, 1992.

SHAKESPEARE, T. (1996) Rules of engagement: doing disability research. *Disability and Society*, 11, pp. 115–119

SIBLEY, D (1995) *Geographies of Exclusion* London, Routledge)

WILLIAMS, G. (1996) Representing disability: some questions of phenomenology and politics, in: C. BARNES & G. MERCER (Eds) (1996) *Exploring the Divide: illness and disability* (Leeds, The Disability Press).

CHAPTER 20

Integrating Models of Disability:
a reply to Shakespeare and Watson

Marie Johnston

(First published 1997)

The WHO model has been widely used as a model of disability and continues to be the implicit model adopted in the delivery of health care. The model has been criticised in a variety of ways with resulting suggestions that it be modified or abandoned. However the model offers a useful starting point by clearly separating the concepts of 'impairment' (limitations of structure or function due to disease or disorders) and 'disability' (limitations in the performance of activities). The model proposes that disability is the result of impairment, but opens up the possibility that other factors may also influence disability. Clarification of these other factors is essential to the viability of this model.

Since disability is defined in behavioural terms, it seems obvious that disability should be influenced by the same variables as influence other behaviours, including physiological, environmental, social, cognitive and emotional factors. I have proposed (Johnston, 1996a) that it is possible to integrate the WHO model with some of the current most strongly validated theories of behaviour. Based on findings from observational, longitudinal and experimental studies, perceptions of control have been found to determine levels of disability, even allowing for level of impairment. For example, one experimental study showed that when individuals were asked to describe occasions when they found it difficult to exercise control, their perceptions of control were reduced and their levels of disability were increased; similarly, describing occasions of successful control resulted in greater perceived control and less disability (Fisher and Johnston, 1996). This study clearly demonstrates changes in disability without changes in impairment and thus challenges the WHO model. I have proposed that, rather than abandoning the WHO model, it should be developed to be more compatible with existing scientific findings and have proposed a fuller model of factors explaining limitations in functional activities. Other psychological models deal with the psychological and emotional *consequences* rather than determinants of impairment and disability.

Theoretic models serve a number of functions. My objective was to achieve a model that more satisfactorily explained the observed phenomena and that allowed the possibility of further testing of the model. For others, such a model can have an applied function, enabling new and potentially more effective insights and methods of clinical intervention; hopefully my paper may serve this end by being reprinted in a journal read by research practitioners (Johnston, 1996b). A third function is to influence social policy and public debate with the aim of persuasion and the possibility of social change. Thus models serve scientific, applied and social functions. It is not clear that the same model can serve all of these functions simultaneously and the rules for each type of model are different. The rules for the development of scientific models are relative clear: such models depend on the generation of hypotheses and testing them with scientific rigour. Scientific models are changed by evidence, whereas applied models are changed by acceptability and usefulness and social models are changed by argument and persuasion.

One can debate the level at which models should be pitched and explanations of human behaviour can be at physiological and social levels. Shakespeare and Watson (this publication) are critical of psychological explanations of limitation of activities, perhaps because they do not believe that what we think and feel influences our behaviour, in which case this is a very fundamental unhappiness with the existence of psychology as a discipline. Alternatively, they may be using a wider definition of 'disability' to incorporate the WHO concept of 'handicap' (limitations in social role) and are criticising the use of a simply psychological explanation of 'handicap'. If so, then they are attacking a straw man as I doubt that anyone has proposed that handicap is exclusively a consequence of individual factors.

Apart from the fact that psychological explanations typically incorporate individual factors in explaining behaviour, there are other virtues in explanations at the level of the individual. As Shakespeare and Watson (this publication) observe, individuals may have widely varying methods of managing impairment. There are major psychological theories of coping and some of these are addressed with reference to impairment and disability in my paper (Johnston, 1996a). As well as individual levels of coping, it is the individual who engages the clinical situation as patient and the professions working with patients need individual level models. A physiotherapist who is aware that perceptions of control may serve to enhance or reduce the range of activities the patient can perform may be able to offer the patient more alternative methods of coping than one who simply believes that activities are determined by impairment.

Of course individual levels of explanation can be interpreted as victim blaming, a view that can be seen as the obverse of 'empowerment'. But all levels of explanation are subject to misinterpretations and the social level can be presented as the 'nanny' or patronising society. Such presentations do not undermine the validity of the approach.

Different levels of explanation of the same phenomenon do not imply that there must be a 'fight' or 'battle' as Shakespeare and Watson (this publication) suggest. A model of social influence does not rule out a psychological model. Social factors undoubtedly influence psychological functioning and therefore, behaviour. Social influences may be mediated by psychological factors. For example, the results I report of patients having different levels of disability when rated by nurses and rehabilitation therapists may be due to the social and interpersonal factors operating; rehabilitation therapists may create a more enabling environment with greater expectations which raise the individual's perceptions of control and therefore the level of performance. Psychological theory clearly recognises the impact of social factors on important psychological variables; for example, perceptions of control are hypothesised to be influenced by persuasion and by the vicarious experience of the performance of others, in addition to the effects of one's own successful or unsuccessful performance.

Social factors may influence the impact of impairment not only on the limitations in activities, but also on the distress experienced by the individual. Stigmatising attitudes could obviously have this effect. Shakespeare and Watson (this publication) are also concerned about pathologising or normalising approaches. But surely any discussion of 'disability', including having journals which address the topic and models which explain it, run this risk.

The model I proposed is not dependent on concepts of impairment and disability and can in fact be generalised to any limitation in activities arising due to any limitation in physical status. Thus the model can equally well explain why a short person cannot get a book from a high shelf and why a tall person cannot walk normally under a low arch. The basic psychological model was designed to explain limitations in behaviour due to lack of intention to perform the behaviour and can therefore account for differences in performance between two individuals of identical physical stature.

Shakespeare and Watson (this publication) argue for the need to take heed of writings of disabled people and contrast these reports with the model I adopt. However, the model I adopt is based on the reports of representative, unbiased samples of individuals with various clinical conditions. While I do not doubt the value of spokespersons, from my empirical standpoint, it is important to gain results which are representative. Thus I describe a cumulative measure of disability not because I 'intended [it] to be a cumulative measure', but because the data from a community cohort resulted in a cumulative pattern.

So rather than defending or attacking any of the existing models, I would like to suggest that we identify the shared and cohesive strands. The WHO model leaves open the possibility that psychological, environmental and social factors may influence the process at the level of impairment, disability or handicap. The psychological models addressed in my paper (Johnston, 1996a) attempt to explain how psychological factors can explain limitations in the performance of activities. I have suggested that such models might be integrated with the WHO model to offer a better explanatory model and one which may have greater relevance in the clinical situation. Social factors can clearly also be integrated with this model.

But this assumes that the purpose of the models is to achieve scientific explanation, a core assumption of the discipline of psychology. If instead the aim is to produce models that achieve social goals, then scientific models may not serve the purpose.

REFERENCES

FISHER, K. & JOHNSTON, M. (1996) Experimental manipulation of perceived control and its effects on disability, *Psychology and Health*, 11, pp. 657-669.

JOHNSTON. M. (1996a) Models of disability. *The Psychologist*, 9, pp. 205-210.

JOHNSTON, M. (1996b) Models of disability, *Physiotherapy Theory and Practice*, 12, pp. 131-141 (Reprint of Johnston, 1996a).

SHAKESPEARE, T. & WATSON. N. (1997) Defending the social model, *Disability & Society*, 12, pp. 293-300.

Index